**BASIC EDUCATION—**
*A World Challenge*

# BASIC EDUCATION—
## *A World Challenge*

Measures and Innovations for Children and Youth
in Developing Countries

**H. M. Phillips**

JOHN WILEY & SONS

London · New York · Sydney · Toronto

157780

Copyright © 1975, by John Wiley & Sons, Ltd.

*Library of Congress Cataloging in Publication Data:*

Phillips, Herbert Moore, 1908–
Basic education—a world challenge.

Includes bibliographical references.
1. Underdeveloped areas—Education (Elementary)
I. Title.

LC2608.P48      372.9'172'4      74–6995

ISBN  0 471 68670 0

Printed in Great Britain at The Pitman Press, Bath

# Acknowledgements

The author gratefully acknowledges his debt to Unesco for much of the source material used, and to the members of its staff with whom many of the themes in the book have been the subject of discussion over long periods of mutual consultation, and especially to Mr. William J. Platt, Director of the Department of Planning and Financing of Education, who has kindly written the Foreword which follows. Appreciation is also expressed of consultations with Unicef and the World Bank, each of these organizations having recently adopted measures of redeployment of their educational assistance programmes favouring basic education. None of the foregoing, of course, necessarily share all of the views expressed in the book.

Thanks are also due to Miss Sarah Waddell and Miss Elena Giglioli, who both typed the manuscript and helped with the collection of the material.

# Foreword

WILLIAM J. PLATT
*Director, Department of Planning and Financing
of Education, UNESCO**

A human being is born with a tremendous potential for learning. Systems of education are dedicated to helping realize that potential. In 1948 the General Assembly of the United Nations agreed: 'Everyone has the right to education' (Article 26 of the Universal Declaration of Human Rights). The fundamental building block for the right to education is primary education. This assertion would seem to hold even though arrangements other than formal primary education are in some use and may deserve a development complementary to that accorded primary education.

What can be said of collective performance and prospect against the world's commitment to the right to education? It is a world in which, as the International Development Strategy for the Second United Nations Development Decade says: 'the level of living of countless millions of people in the developing part of the world is still pitifully low. These people are often still undernourished, uneducated, unemployed and wanting in many other basic amenities of life'.† It is a world of finite, not unlimited resources. In this real world of the 1970s it is becoming clearer all the time that the fundamental building block of primary education has been neglected, that primary education has been inadvertently cast as Cinderella, to use Mr. Phillips's analogy. The International Commission for the Development of Education‡ agrees: 'universal basic education, in a variety of forms depending upon possibilities and needs, should be the top priority for educational policies in the 1970s'.

Thus it is timely to have Mr. Phillips's book. Here, between two covers, is a comprehensive mapping of much of the known and the unknown in basic education for that part of the world in which two-thirds of the world's population and three-quarters of its children live. It is a source book rather than a prescription.

In discussing the challenge of securing basic education for the hundreds of millions of children and adolescents who lack it, the author has concentrated upon school rather than out-of-school education, though he also discusses non-formal

---

* The views expressed here do not necessarily represent the position of Unesco.
† Resolution 2626 XXV, United Nations General Assembly, paragraph 3.
‡ E. Faure, *et al., Learning to Be*, Unesco-Harrap, 1972.

education as a supplement to the school system and has elsewhere presented the case for adult education in *Literacy and Development*, published by Unesco. His reasoning for concentrating on school education here derives from the time factor: whereas non-formal education undoubtedly has a major role to play in the future, the going will be slow. This is due partly to the weakness of governing infrastructure, compared to that existing for formal structures, and partly to the shortage of tested models of non-formal education which are widely known and are seen to be applicable.

Among Mr. Phillips's several contributions here to collective understanding of primary education is his emphasis on primary education as the basic learning cycle and not just as preparation for formal secondary schooling. Mr. Phillips helps us face the realities of the probability of the child in various developing countries completing four to eight or more years of schooling, given population projections, resource constraints, drop-out patterns and educational expenditure. One consequence of looking at this situation is to appreciate all the more how important it is that whatever feasible educational experience the child can have must be a meaningful one—one designed to produce successes, not failures. So long as primary education is viewed only as a screening process for a selective secondary school system, two distortions occur: (a) the screening function tends to operate to produce more failures (or drop-outs along the way) than successes; and (b) the content and ethic of the school are geared to preparation for performance in more schooling rather than for performance in the world outside the classroom.

Mr. Phillips spent many years working closely with Unesco, first as Director of Unesco's office of Analysis of the Role of Education in Development and later as consultant to both Unesco and Unicef in this subject. He speaks here with a clarity that should be helpful to policy makers, administrators, members of the teaching profession and the general public.

# Preface

The subject of this book is the large-scale educational poverty which exists at the primary or elementary level, affecting millions of children and youth in the developing countries of the world who are growing up illiterate.

Its purpose is to focus attention on the need for greater effort than that at present being applied to find solutions, on the size and difficulty of the task and on the possibilities and prospects.

The first part sets out the nature of the challenge and, after putting the problem in a historical perspective, shows the present trends in the quantity and quality of primary education available to the populations of the developing regions.

The second part, under the heading 'The Dynamics of Education Change', discusses the forces which influence the rate of progress in universalizing basic education and the introduction of reforms and innovations. These forces are seen to be social, political, economic and financial, as well as educational.

The third part discusses measures which can usefully be considered to hasten the universalization, if not of the full primary cycle over the next two decades, at least of minimum levels of elementary or basic education to fill the educational gap. Many of the measures would involve important innovations in the organization of educational systems as well as in the content and methods of teaching and learning and in the relation of education to the child's environment.

The conclusion is drawn that there is no technological revolution that can transform the plight of the mass of uneducated children, similar to the revolutions that have occurred in health, where massive declines in mortality have been achieved through modern technology. The task is seen as a long and vast one of educational and social engineering, the skills involved being predominantly those of educational organization. On a world perspective this is the biggest single challenge offered to the educational profession, especially to educational planners, but the effort applied in study, research and experimentation, and in the application of known solutions, is not commensurate.

A future in which this problem remained unsolved would certainly be a grim one for man at a time when material and mechanical innovations, as distinct from educational and social, are advancing so rapidly. The latest figures for Africa and Asia show that in 1971 and 72 the twenty-year trend by which enrolments outpaced population growth has now gone into reverse. The child population aged 5 to 9 grew twice as fast as enrolments for those years. This will lead before long, unless checked, to a massive increase in illiteracy among young adults of marrying age, and because of the link between education and family planning may contribute to a further population explosion instead of the forthcoming alleviation of population growth which the United Nations have estimated.

Prolonged economic recession would doubtless hold up universalizing basic education, in the way financial decisions are made at present; yet it is well to reflect that the whole yearly expenditure of the developing countries on primary education amounts to only about $1 \cdot 5$ per cent of their annual national product and, on a world scale, only a twentieth of the annual sales of the world's two largest automobile manufacturers. The problem has to be seen in a time span of twenty years during which there will be many economic fluctuations. No delay should take place now in planning the organizational changes and starting to create the additional inputs the programme requires.

The book is the result of much discussion, which is deeply appreciated, with educators in the developing countries, an ever-growing number of whom are interested in educational reform and innovation. As many ideas as possible have been brought together from different sources, so as to provide a frame of reference and encouragement to educational policy makers, administrators, staff of teacher training colleges and teachers at all levels.

# Contents

# *Part 1*

## THE PROBLEM

CHAPTER 1

# The Challenge

Of the problems, political, economic and social, which mankind faces, particularly dangerous is the growing gap in levels of living between the richer and the poorer nations. This gap covers all of the main ways in which people live, the level of income they have, the amount of food they get, their health and housing, and the education they receive.

Education alone cannot solve the world's problems; the famous phrase of H. G. Wells, that civilization is a race between education and disaster, went too far. Belief in education as an automatic civilizing force has declined as man's troubles have continued to mount in behavioural areas which education was typically supposed to affect, such as social responsibility and world peace and the reduction of violence and crime—though some will say this is the result of bad education. At the same time recent studies and research also undermine earlier optimistic claims as to the role of education in creating movement between social classes.

Those who believe today that education can change the course of civilization base their view less on automatic gains from education than on the possibilities of fundamental change in education itself; some like Paulo Freire see it as a direct means of intervening in favour of the 'oppressed' against 'oppressors' in unjust societies, though there is no consensus as to how this should be done.

Whatever may be the disappointment with the overall civilizing role of education, few will deny that nevertheless the spread of education to reach the world's illiterate masses remains one of the main hopes of stopping the excessive population growth and low productivity which threaten the future of the world economy as well as one of the chief means of creating a more socially just society.

The United Nations General Assembly in the Special Session in May 1974 reviewed the economic state of the world and produced a 'Declaration on the Establishment of a New Economic Order based on equity, sovereign equality, interdependence, common interest and cooperation among all States, irrespective of their economic and social systems, which shall correct inequalities and redress existing injustices, make it possible to eliminate the widening gap between the developed and the developing countries and ensure steadily accelerating economic and social development in peace and justice for present and future generations'.

This Special Session of the UN General Assembly was called because of the recent large increase of the world price of oil which is a serious setback to the economies of the developing countries other than the small minority which are producers of oil.

Events of this kind take their toll on educational development, but how much cannot now be assessed. However this may turn out, it is obvious that it is not possible in the long term to establish a new order based on equity, on the lines of the United Nations Resolution, if the poorer nations which make up the greater part of mankind continue to have vast numbers of their population growing up and entering adult life without a minimum of basic education. Economically this means a great loss of human resource potential; governmentally it makes much harder the task of administrative and political development which these countries face; socially it means tension between the educational privileged and the deprived; for the individual it means loss of dignity and of opportunity.

At the same time that these tensions about the future of world development have been growing, educational systems have been experiencing their own crisis. Demands for the democratization of education and its adjustment to meet technological progress are in collision with rigidities in educational structure and content in the present systems.

Some changes have been made in both the developed and the developing countries. However, if education is to keep up with the needs of society, let alone provide for the difficult future, much more reform and restructuring is required, especially for the task of creating universal education on a worldwide basis, which is the subject of this book.

The reason for special concern with the first or basic level of education is not only that it is the level which has the role of covering the whole population as their human right, though it fails badly in this at present. A further reason is that, for most of the people in the world, basic education is, and will be for a long time, the only education experience, and that the findings of educational psychologists point to the earlier rather than the later years of childhood as being the key time for learning and personality development.

In the developing countries making up the continents of Africa, Asia and Latin America, there were as at 1970 an estimated 269 million children aged 5–14 who were out of school in the sense of having never attended school or who left before completion. The number is expected on present trends to increase from 290 million in 1975 to 375 million in 1985.[1]

The causes are twofold. First, of the children who become enrolled in school, most drop out in the first two or three years. Secondly, large numbers of children do not attend school at all because there are no schools or school places, or because their parents (particularly in the case of girls) do not send them to school.

In drawing conclusions from these figures it is necessary to make an important distinction. It does not follow that it is necessary to create new places in schools for this number of pupils. To do so would imply that all children should be in school continuously for 10 years. If instead we think in terms of elementary education of 4 years duration, the number of additional places required is diminished to 71 million in 1975 rising to 92 million in 1985 owing to population growth. This would be a rough indication of the additional capacity required in terms of extra facilities to permit every person to have a four year education at some stage in his life between the ages of 5 and 14.

This is the position as regards quantity. But as will be discussed in later chapters, there is also a serious problem of poor quality and lack of relevance of the education given to those who do remain at school and complete the course; which makes the challenge threefold.

When we extend the age group to include young persons over the age of 14 but under the age of adulthood of 18 years we have to add 100 million youth growing up without a minimum basic education. There is thus a further need, namely for programmes in the shape of non-formal education which will recuperate their loss of schooling.

The countries with the largest numbers of children and youth below the educational poverty line are greatly handicapped by a severe lack of economic resources and the present high rates of growth of their school age populations. In the developing countries taken as a whole there is, according to the estimates of the United Nations and Unesco,[2] a major bulge in the rate of growth of the child population 0–4 years of age which began in the last part of the 1960s and which may cause their progress towards universal primary education, if it is envisaged on existing lines, to stagnate for a decade or more. Fortunately, according to the same estimates, the rate of growth of the number of children approaching school age will have dropped by a third by the 1980s from its present size and lightened the task thereafter. But at present African and Asian population growth exceeds that of enrolments.

A stagnation or regression of basic education for this length of time would be a serious blow to these countries' development, and it must be asked whether it is necessary to assume that basic education programmes have to remain on existing lines, or whether they can be reorganized so as to expand even during the population bulge and despite the financial difficulties of the current economic conjuncture.

The question is a fertile one for discussion since the problems of primary education have in general not had the attention they deserve hitherto; though interest in the reform of primary education is now mounting and, as we shall see later, important efforts are already being made in some countries.

The upsurge of popular aspirations in the developing countries on attaining independence led to a strong demand for universal education and in the 1950s and early 1960s long-term objectives were set both nationally and by Ministers of Education working with Unesco in regional conferences. This initial enthusiasm tended to be overtaken by the needs of second and higher level education for nation building and manpower purposes. Further, the long-term objectives were based on European types of educational structure and content which, it was becoming increasingly recognized, were not suited to the conditions of the developing countries. Little effort was made, however, through research and development and experimentation or by actual programmes to set up reformed systems more suited to needs. Thus in the middle and late 1960s, a visitor to the developing countries, whether discussing the educational plans of governments or examining research material, could not help but notice in most cases a poverty of attention to the elementary cycle making it so to speak the Cinderella of education.

However, the overall Development Strategy adopted by the General Assembly of the United Nations for the 1970s (The UN Second Development Decade), which had the active support of most of the developing countries, has since placed a major emphasis upon the better distribution within developing countries of the benefits of development. Increased efforts to universalize basic education are now, therefore, part of a new overall approach to development as defined at the highest international level.

Throughout what follows the words 'developed' and 'developing' countries will appear as in the usage of the United Nations,[1] under which the line of demarcation is 500 US dollars equivalent of national income per head of population. The United Nations themselves are the first to realize the weakness of such a line of demarcation, even as a working rule. The balance of advantage between countries, as between individuals, is obviously not solely distributed by level of income. Moreover, the word 'developing' does not cover the position of countries where income is not rising and development is stagnant. The usage in this case is a diplomatic euphemism since no country likes to be called less developed or underdeveloped.

By 'first level' or 'basic' education will be meant both primary education in school, especially the elementary part of the cycle where the primary cycle is a long one, and recuperative action, through non-formal education for youth who missed the necessary formal schooling. What is in mind is the minimum set of learning needs for the individual for function in his society and his physical environment.

In regard to the universalization of primary schooling, some commentators have taken up pessimistic positions and it is, therefore, necessary right from the start to ask whether this is an endemic situation not susceptible of remedy and whether the children and youth without schooling do in fact need a standard form of primary education in the circumstances in which they live.

The kind of education a child needs depends on the future more than on the present. If by a miracle the educationally deprived children all became literate tomorrow, there would be a shortage of reading material to keep them literate if they live in backward areas, as many do, and there is certainly in those areas a lack of employment in which literacy skills can be directly used.

The time perspective, however, is much further ahead than tomorrow. On the most favourable hypothesis, it would be the next decade or two, rather than the present one, which saw the number of children below the educational poverty line reduced to a small proportion of its present size, except for the least developed countries which cover only relatively small populations. Thus, in speaking of the use to which the education now lacking can be put, we have to look several decades ahead, when the children will be adult, and visualize higher levels of economic development than those now prevailing in the developing regions.

We have to see the issue as a long-term investment as well as a short term response to the individual's aspirations and needs. It is clear that without basic education a person is to a large degree cut off from participation in national society, from opportunities for personal development and from a human right.[3] He also lacks aptitudes for employment and for further education and training.

For the nation, failure to invest in basic education for all means a loss in its human resource potential and an obstacle to its progress. A heavy amount of illiteracy is an impediment to political life and to self-government. In earlier times illiteracy had the effect of keeping populations quiescent; today it is more likely to lead to frustration and tension.

It is true that a number of important production operations do not necessarily call for formal schooling, particularly in agriculture (and most of the educational gap is in rural areas), and that some agricultural economists argued at one time that illiteracy was not an obstacle to familiarizing farmers with the new varieties of production introduced in recent years, known as 'the green revolution'. Time has shown the error of this view, both because illiteracy has tended to limit the gains to the wealthier rather than the poorer farmers and because lack of education has a restraining effect upon what are called the 'second generation effects' of the green revolution (the possible indirect gains in economic activity in the surrounding communities). Numeracy, literacy and the discipline of a primary education are essential to economic as well as social development.

These rewards from basic education would be important but not necessarily urgent unless, as is the case, there were maturation periods involved before they can be reaped. Thus, since more education and the reduction of excessive birth rates tend to go together, education now will help to reduce future population growth, while the reduction of over-rapid population increase will advance the attainment of the target of universal education.

Moreover, in education, as in problems of pollution and exhaustion of natural resources, there are points of no return. Action today takes a long time-span to be fully effective. Today's children without education will in thirty to forty years' time constitute a large part of the citizens and labour force of the developing countries, at a time when their income per head is expected to have doubled and when technology and the means of communication have been greatly extended.

There are also political points of no return. Mr. MacNamara, the President of the World Bank Group, stated to the Joint World Bank—International Monetary Fund Annual Meeting in 1972:[4] 'When the highly privileged are few and the desperately poor are many—and when the gap between them is worsening rather than improving—it is only a question of time before a decisive choice must be made between the political costs of reform and the political risks of rebellion'.

What has been said about the importance of investment in primary education applies to countries and areas which have at least a minimum level of economic activity. The great majority of the world's educationally deprived children do in fact live in such areas and countries. The minority of children live in a number of least developed countries where the population size is relatively small but where, as will be seen later, a form of impasse seems to exist in most cases, both because of lack of resources and because of the almost total unsuitability of the present educational systems as vehicles of popular education.

Within the overall challenge of how to spread basic education for children and youth over the whole population, there is both a pedagogic and a social challenge. The social challenge is how to create at least minimum basic learning opportunities and educational attainments for the mass of the child population who at present leave school without completing the full primary cycle. The pedagogic challenge is how to make the primary level a sound basis for the rest of the educational pyramid. The primary cycles of most of the developing countries are not at present devised for this dual purpose.

The social task consists of meeting the human right to at least a minimum basic education. What is the minimum will vary from country to country, but overall it consists of literacy, numeracy and elementary knowledge of the environment, of health, of civics and of standard moral codes.

The human right extends also, though this is more difficult to define, to at least minimum educational opportunity, causing the social and the pedagogic challenges to overlap even at the level of minimum objectives, an overlap which grows as educational systems become more developed. Thus, however much emphasis is laid on the social objectives of universal basic education, there persists the structural problem of incorporating the two roles of primary education in the same system, since a two-tier system would defeat the right to opportunity. Much of the difficulty of educational reform, as we shall see in Part 3, centres on this issue. At present few educational systems resolve this problem; and the problem itself, as is indicated in Chapters 3 and 4 on current trends, is not yet adequately defined or reflected in the basic statistical data in use.

To many educators a two-stage system of primary education, even with the necessary opportunity ladders, may seem retrogressive and reminiscent of the class system of elementary schools for the poor prevailing in England and France in the last century. In an ideal sense this is undoubtedly so and it should be replaced by a full educational cycle for all as soon as possible. At present, however, as later chapters will show, it is not feasible to universalize the human right to education except by a shorter cycle which provides for the mass of drop-outs. For at least a decade or two the role of UPE (universal primary education) in bringing the mass of educationally deprived children above the educational poverty line probably has to be assumed by UBE (universal basic education), together with supporting services of a non-formal kind for the purpose of literacy retention and recuperation of drop-outs.

The needed balance between the social and the pedagogic efforts will differ according to each country's situation. A series of steps and stages in which rights to education and the supply possibilities have to be confronted, has to be inserted into the educational plan. In these steps and stages many points of view need expression, both scientific and human. The psychology of learning, for instance, argues for an early age of entry into primary education; but the study of local economic and social conditions frequently points to the advantages of later attendance and even intermittent education. Comes the demographic factor (the temporary bulge of the child population travelling up the age scale) and the balance for universalizing formal education is tipped heavily in favour of early age of entry, since the numbers are smaller and can be coped with, whereas the transient bulge cannot and has to be dealt with by other means.

Modern thinking is becoming increasingly interested in the idea of recurrent or lifelong education. In the developing countries progress in this sense will be limited by gaps in elementary education, since the idea presupposes there is a basic education of the individual on which to build. Nonetheless, scope exists for action in this sense in all but the most backward education systems and, as we shall see later, the principle of intermittent learning between formal and non-formal activities is one of the suggestions for reforming and renovating the primary cycle.

Another line of modern educational thought sees the community and the totality of the communications process as the real educational system and formal public education as a subsystem. This is based on research which shows that over half of what a child learns does not come from the school but from the home, other children, the mass media and the community. Studies made in the United States show that the average child spends as much time watching television as he spends in school. By the time he is sixteen he has watched television for 12,000 to 15,000 hours, not always with happy results.

In the developing countries the most influential external force is the community, television being rare though radio transistors are widespread. The need to relate education to the community, and to use it as a catalyst within it, is particularly important; many of the failures of rural primary education programmes are due to their being too much conceived and operated from outside the communities themselves. Interesting examples of efforts by French educational assistance experts in Africa to promote basic education through the forces in the villages themselves are discussed later.

The recent report, *Learning To Be*, prepared by the International Commission on Educational Development, set up by Unesco and presided over by Mr. Edgar Faure,[5] has given an important impetus to many progressive ideas and it has also recommended that basic education should be the top priority for the 1970s in the following terms:

Recommendation

Universal basic education, in a variety of forms depending on possibilities and needs, should be the top priority for educational policies in the 1970s.

Comment

Considerable progress towards giving all people in the world a primary education has already been made. This is a long-range effort, and it must, of course, be continued. However, it would also seem possible to find a remedy for many of the harmful effects of this situation on the present generation by judiciously balancing several solutions: complete, full-time primary education; complete, part-time or 'appropriate rhythm primary education; incomplete elementary education for children and adults; and special teaching programmes for young people aged between 12 and 16, especially for those who have not previously attended school.

Solutions of this kind cannot be applied in the same way in all countries and are obviously of especial economic, financial and social significance to developing countries, although some are not devoid of interest for developed nations as well. Education in alternating periods, for example, can yield very positive results, while appropriate rhythm instruction, the effect of which is usually to spread primary and post-primary studies over a longer period, may help to solve the delicate problem of the age at which a student enters active life, a problem causing concern to educators and governments virtually everywhere.

The rapid expansion of education in the developing countries in the early 1960s coincided with the emergence of a new discipline, contributed to by both educators and economists, namely, the planning of education for economic and social development. The result for primary education was not particularly favourable since secondary education was regarded as a greater contributor to the economy than primary.

The outlook on priorities, however, is changing today in view of unemployment among secondary school leavers and the new emphasis being placed on social factors in development. We find economists reporting that the economic return on investment on primary education is greater than in the second and higher levels in a high proportion of countries studied.

Greater investment in primary education is also regarded as an important contribution to better income distribution in the developing countries, which is one of the main preoccupations of the United Nations Development Strategy. Adler, the Director of the Programming and Budgeting Department of the World Bank, in an article in the journal of the International Monetary Fund and the World Bank Group on means, including education, of attacking the prime causes of the unevenness of income distribution, writes:[6]

> It is clear the considerations of income distribution indicate that rural primary education should receive the highest priority, to be followed by the provision of education and training at the secondary level for the staff of agricultural extension services, and perhaps by non-formal adult education aiming at the rural population. This suggestion runs counter to the preference that in recent years development economists and educational experts have given to secondary education and vocational training.

The rate of return studies are, of course, based upon primary education as it exists with all its weaknesses; and one cannot help but be impressed by its potential if, as is possible, its productivity were greatly improved. It has been suggested that further spread of the present system should be held back pending the improvement of its cost efficiency. But efficiency in economic and pedagogic terms is not the only perspective, nor is it meaningful without a closer appreciation of local living conditions and local aspirations. These can usually only be changed gradually and by education combined with some tangible economic progress.

What education opportunity means in human terms at the local level is clear to anyone who has seen the children left out, and often waiting outside schools, while the fortunate ones go to classes. It is true that the lessons may be taught by simple repetition and that the teachers may fail to evoke curiosity in their pupils. But school attendance is highly prized locally and parents go to great sacrifice to provide for the schooling of their children. It gives prestige and is a form of socialization. Moreover, teaching by the verbal repetition method is frequently the only available means because there are no textbooks; and teachers do not evoke curiosity because their own education is poor and they would be asked questions they could not answer and would lose status. The matter has to be seen not only as a problem of pedagogic efficiency but also as a social and human issue and part of a development conjuncture which educators can influence but not control.

A mixture of the range of influences we have mentioned, pedagogic, economic, social and psychological, together with the pressures of a largely uncontrolled educational expansion on national budgets, have led many Ministers of Education to become much concerned with the need for educational reform and regeneration. Certainly, reforms hitherto have been small and slow and strong pressures are rising for more 'democratization' of the structure of education, of its content and of the opportunities it provides.

Further, it is true that education is one of the sectors where there have not been any major technological breakthroughs like those which have overcome disease or raised agricultural productivity sharply (the 'green revolution', for instance). Is one possible? An increasing number of educators are asking whether the classroom of a group of children of the same age, a blackboard and chalk, and out-of-date text-books are the instrumentalities required, or whether there are not fundamentally new and better educational patterns to be found.

Even if they are right and can be set to work at once to bring about change, the problem does not start with a *tabula rasa*. The past has made heavy preemptions on the future, as we shall see from the next chapters, and much of the difficulty of the challenge is the need for introducing changes in quality, structure and organization at the same time that a quantitative expansion is still needed and the world is facing rapid change. The educational profession is likely to have great demands placed upon its imaginative and inventive skills. The profession has to see itself as taking part in a great endeavour of educational and social engineering and to extend its range of vision.

It is possible to see in low-income countries schools with excellent equipment and highly trained teachers using the latest methods of learning in groups, peer teaching, individualized instruction etc., but within a few yards of the school less fortunate children of the same age working uninstructed, in the fields. These modernized schools represent perhaps 1 per cent of the country's total. In England, where modern methods in primary education have a stronger footing than in most countries, modernized schools are just under half of the total. To achieve this proportion it has taken twenty-five years and considerable local autonomy. Innovators, formed in teacher training colleges as students, manage to put their ideas into practice twenty-five years later when they become headmasters. Innovation is the hardest and most obdurate part of the challenge.

One of the most important fields into which governments and the educational profession will need to extend their vision is to meet the needs of older children and youth who missed primary education earlier. Some of these are in primary schools, although over age, but most need to be catered for by non-formal education such as that given in functional literacy projects linked to the work environment, or in youth clubs and other local out-of-school educational services which can be developed.

Unfortunately, the facilities of this kind are few, though valuable examples exist, and most are for older children and youths who are already literate. There is clearly no easy solution at the youth and adult level to replacing the previous deficiency of primary education.

In *New Paths to Learning*,[7] a study prepared for Unicef by the International Council for Educational Development, it is stated:

> Because of the incomplete development of their formal educational systems, non-formal education falls heir to the mammoth 'unfinished business' of the primary and secondary schools. It inherits a vast clientele of children and youth who have never been to school or have dropped out before finishing, or have completed primary school but have not gone on to secondary. And for a large portion of this clientele, non-formal education has to start virtually from scratch, by providing the 'three Rs'.

The matter is put in proportion in a later statement in the study:

> Yet even these relatively large programmes serve but a fraction—at best no more than 10 per cent—of all out-of-school adolescents and youth in the particular country. This picture remains substantially the same even if the clienteles of other smaller non-formal programmes are added to the total. One estimate suggests that the proportion of rural youth in organized out-of-school activities may be as low as 1·5 per cent.

From the evidence given in the study, non-formal education could play a much more important part than at present in basic education and the present small efforts should be extended and intensified, especially for programmes of recuperation. But to do this on any large scale would take a long time and the children cannot wait that long. There is no escape from the challenge of improving, renovating and extending the formal system; it is to this subject that most of the book is devoted, though non-formal education is also discussed as a means of interlocking support to the formal system.

The problem is larger than can be met by one profession or discipline, and the social worker who can reduce drop-out is reducing the number of illiterates as much as the teacher. The challenge therefore falls heavily upon those concerned with the important aspects of child development, other than education, that closely affect a child's learning power. More equity and opportunity in education means helping to reduce the obstacles of poor conditions of child welfare in the home, of malnutrition and of ill health. Child development should be seen in an integrated fashion. This is difficult to implement since government machinery is not organized in this way, but progress in this direction, notably through Unicef's influence, is on the move. The challenge also falls upon parents, and through them the local communities; parent education and the reduction of discrimination should figure in all programmes for universal primary education.

The problem, especially the need for innovation, also requires resources and information going beyond national boundaries. There is therefore a challenge falling upon the suppliers of educational aid. Although some 2000 million US dollars equivalent moves yearly in educational aid from the developed to the developing countries, it is too much in a standard pattern and insufficiently devoted to catalysing and experimenting with new solutions, and little goes to primary education.[8] There is a major task of redeployment of aid which is a challenge to the suppliers of aid, bilateral and multilateral, and assistance for innovation is required to help the developing countries to experiment and take risks. A similar challenge applies to the voluntary effort by the world's non-governmental organizations, which contribute annually some 400 million dollars to education in the less developed regions. Their projects are sometimes more realistic and closer to local conditions than those of governmental agencies; but they are necessarily scattered in their impact and usually not linked to the country's educational plan. The World Council of Churches administers a substantial programme of its own and also puts out much useful material on educational renovation and regeneration.

Thus we come to the final part of the challenge, the individual educator. In the final analysis, progress depends on the teaching force and, therefore, on the training, status and remuneration which each country confers upon it. An essential part of innovation and renovation must be a new approach to the problems of teachers and to the closely linked financial difficulties posed by the fact that nine-tenths of the costs of primary education are made up by teacher's salaries. The evidence on the use of new media, such as television and radio, is that they do not reduce the need for teachers. They improve quality and cost-effectiveness provided they are accompanied by teacher training.

The difference between a good school and a bad school, even with poor resources, is often to be attributed to the headmaster and his staff, and between the performance of classes and pupils, to the individual teacher. Society is not reflecting in its rewards to primary school teachers the results of the rate of return findings by economists which we have mentioned; too often it is a second-best occupation performed by teachers who would like, but have not received, an adequate training.

We should not leave the present chapter on the challenge of primary education at the world level without some reflections, which are sombre, upon the future.

Few prognostications of the futurologists are optimistic, either for human values or for man's welfare in the light of the rapid growth of population in relation to resources. For a discussion of alternate educational futures at an OECD Conference a background paper states:[9]

Indeed, the very forecasts, whether emanating from Delphi procedures or from more conventional trend extrapolation, which the Syracuse Centre is employing now in the construction of pictures of the future, are so dismal with respect to the likelihood of survival of human values as to call into question society's will and ability to invent the social and political institutions—and to promote changes in underlying human attitudes and behaviours—barely adequate to control and reverse these ecological developments. We are thus confronted with the role and function of educational systems: in what ways might education contribute to the development of attitudes and skills appropriate for supporting, perhaps engendering, fundamental systems breaks and the social, political, and human experimentation which may now be called for?

If we turn to the grandmaster of futurology, who predicted the atomic bomb and whose moving roadways and stationary vehicles we are still awaiting, we find that in several of his books, Wells saw a future in which an elite lived in the luxury of an extraordinarily advanced technology, while elsewhere a great mass of semi-serfs led a restricted proletarian life of servicing the towers in which the elite masters pursued an intellectual and scientific existence, descending occasionally to the intermediate pleasure cities.

This gives us a future perspective for the world similar to that Disraeli found for England in 1870 when he described the country as consisting of two nations, the rich and the poor, one of the subsequent pieces of corrective action to which was the introduction of universal public primary education a year or two later.

The basic cause of this perspective is the ever-growing gap between the richer and the poorer nations of the world. But there are also educational factors since, as we saw, primary education affects both economic growth and population increase and could greatly affect value systems.

In the *Unicef News* of April 1973 there is an article by Balcomb of Unicef in which he writes:

> According to a brilliant analysis presented by Mr. Feroze Rangoonwalla (of *Film* magazine) at a recent panel meeting on satellite television, the hero of the typical Hindi film is a likeable, passive young man. The heroine is a likeable, passive (and very good looking) young woman. The villain is the active type—the only person who practises 'scientific method', according to Mr. Rangoonwalla—and for about the first hour and a half of the film he does very well for himself. Scientific method loses out in the long run, however, for in the last reel the hero always triumphs through some completely gratuitous stroke of luck or fortune. It is all very good as wish-fulfilment fantasy, but wish-fulfilment fantasies are about the last thing India needs at this stage of its development.

The final comment is, of course, justified in the sense that if scientific method remains the villain there will be little economic development, the real villain being poverty. But prejudice against the scientific method does not exist without reason.

The scientific method is too often presented in the form of violent films and other crude expressions of emotional frustration. The increase in violence and antisocial behaviour which has appeared in many school children in developed countries has not yet reached an equal magnitude in the developing countries, though much child delinquency of various kinds exists in cities and shanty towns. There is a greater sense of non-material values, which, as recent trends have shown, is having considerable appeal to children of the technologically advanced countries. The persistence of this appeal shows that it is not simply a temporary cult or fashion, but reflects a need. (It is interesting to note that in a recent year more than half of the US Peace Corps volunteers in Thailand decided to stay and make their homes in the rural villages.)

Thus there is a challenge to educators both of the West and of the East of how to assist western children to experience the values of the great historical cultures of the East and of how to help children of the East to adopt motivations for a wider economic and social progress and the use of science to overcome poverty, without destroying important value systems.

A number of people in the industrialized societies, disappointed by the contradiction of development policies with the teachings of the great religions and philosophies, and conscious of the over-expending of the resources of the biosphere and the problems of pollution, are now aspiring to more value-pervaded lives conducted within the conditions of limited economic growth. But while limited economic growth may be good for the rich countries it is anathema to those which are still plagued by poverty.

New approaches to global development have therefore to be found in which the removal of poverty and the limitation of abundance involving waste are joint objectives. Since the bulk of the population who will have to resolve these problems is still at school, education faces a special challenge, unlike any it has yet met. Of course, how far education can play a dominant role in society is a question to which there has been as yet no universal answer.

The future will no doubt increasingly bring electronic devices to the aid of education. In a book published by the OECD (CERI),[10] results are given of a research and design project of the educational facilities laboratory at Rice Institute. It states:

Technology will exert an influence on education out of all proportion to the influence it present exerts. Among the technologies designed were drive-in education, the motorized carrel, the shoulder carrel, and the town brain. All of these technological innovations and developments were explored quite free of possible constraints imposed by social, political, and economic modalities in the future.

The shoulder carrel, for example, is a private, air-conditioned, electronically-controlled booth, mounted on the student's shoulders and designed for use either at home or in school. The carrel would bring to the student a vast library of data, electronically retrieved and individually controlled, thus in direct competition and contrast with person-to-person teaching. The carrel weighs about 20 pounds, and incorporates such instruction media as UHF–VHF TV, tapes, records, computer connection, two-way radio, telephone, slide projectors and screens.

On the other side of this individualized electronic man–machine symbiosis is the town brain for transmitting 'learning' to town residents of all ages. The town brain is a central computer bank, monitoring and programming centre which is electronically hooked up with a variety of audio-visual, computer-assisted communications links ranging from individual, hand-carried consoles, to home installed consoles, to portable conference units and mobile teaching units which permit the development of a total, comprehensive education system, independent of classrooms, lecture halls and permanent school buildings.

Some experts have gone so far as to see a golden age for education dawning through electronics. It seems more probable, however, that, while there will be an increase in knowledge-communicating machines of this kind, there is unlikely to be any general acceptance of educational methods which run contrary to a humanist conception of education based on person-to-person contact. This contact will no doubt be very heavily aided by audio-visual measures. But a future in which a data bank on a child's shoulder is a major educational instrument rather than an occasional interesting aid seems unlikely.

Soviet pedagogues are sceptical of mechanical educational technology even of a less 'futuristic' nature, partly, it would appear, for social reasons. Markouchevitch and Petrovsky in their paper[11] for the International Commission on Education write:

> With all respect to those who have drawn attention to the possible uses of computers, television sets with feedback, etc., it seems to us that there is room for considerable scepticism as concerns the very widespread notion of 'technological determinism', according to which the widespread use of technical innovations would of itself bring about a peaceful solution of the most acute social problems of education, such as those pinpointed by highly qualified experts like Skorov, Shubkin, Coombs and others.

A long period of time would, in any event, be required for such technologies to develop and take root in the developing countries. It would seem clear that there is no *deus ex machina* to be wheeled onto the stage in the form of modern technology, at least for a long time, and that education must raise itself up by its own bootstraps. The main leverage is likely to remain for many years the reorganization of educational objectives, content, structure and methods, the training and re-education of teachers, the use of current types of audio-visual media and the improvement of educational management in order that the existing systems may function more effectively and that no opportunities for reform and innovation be overlooked.

Education is the process which bridges the generations; it both passes on old values and creates new ones. The educational planner, therefore, has to be alert both to the causation of the past and the aspirations of the future. Like a centre-forward he has to move towards the goal but also to glance backwards to see where the passes are coming from. We will therefore in the next chapter take a short look at the historical picture to see how and why the developing countries are in their present educational predicament.

The look backward should not obscure the extent of the change taking place today in the prevalent notions both of development and of education. The dominant idea of the 1960s had been that the emerging countries should follow the western model of capital accumulation, both material and human, and technological progress which would bring about more or less automatic changes in their social and economic structures. In this effort education gave the basis for human capital formation, social mobility and increased opportunity for the population.

As we shall see in later chapters this notion is being challenged by the view that with the present way the economies and social structures and educational systems in most of the developing countries work, no such automatic progress is taking place. Employment is not growing as hoped and basic education for conditions outside the wage sector, as well as within, is needed.

Behind many of the purely technical and educational factors there looms the search for new objectives and models different from those at present existing either in developed or developing countries. Julius Nyerere, President of Tanzania, who is both a politician and an educator, stated at the Dag Hammarskjold seminar held in May 1974 in Dar-es-Salaam:

> But I sometimes suspect that for us in Africa, the underlying purpose of education is to turn us into Black Europeans, or Black Americans. I say this because our educational policies make it quite clear that we are really expecting education in Africa to enable us to emulate the material achievements of Europe and America. This is the object of our activity.
>
> We have not begun to think seriously about whether such material achievements are possible. Nor have we begun to question whether the emulation of European and American material achievements is a desirable objective. I believe that these two matters are now in urgent need of our consideration.

Many of these ideas are only in the formative stage and have not permeated opinion in the developing countries let alone been implemented on a large scale. In the same speech the President stated: 'Parents, politicians, and workers, as well as educators, are suspicious of, or hostile to the educational innovations required. But the total result is that few of our schools are really an integral part of the village life, except in the sense that they occupy village children for so many hours a day'.

If this is true of Tanzania which is one of the few countries where a major effort has already been made under high leadership for seven years, how much more is it true elsewhere? It is becoming increasingly clear that the key to development lies in social factors and the commitments of individuals and that without this, material capital and technology benefit only the more privileged sections of the economy, as well as incurring a good deal of inefficiency and waste. If basic education is not itself the prime agent of such commitment, it is at least a necessary condition for it.

The concern of the book is with 93 different countries and everything that is said cannot be applicable to all of them. There are both resemblances and considerable variations in their educational systems and in their states of development and cultural and political history. To enable the reader to see the position of the different countries in a broad perspective there is set out at the end of the book an appendix which gives the 15 main educational, economic and fiscal indicators available for each country and which puts them in the order of rank for basic education. This gives the statistical position, but behind the statistics lies each country's particular education history and its own internal dynamic or hesitancy on the cultural and sociopolitical issues involved, of which some principal variations between countries are discussed in Chapter 5.

Some will feel rightly that great emphasis must be placed upon the integration of education with local work possibilities and on change in educational content and methods to meet new needs. Stress has been placed upon getting as many children as possible into school and retaining them long enough to acquire an adequate minimum education because it is useless to worry about what to teach in school unless the schools are there and the children attend. It does not mean that an all-out attack is not also needed on improvement of content and method, both because restructuring the system to increase quantity means changed content, and because of the irrelevance of much current teaching to local needs. Local learning needs have to be diagnosed and met in new ways, as discussed in Chapters 9 to 12.

Some, too, will wish to stress that a nation cannot be built on minimum education. The upper part of the primary cycle and lower secondary, which provide the manpower for the skilled trades are indeed very important. What is required is a balanced educational expansion related to development. But at present the balance seems, in most developing countries, to be tilted too little towards improving and extending elementary education. In our later chapter on planning we suggest some ways and means of reconciling these two needs in each country. Our proposals for universalizing minimum basic education do not damage the upper part of the cycle, but restrict when necessary its rate of growth relative to the elementary part in the interest of universal basic education.

Others may feel that the work of the educational philosophers, and of Illich and Freire who wish to revolutionize education, or society through education, are dismissed too readily in the chapter on innovations where their theories are described as impracticable and coming either too late or too soon upon the world scene. If this is true it is because our immediate concern in this book is with children here and now under a variety of educational and political systems, since as we saw earlier population is mounting and time is running out. We have therefore tried to keep our eye on the unhappy child standing outside a school in which there is no place, the over-burdened and untrained teacher struggling to educate in poor premises and lacking teaching materials, and the Minister of Education arguing for a large allotment, rather than on long-run philosophical issues.

Some will feel, and they will be justified, that not enough has been said in the book of the contribution to be made by modern educational psychology. To some extent this is because of the prior need to solve the macro-educational questions of policy and administration. However, the findings of modern psychologists should also influence macro-educational plans on such matters as the best age of entry, the layout of schools, the structure of the curriculum, and whether as in the USSR a three-year rather than a four-year elementary cycle is possible, the application of the three-year cycle having been preceded by intensive research. More studies of these questions in the context of the developing countries are greatly needed and Chapter 11 outlines a number of these requirements.

## REFERENCES

1. These figures are based on the age-specific enrolment percentages (i.e. the percentage of children in each of the years 5 to 14 who are at school) shown in the *Unesco Statistical Yearbook* for 1972. The existing provision of a continuous education of at least four

years, and the deficit, is shown by the size of the highest continuous four-year percentage peak over the range of the years 5 to 14.

2. *The World Population Situation in 1970* (UN Sales No. E. 71. XIII 2); and *Towards Accelerated Development* (UN Sales No. E. 70. II A 2).
3. *The Universal Declaration of Human Rights* proclaimed by the United Nations General Assembly in 1949; and the *Declaration of the Rights of the Child* (General Assembly Resolution 1386 (XIV), 1959). See also *The Right to Education* by Louis Francois, Unesco, 1968.
4. 'Finance and development', *World Bank and International Monetary Fund Review*, September 1973.
5. *Learning To Be: The World of Education Today and Tomorrow*, Report of the International Commission on the Development of Education, Unesco-Harrap, 1972, p. 192.
6. See Reference 4.
7. *New Paths to Learning*, Philip H. Coombs with Roy C. Prosser and Manzoor Ahmed; Barbara Baird Israel, editor. Prepared for Unicef by the International Council for Educational Development, 680 Fifth Avenue, New York, 1973, pp. 26 and 56.
8. *Planning Educational Assistance for the Second Development Decade*, H. M. Phillips, Unesco: IIEP, 1973, pp. 23–29.
9. Background papers for the *OECD Conference on Policies for Educational Growth*, OECD, 1970.
10. *Alternative Educational Futures in the United States and Europe*, OECD (CERI), 1972, p. 96.
11. *Where is Education Heading?*, A. I. Markouchevitch and A. V. Petrovsky, Unesco, International Commission on the Development of Education, Series B, No. 4, 1971, p. 8.

## SELECTED FURTHER READING

*Our Moral Involvement in Development*, Jean-Marie Domenach, United Nations Centre for Economic and Social Information, New York, 1971.
*The Challenge of World Poverty*, Gunnar Myrdal, Penguin Books, 1970.
*The Quality of Education in Developing Countries*, C. E. Beeby, Harvard University Press, 1966.
*The World Educational Crisis*, Philip H. Coombs, Oxford University Press, London, 1968.
*International Targets for Development*, ed. Richard Symonds, Harper and Row, New York, 1970.
*International Development Strategy*, United Nations, New York, 1970.
*Partners in Development*, Lester B. Pearson, Praeger, New York, 1969.
*Strategy for Children*, Unicef, 1969. United Nations Publication 67. IV. 29.
*Initiatives in Education, A World Profile for 1971–72*, International Bureau of Education, Unesco: IBE, 1972.
*The World Social Situation*, United Nations (E/CN5/456/Add 13), 1971.
*The Case for Development*, six papers by the United Nations Centre for Economic and Social Information, Praeger, New York, 1973.
'Education and the making of modern nations', ed. Frank Sutton, in *Education and Political Development*, ed. James S. Coleman, Princeton University Press, 1965.
*The Rise of the Schooled Society*, David Wardle, Routledge, and Kegan Paul, London, 1974.
*The World Development Plan, A Swedish Perspective*, Ernst Michanek, Dag Hammarskjold Foundation, Uppsala, Sweden.
*Literacy and Development*, H. M. Phillips, Unesco, 1970.

20

*Let My Country Awake,* Malcolm S. Adiseshiah, Unesco, 1970.

*Report on Children,* United Nations, 1971.

*Education and Development Reconsidered,* The Bellagio Conference Papers, Ford Foundation/Rockefeller Foundation, ed. F. Champion Ward, Praeger, 1974.

*Education,* Sector Working Paper, published by World Bank, December 1974.

*Attacking Rural Poverty, How Non-formal Education Can Help,* Philip Coombs with Manzoor Ahmed, A World Bank publication, The Johns Hopkins University Press, 1974.

*Education in Africa. What Next?* Dragoljub Najman, Foreword by Amadou Mahtar M'Bow, 1972.

CHAPTER 2

# The Historical Perspective

A hundred years ago primary education was far from universal among the child population of the advanced countries, although it was widespread in the states of Prussia, Denmark, Norway and the Netherlands, which had established systems of universal primary education in the earlier part of the century. Education had been traditionally in the hands of religions, guilds or philanthropic organizations, except where it was part of the business of private schools, and many children were unable to profit from these facilities. The basic doctrine was that education was the responsibility of parents and that charitable organizations helped parents who could not afford education for their children.

In France, the United Kingdom and the United States, and in the other advanced countries, there had been a good deal of heart-searching about public responsibility for primary education, but it was not until the last decades of the century that systems of universal, publicly financed, primary education were made operative.

The causes of the delay in those countries, compared with the progress in Prussia and Denmark are clear from the historical material on the subject, particularly rich in the case of England, though there are also interesting indications from other countries.

Various points of view appear. Some regarded mass education as a threat to privilege; others saw in it a means of averting threats to the existing order of society by making the population more orderly and unified (this view was connected with the pressure for the universal right to vote); still others saw in it a positive means of raising national prosperity and increasing the welfare of the population.

The 'threat to privilege' viewpoint is illustrated by the comment of Robert Lower on the legislation introduced in the first part of the century to provide education for poor children, which stated: 'We do not profess to give these children an education that will raise them above their station and business in life—that is not our object—but to give them an education that may fit them for that business'.

The view that mass education was needed to create a healthily unified population is reflected by James Mill writing in the earlier part of the century: 'The minds, therefore, of the great body of the people are in danger of really degenerating, while the other elements of civilization are advancing, unless care is taken, by means of the other instruments of education, to counteract those effects which the simplification of the manual processes has a tendency to produce'.

Adam Smith in his Wealth of Nations, written at the end of the eighteenth century stated that, 'An instructed and intelligent people are always more decent and orderly than an ignorant and stupid one . . . they are more disposed to examine, and more capable of seeing through, the interested complaints of factions and sedition, and they are, upon this account, less apt to be misled into any wanton or unnecessary opposition to the measures of the government'. Diderot in the eighteenth century in France wrote: 'A peasant who knows how to read and write is more difficult to oppress'.

The exceptional progress by Prussia and Denmark can perhaps be explained in two ways; first, by the strong influence of the Reformation and the Protestant emphasis on education as a means of Bible-reading and self-improvement, in material as well as in spiritual matters; secondly, by the Toynbeean challenge and response situation which the two countries experienced.

In the case of Prussia, the loss of large territories, following Napoleon's victories, and the terms of the peace treaty, restricting the size of her army and imposing a heavy debt, caused a sharp patriotic response. This included the establishment of universal primary education under secular control—an asset which later influenced the superiority of the organization and discipline of the Prussian armies when in 1870 they defeated France, which was still without universal primary education.

In the case of Denmark, the challenge followed her defeat by Prussia in the 1860s and was also of an economic nature. The opening up of the farmlands of the North American continent threatened Denmark's traditional form of agricultural exports and it had to reorganize and redevelop its economy in the direction of the non-concentrated type of agriculture (dairy farming, etc.) which has been the base of its remarkable prosperity since. Danish leaders in their response to this threat attached, with much foresight, great importance to the spread of education to raise the productive capacity and adaptability of the population.

In the Netherlands, a state plan for primary education had been adopted in the Republic of Batavia in 1806 which was later extended in 1815 to the whole of the newly created kingdom, which included Belgium. The system consisted of parallel Protestant, Catholic and secular schools, as it still exists in the Netherlands.

In Italy in 1859, the Kingdom of Savoy, in the process of throwing off foreign rule and annexing much of Italy, adopted the Casati Law and four years of primary education was made compulsory in all towns with a population of over four thousand. The state, however, gave no financial support and public opinion was not roused to the need; in fact, the little achievement there was fell short of Casati's ambition and illiteracy remained a serious problem down to modern times, especially in the south.

At the time of its defeat by Prussia in 1870, France, as we have mentioned, still had a limited system of primary education despite the Daunou Law, passed by the National Assembly in 1795. This had required secular primary schools to be set up in the larger centres of the population, but Napoleon, when he came to power, allowed primary education to remain with the churches and private societies. In 1833 a law was passed establishing a national system of primary schools of an elementary kind and not integrally related to secondary and higher education. As in

England, the tendency was for there to be one type of education for the privileged and another for the poor. By the end of the century, however, a complete primary system was in existence, springing from the primary education laws of 1881 and 1886 which included optional programmes after the sixth and seventh school year to prepare for progress up the educational ladder into the second level or into employment.

In the United Kingdom the growth of commerce and empire had been matched by the development of a private upper and middle class education which served its purpose effectively. For the mass of the working class, however, in the early years of the nineteenth century, there was no form of public provision, except in a few areas, and the schools which existed were run by the church or philanthropic organizations. The prohibition of child labour under the Factory Acts imposed on the community the problem of what to do with the children who no longer worked; the first primary education legislation to attack this problem was passed in 1833. It was not until 1870 that the basis for modern secular public education was laid by the Education Act of that year, which created local school boards assisted by government grants and made universal elementary education compulsory, allowing the private schools to retain their place in the system, subject to regular official inspection. Scotland, which had separate provisions of its own for education, was considerably in advance of England and Wales throughout the century.

In the United States the first settlers gave high priority to education, both for religious reasons and because of its clear role in aiding the establishing of a new society—the church and the school being usually the first centres of the new settlement. Thomas Jefferson submitted to the state legislature of Virginia in the eighteenth century *A Plan for the Diffusion of Knowledge* which pleaded for universal primary education. Support for education at public expense was organized by volunteer groups and schools were set up, as in England, by private societies with supplementary funds supplied by local authorities. By the end of the nineteenth century every state was providing free secular primary education at public expense.

In Russia there had been the curious episode of the imperial sanction given by Catherine the Second in 1786 to a plan which a government commission had prepared for a system of primary education in all cities and large towns, with provision for teacher training and educational aids. This came to nothing and it was not until the freeing of the serfs in 1861 that some effective steps were taken with the establishment of elected district bodies with power to set up schools on the basis of funds raised by local taxation. This effort, however, only touched the fringe of the matter, and a massive national problem of 70 per cent illiteracy was allowed to continue into the twentieth century until the Soviet regime took over.

The Soviet viewpoint was expressed vividly in a statement issued in 1920 by the Perm Guvernia Extraordinary Committee of the USSR for the Elimination of Illiteracy, which said, 'An illiterate person has hundreds of enemies: epidemics, hunger, disorder, humiliation'. Education was also seen, as it also had been earlier in Prussia and in Japan, as an instrument of political influence.

There followed an education programme of remarkable dimensions which not only brought a system of compulsory four year primary education into operation very rapidly, but also eliminated adult illiteracy among the working population over a period of some fifteen to twenty years. It included most of the Asian populations in the former Czarist colonies with their multiplicity of mother tongues. This was achieved by giving education priority over other claims on social development, notably housing and health, to which funds were switched progressively as educational expansion was achieved.

In Japan in the 1870s the Emperor, restored to power in 1868, was already beginning to use education as an influence for national unity and to face the prospect of opening up Japan, hitherto a closed society, to the rest of the world. A series of laws were enacted, based on the Imperial Oath of Five Articles, to which the Emperor was to adhere. The educational article read: 'Knowledge should be sought throughout the world so that the welfare of the empire may be promoted'. A Department of Education was created in 1870 and the 1872 Fundamental Code of Education stated: 'There shall in the future be no community with an illiterate family, or a family with an illiterate person'. The *Imperial Rescript on Education*, issued in 1890, defined the basic purpose of the elementary school as character building, piety to family and state, and emperor worship. Six year compulsory schooling was introduced in 1907, the previous course being of four years. Children receiving elementary education made up 25 per cent of the population of those of school age in 1870, 46 per cent in 1886, 81 per cent in 1900 and 95 per cent in 1906.

In other parts of Asia the situation was largely static, owing to the failure of most areas to achieve identity in the form of national states and to the influence of colonialism, while China was still living in a mature form of feudalism. Primary education in Asia was in the hands of the religions, some of which, as in the case of Buddhism and Islam, made an impressive impact on literacy through teaching conducted in schools designed primarily to expand the religion and permit the reading of the sacred texts; or it was the prerogative of the law-makers, the nobles and the servicing groups they retained' or of the small class of merchants and businessmen engaged in commerce.

In Africa, education was extremely limited and associated with the very small numbers who were in contact with Islam over the land routes and later with Europeans in the ports or administrative centres already starting to be set up in those parts of Africa which were colonized. But basically the continent as a whole was still completely underdeveloped and tribal. African potential, though great, was late in being mobilized.

In Latin America the attainment of liberation early in the century gave rise to the same type of aspirations as emerged at the time of the French Revolution. As in the case of the Daunou Law in France, implementation of these aspirations proved difficult because of internal political problems. During most of the century, colonial subjection was replaced by internal domination by the landed classes of European origin which had declared their independence. Little, accordingly, was done to secure education for the mass of the population, great numbers of whom spoke indigenous languages and were living in extremely poor conditions. As the century closed and the twentieth century developed, many efforts by central governments to spread primary education encountered structural problems which they were unable to resolve because programmes initiated centrally had to be implemented in localities where the distribution of political and social power distorted their implementation. The story of Latin American primary education was really a twentieth century process which took place most rapidly in the countries which received large numbers of European immigrants, such as Argentina and Chile, and in Mexico when the results of the Revolution became consolidated.

It will be seen that what history shows is that among the advanced countries the idea of universal primary education has emerged at various times in different countries as a response to religious, social, economic or political challenges felt by states and governments, rather than to pressure by parents. It led to legislation making it at first an obligation on towns or communities to provide schools, followed in due course by further legislation to make it free and secular.

In France and the United Kingdom, both relative latecomers to universal and free primary education, the availability of education and the structure of what primary education existed had had a strong class differentiation, which received corrective action more slowly in France, where the social structure was more rigid. In Japan too, the extension of primary education was unaccompanied by social mobility until the twentieth century, the type of education given being appropriate to position in the social and economic class structure and the channels to higher education being restricted.

In many countries where voluntary schools were numerous and industry relied on apprenticeship, as in the United Kingdom and the United States, the full legislation for free and compulsory primary education came late. In others, like Saxony, Prussia and the Netherlands, where there were better-integrated societies and the problem was manageable, it came early. In still others, like France and Italy, legislation came and went as the political scene changed. All, by different methods, achieved their quantitative goal by the end of the nineteenth century.

The restraining factor in most countries was the means to implement the legislation, with the result that progress was spread over some twenty to thirty years before full systems were in operation; content and methods also left much to be desired.

This picture is very much the same as that obtaining in the less developed regions of the world today. Aspirations and legislation have run ahead of means and results. A difference has been that the systems in most developing countries today are imported rather than national in origin. Also the political challenge and response came later in Asia and Africa than it did in Europe and Latin America, owing to colonial conditions. There were no nineteenth century Gandhis and Nehrus, nor Asian or African Bolivars.

The broad answer to the comparison with a hundred years ago is, therefore, that there is a certain statistical resemblance as regards the proportion of children enrolled, but there are important differences in conditions. The developed countries a hundred years ago were more mature than today's developing countries, and economically much richer. There was less outright poverty and therefore less dropout; content was better geared to environmental and employment needs. There was a longer established machinery of government and the mass of the population were more ready for developmental ideas and technological change owing to their long exposure to a succession of continental wars, and to active religious systems. Their populations were growing at a much slower rate than those of today's developing countries.

On the other side of the equation, the economic growth rates of the developing countries today are higher than those of the developed countries a hundred years ago, although their *per capita* incomes are about what the developed countries had two or three hundred years ago. Moreover, there are the possibilities, which did not exist earlier, to profit from the great extension of the communication media and of international cooperation programmes in education.

It is interesting to reflect upon what might have been the position in Asia and Africa if there had been no colonialism and they had developed their educational systems under their own influences. Would Gandhi's system of basic education have succeeded instead of being shelved? Was it a reaction to colonial influence, including Gandhi's own British education? Or was it an innate Indian development with its sources in India's real needs and religious past? Certainly the adoption by the developing countries of European-type education, and their insistence on clinging to it rather than developing new patterns of their own, is a major difficulty when it comes to extending primary education throughout their rural areas.

To conclude this chapter on the historical perspective, there is an optimistic note which may be struck. In 1850 the gap in average product per head between the poor and the rich countries was of the order of 100 to 200 US dollars equivalent. This gap increased to 1000 in 1950 and to over 2000 in 1970. The educational gap, on the other hand, is being closed and not extended, as will be seen from the chapter which follows on current trends. While a world with equal or near equal levels of living among the nations is a mirage, the possibility of a world with minimum basic education on a universal scale is a real possibility which could be attained by the present generation; though quality of education is likely to remain a continuing educational differential owing to the great disparities between educational expenditure per head between the two sets of countries.

Lessons from the historical picture, however, have to be drawn with due caution, particularly for two reasons. First, the developing countries have been greatly influenced by the developed during the colonial period, both initially and later with continuing connections and educational assistance. Secondly, the solution that appears to be required at present in the developing countries runs contrary in certain respects to the process taking place now in the developed countries.

In the developed countries the issue is, and has been for some time, that of replacing an elitist system under which the primary schools were designed to take care of the poorer sections of the population, while the flow up the educational system was mainly for the more economically favoured. Most European reforms are directed at longer cycles and the establishment of comprehensive type schools as means for the 'democratization' of education.

What is a good democratic approach in one set of circumstances, however, may not be so in another. In particular it is not possible to regard it as 'democratic' to concentrate upon widening the upper part of the educational pyramid at a time when the country has large numbers of children who are not even on the first rung of the ladder, as is the case in the developing countries.

A whole set of complications, as later chapters will show, flow from the impact in the developing countries of educational thinking which springs out of the historical development of Western countries, which does not take into account that, in terms of educational coverage of the population, most developing countries have a long time lag behind the developed countries.

## REFERENCES

For much of the historical material and quotation (though not necessarily the interpretation of these) in this chapter, the author is indebted to *Educational Patterns in Contemporary Societies*, by I. N. Thut and Don Adams (McGraw-Hill, New York, 1964); *Education, Economics, and Society*, by A. H. Halsey, Jean Floud and C. Arnold Anderson (Free Press of Glencoe, New York, 1961); *Education and Economic Development*, edited by C. Arnold Anderson and Mary Jean Bowman (Aldine Publishing Co., Chicago, 1965)—see especially the chapter entitled *Literacy and Schooling on the Development Threshold: Some Historical Cases*, by C. Arnold Anderson; and to *Readings in the Economics of Education*, edited by Mary Jean Bowman, Michel Debeauvais, V. E. Komarov and John Vaizey (Unesco, 1968)—especially *What Some Economists Said About Education*, by John Vaizey, *The Significance of Education: Excerpts from Socialist Writings*, by V. E. Komarov, ed., and *Economic Development and Educational Investment in the Meiji Era*, by Koichi Emi. See also 'Educational distance between nations, its origin and prospects', by S. J. Patel in the *Indian Economic Journal*, July/September, 1965.

# CHAPTER 3

# Present Trends—Quantitative

The number of children reaching school age and the number who become enrolled vary from year to year and it is necessary to base projections on trends, usually of a five-year duration, rather than on any individual year. At the same time, educational statistics have a considerable time lag. Thus *Unesco Statistical Yearbook* for 1973, issued in 1974, gives the 1971 figures; and that for 1974, which will appear at the end of 1975 will give those for 1972. The trends and projections discussed in this chapter are those provided by the Unesco Statistical Office for the World Population Conference of August 1974, and those in the *World Bank Sector Working Paper* of December 1974, which are based on figures up to and including 1971.

This point has particular importance at the present moment because the figures for 1971 reverse the trend of the last 20 years, during which the annual rate of growth of primary enrolment in the developing countries as a whole has well exceeded that of the child population of school entry age. In 1971 the enrolment growth rate was only 2·8 per cent, whereas the population aged 5 to 9 was estimated to be growing at 3·3 per cent a year over the period 1970–75. Preliminary figures coming forward for 1972 show a further regression.

Thus the two-year trend 1971–72 is for universal primary education to become more distant rather than nearer. Whether this will become more than a particular two-year trend will not be known until a few more years have passed. But even on the more favourable 1960–70 trends, Unesco projections indicate stagnation up to 1985 to population growth. Further, both the 1972 and 1973 figures relate to the period before the oil crises and the current economic recession. The projections of out-of-school children in what follows are therefore likely to be underestimates. But it is not possible to do more than set out the existing Unesco and World Bank projections cited, with the warning we have given, as they are the only ones which have been made at present.

As of 1970 there were 836 million children in the world aged 5 to 14. Of these only 196 million were in the 'developed' countries, the remaining 640 being in the 'developing' countries, including China's 173 million. By 1980 the 640 million in the developing countries will have grown to 822 million, a rise of 28·5 per cent, and the 196 million in the developed countries will have increased by only 1·5 per cent. China will be responsible for only about 11 per cent of the increase of the 640 million since it is in process of achieving population stability and over the five years 1980–85 the Chinese increase will be only just over 2 per cent of its 1980 figure. In what follows, China, North Viet-Nam and North Korea are excluded from the statistics of enrolment and population because they have not hitherto supplied to Unesco the necessary educational data.

The following table shows the situation as at 1970 and projected until 1980 and 1985 on the basis of the trend of enrolment growth for 1960—70 and estimated population growth rates for 1970—85.

Table 3.1* School enrolments (millions) developing countries

|  | 1970 | 1975 | 1980 | 1985 |
|---|---|---|---|---|
| 5 — 14 age group | 481 | 550 | 630 | 725 |
| In school | 212 | 260 | 300 | 350 |
| Out of school | 269 | 290 | 330 | 375 |

*Source: World Bank Sector Working Paper, *Education*, December 1974.

The 269 million described as out of school had either never attended school, or had attended and dropped out. If we take the age range 6 to 11 the out of school number is reduced and is as in Table 3.2.

Table 3.2* Out of school children and youth, age-range 6—11 (millions)

|  | 1965 | 1975 | 1985 |
|---|---|---|---|
| Less developed regions (excluding China) | 114 | 128 | 165 |
| East Asia (excluding China) | 0·8 | 0·1 | 0·1 |
| South Asia | 71 | 80 | 98 |
| Africa | 29 | 34 | 49 |
| Latin America | 14 | 13 | 17 |

*Source: *Educational Development, World and Regional Statistical Trends and Projections until 1985,* Unesco Office of Statistics, Paper for World Population Conference 1974. (The term 'less developed regions' used in this and other tables is not strictly the same as 'developing countries' used in other tables because of the way the UN population data is presented. Temperate South America (Argentina, Chile, Uruguay and Paraguay) is excluded, but the orders of magnitude are little affected at the world and regional levels).

The rates of increase in enrolments in 1970–71 as compared with 1965–71 are shown in Table 3.3. In Africa the heavy decline in the annual growth rate of the first level as compared with 1965–71 was accompanied by a substantial decline in the second level growth rate while the third level growth rate more than doubled. In Asia the second level growth rate rose considerably and the third level more than doubled at the same time the rate of growth of the first level was more than halved. Latin America showed nearly a doubling of the growth rate at the second and third levels and little change at the first level. In the Arab States the growth rates increased strongly at the first and the third levels, and fell off slightly at the second.

**Table 3.3**   Annual percentage increases in enrolment by level

| Region | 1970–71 | | | 1965–71 | | |
|---|---|---|---|---|---|---|
| | 1st | 2nd | 3rd | 1st | 2nd | 3rd |
| *Africa* (excluding Arab States) | 1·6 | 3·4 | 19·8 | 4·4 | 5·0 | 8·6 |
| *Arab States* | 8·9 | 7·2 | 17·5 | 4·6 | 8·8 | 9·0 |
| *Asia* (excluding Arab States) | 1·6 | 4·6 | 17·7 | 3·6 | 3·5 | 9·4 |
| *Latin America* | 4·7 | 7·6 | 17·3 | 4·6 | 9·5 | 12·3 |
| *Developing countries* | 2·8 | 7·1 | 19·5 | 4·4 | 7·6 | 10·2 |

*Source: *Unesco Statistical Yearbook,* 1973

It is normal for the second and higher levels to increase at a greater rate than the first level as development takes place, the starting base for the percentage increases being smaller, but the disparity in growth rates between the primary and the other levels is particularly large in relation to the number of children not receiving primary schooling, the higher unit costs of the other levels, and the growing shortage of employment outlets for second and third level graduates.

Preliminary figures for 1972 indicate a continued decline in the growth rates of primary education in Africa and Asia.

In order to assess how the longer-term trends have been moving towards the universalization of primary education it is necessary to look now at the changes in the percentages of children in school (enrolment ratios). Enrolment ratios balance the increase in enrolment against the growth of the child population.

We show first the standard enrolment ratios as used in the *Unesco Statistical Yearbook* which indicates the percentage of children at school at any level who are within the age group prescribed for the national primary educational cycle. These ratios do not give a picture of the proportion of children receiving basic education of 4 or 6 years because many countries have longer cycles. In such cases the ratios are over-pessimistic, if by basic education is meant what can be learned in 4 or 6 years. The longer the prescribed national cycle the smaller the ratio. Further, they do not show the system's real capacity to provide such basic education since its capacity, as well as the enrolment ratio itself, is influenced by the length of the cycle. The analogy is with a train. The capacity of the train may be 500 people and if it makes a 200-mile journey non-stop this is the actual capacity for that journey. But if it stops at a station during the journey, and people get in and out, it can carry more than 500 people.

The standard enrolment ratios have grown as shown in Table 3.4.

**Table 3.4**  Percentage enrolment of children of primary school age (attending school at any level)

| Region | 1960 | 1970 |
|---|---|---|
| *Africa* | 34 | 48 |
| *Asia* | 50 | 59 |
| *Latin America* | 60 | 78 |
| *Arab States* (included in figures for Asia) | (38) | (61) |

A more significant index of a country's education achievement is how much time is actually spent at school by how many children. The years of attendance achieved and the amount of drop-outs can be derived from the age specific enrolment percentages (i.e. those for each individual year) which Unesco publishes separately for many countries though they do not indicate the number of school days per year, which varies, e.g., in Asia, from 178 in Thailand to 250 in India and Indonesia, while there is also considerable variation in the number of hours worked per week, e.g. between 14 for Grades 1 and 2 in Indonesia to 28 in the Philippines.

If we look at the age specific enrolment percentages we see that at their maximum peak they rise to just over 70 per cent for Asia as a whole, while for Latin America they are nearer 80 per cent and for Africa nearer 60 per cent. But there are great variations between individual countries. Table 3.5 illustrates the position.

It can be seen from Table 3.5 that the actual (or, as it were, natural) cycle when attendance is at its highest is around four years. This fact, and the notion that there is a natural cycle produced by drop-out which indicates what local conditions can bear educationally at any given moment, should be kept in mind since it plays a major role in the later chapters on the planning of primary education and the reform of its structure.

The special study made by Unesco for the World Population Conference which we have already cited, sets out the percentage of pupils aged 6 to 11 and aged 12 to 17 who remain in school six years later in the less developed regions in Table 3.6, in-dicating that, except in the case of girls, retention rates have shown little improvement.

32

**Table 3.5** Percentage enrolment by age cohort in primary education

| Age | Asia (1970) | Indonesia (1971) | Brazil (1970) |
|---|---|---|---|
| 5 | 29·9 | — | — |
| 6 | 61·6 | 14·4 | 16·6 |
| 7 | 71·3 | 44·4 | 66·2 |
| 8 | 70·2 | 62·4 | 76·2 |
| 9 | 63·8 | 66·3 | 81·0 |
| 10 | 57·0 | 64·6 | 82·8 |
| 11 | 47·3 | 60·7 | 69·7 |
| 12 | 39·8 | 48·8 | 58·1 |
| 13 | 33·5 | 34·7 | 41·8 |
| 14 | 27·9 | 18·7 | 25·2 |

| Age | Egypt (1971) | Cameroun (1971) | Central African Republic (1970) | Niger (1972) |
|---|---|---|---|---|
| 5 | 6·3 | 22·3 | 5·2 | — |
| 6 | 60·0 | 74·4 | 58·3 | 4·5 |
| 7 | 70·1 | 77·0 | 80·9 | 14·5 |
| 8 | 70·5 | 77·2 | 73·4 | 15·0 |
| 9 | 67·7 | 74·1 | 44·0 | 13·6 |
| 10 | 62·3 | 73·6 | 49·8 | 11·8 |
| 11 | 55·3 | 69·9 | 35·1 | 10·0 |
| 12 | 21·9 | 64·8 | 36·0 | 10·7 |
| 13 | 6·1 | 53·1 | 38·1 | 6·5 |
| 14 | — | 34·4 | 19·7 | 3·6 |

**Table 3.6** Percentages of pupils who remain in school six years later

| | 1960 | 1970 | 1980 |
|---|---|---|---|
| Aged 6 – 11 | | | |
| Boys | 62 | 60 | 60 |
| Girls | 52 | 54 | 54 |
| Aged 12 – 17 | | | |
| Boys | 28 | 28 | 29 |
| Girls | 23 | 24 | 26 |

The regional figures obscure many variations between countries, as can be seen from the indicators for the 93 developing countries shown in Appendix 1 at the end of this book. There are also great disparities within countries between urban and rural primary education and in many countries between the enrolment of boys and girls. The value of the regional figures is for the observation of trends for the developing countries as a whole and also for the measurement of progress towards, and the setting of objectives for, the goal of universal basic education.

According to the objectives adopted at Unesco's Regional Conference of Ministers of Education and Overall Planning in the 1960s, universal primary education was obtainable in most of the developing countries by 1980 and in the rest around 1985. These objectives were included in the United Nations strategy for the Second Development Decade, but now need adjustment.

The latest contribution to this subject is a paper prepared by Unesco's Statistical Office for the World Population Conference of September 1974. This paper regards the prospects for universal primary education much less optimistically than the present regional objectives do and states: 'demographic factors seem likely to continue to dominate the ability of states to provide places for potential students, unless national and international policies, towards education, change'. It adds: 'A combination of even greater efforts and more imaginative interventions in the conservative practices of educational systems would appear to be required'.

This reassessment is the result of Unesco using the latest estimates by the United Nations of population growth, as shown in Table 3.7.

**Table 3.7** Population growth, less developed countries, excluding China, North Viet-Nam and North Korea. Average annual percentage increase

| Age | Period | | | |
| --- | --- | --- | --- | --- |
| | 1965–70 | 1970–75 | 1975–80 | 1980–85 |
| 0–4 | 3·1 | 2·6 | 2·2 | 2·0 |
| 5–9 | 2·6 | 3·3 | 2·8 | 2·3 |
| 6–11 | 2·5 | 3·2 | 3·0 | 2·5 |

The regional objectives (which also excluded China, North Viet-Nam and North Korea) had been calculated on lower population growth ratios, that for Asia having been estimated at 2·4 for the period 1965–80 for the group 6 to 12 years of age.

The estimates of population growth including China, North Viet-Nam and North Korea are shown in Table 3.8.

**Table 3.8** Population growth, less developed countries, including China, North Viet-Nam and North Korea. Average annual percentage increase

| Age | Period | | | |
| --- | --- | --- | --- | --- |
| | 1965–70 | 1970–75 | 1975–80 | 1980–85 |
| 0–4 | 2·8 | 2·1 | 1·8 | 1·7 |
| 5–14 | 2·0 | 2·4 | 2·6 | 2·1 |

These present a more favourable picture because of the much lower rate of population growth in China than in most of the rest of the developing countries.

The enrolment ratios projected on the basis of the rate of progress attained in the 1960s and the new population forecasts for the 1970s are as shown in Table 3.9.

These figures are disturbing since they show, on the basis of the population estimates, that the proportion of the children aged 6 to 11 in school is likely to virtually stagnate until 1985.

The growth of enrolment of children aged 6 to 11 years was almost linear for the developing countries during the last decade, implying declining annual growth rates of enrolment. As population grows exponentially, an enrolment increase of constant numbers each year will, if maintained, sooner or later be insufficient to keep pace with the population growth as well as increase the enrolment ratios. This is the main

**Table 3.9**   Enrolment ratios 6 to 11 years

|  | 1970 | 1975 | 1980 | 1985 |
|---|---|---|---|---|
| Less developed regions (including China) | 70·2 | 71·1 | 70·5 | 70·3 |
| Less developed regions (excluding China) | 60·2 | 61·6 | 61·6 | 62·3 |

reason behind the relatively pessimistic results presented by the above-mentioned report, whose purpose has been to derive the implications of continuing until 1985 the education trends observed during the period 1960–1970.

The estimates which the study makes for the different regions are given in Table 3.10.

**Table 3.10**   Enrolment Ratios 6 to 11 years by regions

| Region | 1970 | 1975 | 1980 | 1985 |
|---|---|---|---|---|
| Africa | 44·2 | 45·8 | 45·6 | 44·3 |
| Latin America | 72·4 | 74·8 | 75·3 | 74·7 |
| Asia (excluding China) | 64·6 | 65·6 | 65·1 | 67·0 |

The sombre picture is in the African region and in South Asia (where the corresponding figures are 60·9, 62·2, 62·3 and 64·1, the situation being particularly influenced by the low enrolment ratios in Pakistan and Bangladesh and the high rates of population growth over practically the whole of the area).

The conclusion of the Unesco study submitted to the 1974 World Population Conference is:

There is little evidence that South Asia and Africa will succeed in doing more than maintain the present relative level of provision in response to the increasing numbers seeking admission to education. The prospects are somewhat brighter for Latin America. . . . By 1985 the less developed regions as a whole will only be slightly nearer universal education for children aged 6 to 11 than they were in 1970. To reach universal education for this age range by 1985 would require that the less developed regions treble their average annual enrolment increase attained during the 1960s. . . . As education already is consuming a large proportion of the national income and, as there are many competing demands on public funds, one might question whether or not universal primary education is a realistic target for 1985 for a large number of developing countries.

In commenting on these forecasts the following points can be made. They interpret universal primary education as a six year cycle, which is longer than normally required for a minimum basic education. If the amount of education required is reduced from six years to four, the resources needed will be considerably less.

Secondly, the average annual economic growth rates postulated by the United Nations for the 1970s, and achieved in the first three years of the decade, are 20 per cent higher than those for the 1960s, though this was before the oil crisis, and for Africa and Asia nearly 50 per cent higher. The study uses the United Nations projections for population increase after 1970, but not those for increase of economic growth. The increase in resources from raising an economic growth rate from 5 to 6 per cent is in effect more than 20 per cent. Since about 3 per cent of economic growth is needed to take care of population increase, an addition of from 5 per cent to 6 increases by about a third the disposable income after taking care of population increase. Further, some of the countries with low primary enrolment ratios and large populations are spending unduly low proportions of their income on education compared with other countries with similar income but higher enrolment ratios.

Thirdly, the population forecasts show the growth of the child population aged 0 to 4 in the less developed regions, including China, as falling drastically by 1980–85 to one half of what it was for 1965–70, i.e. 1·7 as compared with 2·8, or from 3·12 to 1·96 excluding China. If the study projected the population trends towards the end of the period 1970–85, it would be shown that relief from high pressure of population growth was on the horizon. If the forecasts can be taken as a guide for policy, this would permit governments to decide to make a heavy investment on education in the 1970–85 period on the understanding that declines would set in in the 1980s. This was in fact the policy followed by the USSR in bringing its Asian republics to standards of minimum basic education; though in unplanned economies the task would be more difficult, since it involves delaying other forms of investment.

Fourthly, a positive factor which should be taken into account is that the urban population is rising more rapidly than the rural and that the extension of primary education is normally easier in urban than in rural areas, though there are the serious problems of shanty towns.

Fifthly, the quantitative situation has to be seen, as we suggested earlier, in terms of increasing the chances of children of 6 years of age to have had a minimum basic education before becoming adult, rather than in terms of increasing the block of children of a particular age group attending particular types of schools. The major issue is the reduction of drop-out in the first four years of school and the devising of simpler and more effective types of education, both formal and non-formal, than the present systems provide. Some steps are already being taken in this direction, as we shall see in later chapters.

In the foregoing we have been discussing the developing countries at the global and regional levels, with some references to particular countries with the largest populations. This is necessary because statesmen and educators have to see what the trends are, and the attitudes they form are important for their influence on international policy. But, in reality, the problem can only be dealt with country by country and we therefore now look at the countries with the largest populations (UN estimates for 1971), in snapshot with further details later.

*China* (787 million) appears to be moving steadily towards the goal of at least minimum basic education for its whole population. Its rate of population increase is relatively low and it is using non-formal as well as formal methods.

*India* (550 million) is experimenting with non-formal methods but relies fundamentally on the formal system. It had 83 per cent of its children aged 6 to 11 enrolled in 1972 and 37 per cent of those aged 11 to 14. This is a remarkable achievement in such a diverse country as India with different languages and cultures, great variations in topography and local degrees of development, and with difficulties in some areas in obtaining the enrolment of girls. However, the increase of primary enrolments declined sharply in 1971 and 1972 to below child population growth.

The percentage of boys aged 6 to 11 enrolled in 1969 was 95·2 per cent and for girls 58·5. The quantitative solutions for India appear to be (1) reducing drop-out and continuing experimentation with innovatory approaches (such as part-time schooling, links with non-formal education, multi-entry and non-graded schools), (2) greater enrolment of girls and (3) expansion to keep pace with population growth, which fortunately, though high, is not among the highest in Asia.

*Indonesia* (125 million) has a somewhat higher rate of population growth than India and the age specific peak enrolment for the four years 8 to 11 was 60 per cent in 1971. Outside these years drop-out rates are high. The increase of the chances of children of 6, 7 or 8 years of age to have at least four years of education is restricted by the cost to parents of fees, uniforms etc., as well as by rapid population growth, since education is not free. The main task is to allocate more than the present low proportion of revenue devoted to education in order to reduce the cost to parents, to adopt other measures to increase the holding power of t e school, and to diminish, as in the case of India, the disparity between the enrolment of boys and girls. Population growth has now exceeded enrolment.

*Brazil* ( 3 million) shows an enrolment ratio of 128 for its four year cycle 7–10, the excess over 100 being due to over-age and under-age pupils. The four year peak of enrolment for the 8–11 group is around 70 per cent. Population growth is very high. The country is booming economically, but progress is mal-distributed.

Bangladesh (72 million) shows a similar inequality of enrolment as between girls and boys as many other Asian countries, which affects the enrolment ratio. Progress towards universal primay education was faster in the latter part of the sixties than in Pakistan, the annual rate of increase of primary enrolment having been 7·0, 11·8 and 14·5 per cent for 1967, 1968 and 1969, compared with 5·9, 6·1 and 10·5 for Pakistan in those years. The enrolment ratio in 1969 was 56 for Bangladesh and 48 for Pakistan. Population growth rates are very high.

*Pakistan* (63 million) had only one girl enrolled for every three boys, and the enrolment in 1969 for both sexes together did not reach more than 45 per cent for any year of childhood. The enrolment ratio was 40 for the first five years, but over-age pupils brought it up to 48. The government of Pakistan is at present making a special drive to spread and improve primary education. It has a population growth rate of 2·9 per cent for 1969–71 and a *per capita* GNP growth rate of 3 per cent.

*Nigeria* (57 million) has adopted a major programme to universalize free primary education. It has a high population growth rate. The enrolment ratio is 34, for 1971 for a seven-year cycle. The problem is to keep pace with population growth and at the the same time to push education into the less economically favoured or remote areas, as well as to reduce drop-out.

*Mexico* (50 million) has an exceptionally high population growth rate but also a high rate of growth of GNP though it is not distributed as evenly as in other countries. Its enrolment ratio for a six year cycle is 104, or 81 excluding children outside the 6–11 age group who are attending school. The problem, apart from keeping pace with population increase, is the extension of education into the more backward areas of the country.

Following these large countries in population terms come 10 developing countries with over 20 million population, 30 between 20 million and 5 million, and 48 with under 5 million, covering in all a variety of conditions and degrees of educational development, and of rates of population growth (see Appendix 1).

Some highlights will now be given of the position in the different regions, showing more details.

## THE ASIAN REGION

The situation in Asia is dominated by the presence of the three most populous nations among the developing countries, namely China, India and Indonesia, and the fact that Asia covers a third of the world's population.

In the Asian model[2] adopted by Ministers of Education and Ministers Responsible for Economic Planning at the Unesco Conference of 1965 (which excluded mainland China, the Arab States, North Korea, and North Viet-Nam) Asian countries were divided into three groups as follows:

*Group A.* Those countries likely to achieve at least seven years of universal compulsory education after 1980 (Afghanistan, Laos, Nepal).
*Group B.* Those likely to achieve it around 1980 (Burma, Cambodia, India, Indonesia, Iran, Mongolia, Pakistan).
*Group C.* Those likely to achieve it before 1980 (Ceylon, Republic of China, Republic of Korea, Malaysia, Philippines, Singapore, Thailand).

Some Asian countries, e.g. the Republic of Korea, Malaysia (West) and Singapore, have already achieved or are near to universal primary education. However, the region as a whole experienced in 1970–71 a decline in the rate of growth of enrolments to 1·6 per cent which fell below the increase of new entrants to the primary school age group. Unless this fall in the increase of enrolments is corrected, the number of children growing up without primary education will increase rather than be reduced.

This slackening of progress is partly due to the fact that in those countries education is now pushing out in the less advanced area. The Unesco Regional Office[3] (Bulletin XIV) reports:

> The 'traditional' pattern of educational expansion typically runs into a barrier when it has reached 50–60 per cent enrolment ratio. Further expansion, which means expansion into remote areas or to deprived sections of the population, becomes slower and more difficult to implement. A well-designed strategy has yet to evolve which will counter the 'traditional' pattern with its built-in unevenness and use the instrumentality of education to transfer opportunities to those who are deprived.

The enrolment ratio in mind is the unadjusted ratio (i.e. the age group 5–14). Both India and Indonesia have well passed the barrier on the basis of enrolment ratios adjusted to the length of their primary cycles, i.e. their own current interpretations of what constitutes primary school age. Thus, as we saw earlier, India had in 1972 83 per cent enrolment of children aged 6 to 11. In Indonesia the enrolment ratio in 1970 was 71 for the age group 7 to 12.

The task in regional terms is to create school attendance for the 30 per cent who do not get enrolled at any time during their childhood, to reduce drop-out so as to make attendance effective for at least four years for the 70 per cent who do get enrolled and to keep pace with population increase. This is becoming of ever increasing difficulty as action has to cover areas with less favourable economic and social conditions and growing populations of the less developed rural areas have to be incorporated.

Asian Ministers of Education and Those Responsible for Economic Planning at the conference held in June 1971 in Singapore noted,[4] 'the remarkable convergences between the total enrolments actually recorded by the countries of Asia and the targets laid down in the Asian Model'. This was before the 1970 figures of enrolment were available and the new population growth rates had been assessed.

At the same time the Ministers declared, 'short of a thrust in favour of innovations leading to a regeneration of education in the region, solutions to the quantitative demand will be increasingly difficult to find' (see Unesco Final Report of the Conference).

The authors of the Asian Model, who based their findings on the then UN estimates, were of course aware of the danger of population growth upsetting their picture and they stated:[5] 'Any change in the growth rate of population would have important consequences for the enrolment figures shown in the projections'. The danger is now evident as the latest Unesco study, which we have discussed above, has demonstrated.

# THE AFRICAN REGION

Africa is in the worst position of the developing regions and has the largest proportion of the world's least educationally developed countries. African objectives for universal primary education were established at Unesco's Regional Conference of Ministers of Education at Addis Ababa in 1961, but were over-ambitious. They were the first attempt in this field by Unesco and the improved method of establishing objectives, which became incorporated four years later in Unesco's Asian Model, had not yet been evolved.

Thus while the Ministers of Education of Asia and Latin America have been able recently to declare that the quantitative objectives are being achieved on time, the African Ministers at their last conference in Nairobi in 1968 reported,[6]

In secondary education, in 1965–1966, there was a shortfall of 272,000 pupils on the basis of the proportion of secondary school pupils to primary school enrolment. . . . Much more serious was the situation at the primary level where enrolment in 1965–1966 was 1·1 million short of the total foreseen and where it appeared that unless the trend was reversed, the primary schools of Africa would be in danger of losing the battle against illiteracy.

The conference noted that, . . . the enormous wastage at the primary school level is measured by the fact that for the continent as a whole, only 32 per cent of pupils enrolled in the first year complete their sixth year'.

Two adverse features affecting the prospects for attaining primary education in the region are, firstly, Africa's high rate of population growth, which means that the heavy task of meeting the backlog has to be accomplished at the same time that a large number of new places has to be formed. Between 1970 and 1975 the African population was expected by the United Nations to grow at 2·8 per cent a year. Enrolments in 1971 grew at only 1·6 per cent. Secondly, the educational backlog is higher than in any other region, since it was the last of the world's great regions to embark on the development process. In 1950 enrolment in primary education was equal to about 18 per cent of the African population aged 5 to 14 as compared with 24 per cent in Asia and 38 per cent in Latin America.

The severity of the African educational scene can be seen from the average annual increase of enrolments required under the projections in the new Unesco study to attain 100 per cent enrolment of the 6–11 age group. It would have to be four times that of 1960–65 during the period 1970–85. Resources, of course, will also be very much larger in the period 1970–85, but the extent of the task on the basis of a six year cycle is clearly prohibitive in regional terms.

There are, however, very wide variations between African countries in their primary enrolment ratios, even between those which are least developed, due, as will be discussed later, to great disparities in unit costs. Some countries have a much higher enrolment than others and their task will be easier.

A positive factor is that Africa has been the main focus of educational assistance mostly from the ex-colonial governments following independence, but also from the newer bilateral donors such as Sweden, Canada and the German Federal Republic, and from the International Agencies such as Unesco, the World Bank Group, the United Nations Development Programme, Unicef and the Development Fund of the European Community. Little of this aid, however, has gone to primary education, although it can be argued that aid to second level and higher education has partially released domestic funds for the growth of primary enrolments. The total public expenditure on education in Africa has been recently around US $ 2850 million.

Africa has received twenty times per head of population the amount of educational assistance given to Asia and six times that assigned to Latin America. The Addis Ababa targets of 1961 postulated a requirement of US $ 970 million of external assistance by 1970, falling to $ 600 million by 1980 as the continent became educationally more self-sufficient. The amount of educational assistance to Africa was in 1970 running at about $ 700 million a year, or a quarter of their total budgets, unequally distributed between countries. Thus in Africa, as in Asia, regional figures can be misleading and not applicable to a number of countries, as can be seen from the data in Appendix 1.

## THE LATIN AMERICAN REGION

Latin America has an estimated annual average population growth rate of 2·9 per cent for 1970–75. Variations between countries over the period 1965–70 ranged from 1·4 per cent for Argentina to 3·4 per cent for Mexico and Columbia. Latin America's *per capita* income and primary enrolment ratio well outstrip those of the other developing regions, the proportion of trained teachers is greater, the pupil–teacher ratio is 31, well below those for Africa and Asia (39 and 40), and teacher salaries are five times as high as in Asia and two and a half times as high as in Africa.

On the other hand drop-out rates and the number of over-age children are particularly high, and there exist large-scale maldistributions of educational progress, between countries, between urban and rural areas and between social groups. Some 8 million children are unenrolled. The educational facilities in the great Latin American cities are very different from these available to the Quechua-speaking Indians in the Altiplano of Ecuador, Peru and Bolivia, or the poor populations in the shanty towns surrounding the cities.[7] About half of the total population of Latin America has a *per capita* income little different from the Asian or African average, while the other half are considerably better off.

## THE ARAB STATES REGION

The Ministers of Education of the Arab States held their last meeting under the auspices of Unesco at Marrakesh in 1970. The information before them showed that for the sixteen Arab states the enrolment ratio for the 6–11 age group of children had advanced from 50 per cent in 1961 to 62 per cent in 1968. This represented an annual growth rate of 6 per cent. For 1970–75 the estimated population growth rate is 3·3 per cent. In 1971 enrolments increased by 8·9 per cent.

The Conference stated,[8] 'by now means all countries feel that they will be able to achieve universal primary education by 1980', there being considerable variations in the position of different countries. Jordan, for instance, has a remarkably high enrolment ratio and Yemen a remarkably low one. The position as regards access of education to girls was improving but 'is still a long way' from equality with boys.

Concern was expressed, as in the other regions, for the need for more educational progress combined with change. The conference report states:

> The expansion of education still has a long way to go. Although the extension of primary education has been impressive during the last years, there are still serious deficits: out of 19 million children of primary school age, some 8 million were out of school in 1967; the rate of expansion has slowed down in recent years; the total drop-out rate reaches 50 per cent in some countries and less than a quarter of the children in several countries go through the first level without repeating a grade.

The Conference Resolution on the universalization of primary education stated:

> The Conference recommends that Arab States whose legislation does not include an explicit provision for compulsory education should enact such a provision and that all Arab States should commit themselves to the implementation of their legislative provisions concerning compulsory education at the earliest possible date.

The Conference also reaffirmed 'the recommendation of previous regional educational conferences concerning the prohibition of repetition in the first four years of primary education, accompanied by measures to ensure the continuity of the pupil's progress and enable him to pursue his studies with success'.

## THE LEAST DEVELOPED COUNTRIES

A category of countries which cuts across the different regions has been set up by the United Nations. It consists of the 25 least developed countries based on a criteria of low income, high illiteracy and lack of industrialization. Sixteen of these countries are in Africa, seven in Asia and one each in Latin America and Oceania; the designated countries are: Afghanistan, Bhutan, Botswana, Burundi, Chad, Dahomey, Ethiopia, Guinea, Haiti, Laos, Lesotho, Malawi, the Maldives, Mali, Nepal, Niger, Rwanda, Sikkim, Somalia, the Sudan, Uganda, Tanzania, Upper Volta, Western Samoa and Yemen.

Although one of the criteria of this category of countries is high adult illiteracy, there are very great variations between them as regards primary school enrolment today. This grouping has therefore little utility from an educational standpoint. While there is very general relation between average income level and the average primary enrolment ratio, these countries also show much variation in the percentages of their total public expenditure devoted to education.

Rwanda, for instance, had 74 per cent primary enrolment for a six year cycle in 1970, whereas Niger had 10 per cent for a cycle of the same length. Malawi had 37 per cent enrolment for an 8 year cycle, whereas Somalia had 10 per cent for a four year cycle.

## CONCLUSION

To conclude this chapter we now try to draw from the conventional statistics the type of data which illuminates the deficiency in minimum basic education and indicates the future gap to be filled, so that in Chapter 6 on financial and economic factors we can assess the feasibility of the task.

For convenience, 4 years of continuous enrolment in school is taken as an index of basic education, though in some circumstances it may be five and in the USSR the elementary cycle is of three years duration. It is also assumed in future projections that policies of automatic promotion will be followed as already in many countries in order to facilitate pupil flow.

The capacity of the educational systems of the developing countries to provide four continuous years of education can be assessed by examining the four-year continuous peak periods in the age specific enrolment ratios, (i.e. the percentage of each yearly age cohort who become enrolled). While it is operationally unrealistic to treat the developing countries as a whole because action takes place at the level of each individual country, it is a useful exercise in order to see the size of the problem, and to show the method suggested for use at the country level.

As at 1970 the peak four year continuous enrolments came to 120 million out of 457 million children aged 5 to 14 in the developing countries (excluding China, North Korea and North Viet-Nam). In the same year the size of the average four-year age group within this total was 183 million children, thus enrolments were some 66 per cent of the total. By deducting 120 million from 183 million for 1970 we derive a deficit of facilities to provide 4 years of continuous education for 63 million children.

The comparable deficit on the basis of applying UN population growth estimates and the same rate of expansion of primary education as in the 1960s is 71 million for 1975, 78 million for 1978, 83 million for 1980 and 92 million for 1985. This rise in absolute numbers despite a 5 per cent rate of growth assumed for primary enrolments and a rate of around 3 per cent for the growth of the school age population is due to the exponential nature of population growth.

The task of universalizing a four-year education cycle seen statistically is to raise from 66 per cent to 100 per cent the present capacity in the peak four years. This peak varies from country to country, but for most it covers the children 7 to 10 years of age.

The basic minimum human right to education, under this conception, is not to have access to education starting at the prescribed school entry age, but to have delivered a continuous period of at least four years of education at the best suited point of time in the child's passage from 5 years of age to 14. In addition there is the right to educational opportunity going beyond minimum basic education, the progressive implementation of which we discuss in Chapters 8 and 10.

Table 3.11 sets out the situation for the developing countries as a whole (excluding China, North Korea and North Viet-Nam) at present and projected until 1985. The population projections are those issued by the United Nations and the enrolment projections are based upon the same rate of expansion of primary education as took plece in the 196;s continuing until 1985. There has in fact been a serious fall in the rate of expansion during the last few years, but there is plenty of time before 1985 for it to regain its previous pace or exceed it.

**Table 3.11**

|  |  | 1970 | 1975 | 1980 | 1985 |
|---|---|---|---|---|---|
|  |  |  | (millions) |  |  |
| (1) | 5–14 age group (excluding China, North Korea and North Viet-Nam) | 457 | 530 | 617 | 706 |
| (2) | Portion of (1) not receiving four-year schooling | 230 | 266 | 300 | 340 |
| (3) | Size of average four-year age group within (1) | 183 | 212 | 247 | 282 |
| (4) | Portion of (3) enrolled in four-year peak-enrollment age group (ratio) | 120 (66%) | 141 (66%) | 164 (66%) | 190 (67%) |
| (5) | Portion of (3) out of school | 62 | 71 | 83 | 92 |

The projections indicate a stagnation of the universalization of four-year minimum basic education until 1985 unless special steps are taken, and the 1971 and 1972 figures show actual regression. In reality of course the situation will vary in each individual country but there is a general lesson to be drawn. This is that in addition to the allocation of additional resources, as discussed in Chapter 6 on finance, means should be found of reorganizing the efficiency of the cycle so that, while an adequate flow towards the second educational level is maintained, the pupils who at present constitute the heavy wastage of the primary cycle through drop-out and repetition because they fail to complete a longer cycle should instead be given a terminal four-year course.

## SOURCES OF STATISTICS

The *Unesco Statistical Yearbooks* for years 1968 to 1973. (Note: The figure showing the growth rate for the 0–4 age group for 1965–70, which is given as 1·6 on p. 29 of the Unesco Yearbook (1972) is a misprint for 2·8—an important difference.)

*A Summary Statistical Review of Education in the World in The Sixties* (Unesco, ED/IBE/CONFINTED 34/Ref. 1, 1973).

*Population and Development in Perspective: World and Regional Population Prospects*, prepared by the United Nations Secretariat for the World Population Conference, 1974 (Document E/Conf. 60/BP/3 and PB/3 Add 1).

*Educational Development, World and Regional Statistical Trends and Projections Until 1985*, background paper prepared by the Office of Statistics, Unesco, for the World Population Conference, 1974.

'First-level education in the Asian region', *Bulletin of the Unesco Regional Office for Education in Asia*, No. 14, June 1973.

*Education*, Sector Working Paper, World Bank, December 1974.

44

## REFERENCES

1. The figures in Tables 3.4 and 3.5 refer to years in the late 1960s and are taken from *Development of Education in Asia*, UNESCO/MINEDAS 3, 1971, tables on pp. 21–22.
2. *An Asian Model of Educational Development, Perspectives for 1965–80*, Unesco, 1966.
3. *Bulletin of the Unesco Regional Office for Education in Asia*, No. 14, 1973, p. 44.
4. *Report of Third Regional Conference of Ministers of Education and Those Responsible for Economic Planning in Asia*, Singapore, 31 May–7 June, 1971, pp. 50 and 58.
5. *An Asian Model of Educational Development, Perspectives for 1965–80*, Unesco, 1966, p. 46.
6. *Report of Conference on Education and Scientific and Technical Training in Relation to Development in Africa*, Nairobi, 1968, p. 8.
7. *Report of Conference of Ministers of Education and Those Responsible for the Promotion of Science and Technology in Relation to Development in Latin America and the Caribbean*, Caracas, p. 2.
8. *Report of Third Regional Conference of Ministers of Education and Ministers Responsible for Economic Planning in the Arab States*, Marrakesh, 1970, pp. 11 and 18.

## SELECTED FURTHER READING

Statements made by delegations at, and country documents submitted to, the various Regional Conferences of Ministers of Education and Those Responsible for Overall Planning cited above. Reports of the biennial Unesco General Conferences and the annual conferences of the International Bureau of Education/Unesco.

Document of 14 August 1972 ED/WS/344, prepared for Inter-Secretariat meeting of Unesco, the Organization of African Unity and the United Nations Economic Commission for Africa, on the Revision of the Educational Objectives of the Addis Ababa Conference.

*Challenges of the Population Issue for Educational Planners; Introduction to a Methodology*, Unesco ED/WS/425, August 1973.
*Regional Seminar of Experts on Population Dynamics and Educational Planning. Final Report*, Bangkok, 10–18 September 1973, Unesco Regional Office for Education in Asia, Bangkok, 1973.

# CHAPTER 4

## *Present trends—Qualitative*[1]

In educational systems quantity and quality are interlocked. Some aspects of quality can be quantified, others cannot. Examples of quantifiable aspects are the size of classes, the amount of time spent in school, the proportion of trained men and women in the teaching force, the number of textbooks and teaching aids in use, and the distribution of school hours among the different subjects in the syllabus.

However, the quantitative link cannot be pushed too far. An optimum size class is negated if content and curriculum are poor. Large numbers of trained teachers are an impediment rather than an asset if they are trained in counter-productive methods. Nor can trained teachers operating in optimum size classes be fully effective if the textbooks and teaching aids are ill-conceived and the school premises are bad, or if the curriculum lacks relevancy and is badly structured. Structure is vital to quality.

Moreover, quality in education does not only consist of good teaching. It consists also—and indeed primordially—of the quality of the learning which is achieved, assisted by teaching. For this reason a country's capacity to produce good learning situations also has a key place in educational quality.

Quality of learning is greatly influenced by the conditions of school attendance, such as length of distance children walk to school, whether they have a midday meal, the living levels of their families and their health and nutrition, and whether the attitudes of their parents are positive towards education. It is also affected by the cultural and religious views prevailing in the local community and the state, by the influence exercised by other children and by the younger generation as a group, and by the economic and social environment.

Planning and administration, efficiency of inspection, and the reliability of the examinations in use are also important as major factors in quality.

All of these items influence the efficiency of the functioning of the system as a whole and its capacity to keep down drop-out and repetition of grades.

Current trends show that it is more difficult to bring about qualitative change than quantitative increase. Whereas enrolments have doubled over the last ten to fifteen years, there has not been comparable progress in quality. Indeed, many educationalists are inclined to say that quality has actually declined over the period. This may well be true of Africa, though in respect of the other regions it is debatable.

In a recent essay,[2] one of the Directors of Unesco's Department of Education, Najman, states: 'From a qualitative point of view, not only is education in Africa failing to achieve the result which governments and people expect, but in practically all countries, and certainly on the continent as a whole, it has undergone a permanent process of worsening'.

In an article in Teacher Education in New Countries[3] J. Cameron summarized the weaknesses of primary education in Tanzania in 1968, shown in a study made by the Netherlands Centre for the Study of Education in Changing Societies. Educational progress since in Tanzania has been considerable under the inspiration of President Nyerere and a major educational reform is under way. Nonetheless, the weaknesses described are true of much of Africa today:

> inadequate financial provision, resulting in sub-standard school buildings and the bare minimum of basic furniture and equipment, especially textbooks; subject-oriented syllabuses which are dominated by rigid and rigorous examination requirements, whereby a small minority is selected for admission to secondary schools; the low educational standards, poor professional performance, and declining social status of the teachers; the inefficiency of the administration and the inspectorate; and last and not least the wide gap between the schools and the communities they purport to serve.

An important aspect of quality is the relevance of the education given to the child's needs as he grows up in his environment. On this, Harold Houghton and Peter Tregear, who have worked many years in the less developed countries have written in a publication[4] of the Unesco Institute for Education, Hamburg, called *Community Schools in Developing Countries*:

> Why is so much of the schooling offered to an African, Asian or Latin American child so unrewarding, to himself and to his community? First and foremost, because it is the result of a quest for quantitative expansion without too much regard for quality. Most developing countries know that when they commit themselves to an annual increase in school enrolment of four, five or six per cent, they are equally committing themselves to a corresponding increase in the number of class teachers, unable though they may be, and usually are, to offer these teachers any thing like adequate preparation, academic or professional, for the work they will be doing. There is therefore a constant lowering or at any rate no rise in the efficiency of the process of instruction. But no less important, though less apparent, is the unsuitability of the educational diet on which most children in developing countries are fed . . . the original intention underlying the provision of education in the great majority of the countries with which we are concerned was not to educate a nation but to educate the carefully chosen few who would sometime run the nation's affairs, and the larger numbers, still small in proportion to the whole population, who would become the doctors and the lawyers and at a lower level the clerks, salesmen, nurses, teachers and so on. Admittedly this restriction of educational opportunity was not always deliberate or even conscious, but the rigid process of selection on which progress from one level of education to another was based on reduced primary schooling to a period of preparation for the secondary schooling which most children would never enjoy.

On the problem of relevance in the context of francophone countries, Ki-Zerbo writes in the Unesco journal, *Prospects:*[5]

but today the school has sometimes aggravated certain faults in the colonial school without preserving some of its qualities . . .. As for the syllabus, the methods and the structure, this is a huge subject; it is in primary education that the work began. Quite often reforms were superficial. Certain publishing houses, yielding to easy solutions, thought that in order to Africanize a text-book, it was enough to alternate Mistral and Camara Laye, or else Abraham Lincoln and Soundiata, or that it was enough to replace the apple tree with a mango tree and to put under the tree a little Traore instead of a little Dupont. I do not believe that this is the real way of adapting textbooks . . .. In history and geography, the Ministers decided upon considerable work in secondary education with the cooperation, one must admit, of our French colleagues who helped us create new syllabi in which about 30 per cent of the credit timetable is devoted to the history and geography of Africa. I can tell you that I have lived through this experience: it was a veritable deliverance for our students, African pupils who until then were forced to rack their brains in trying to follow the details of the geography of the Massif Central or the troubles of one Merovingian king or of Louis VI the Fat.

An account of the progress in introducing local African material to replace European style textbooks is to be found in a study by Kelly.[6] Kelly points out that in the anglophone countries examination options for texts by African authors had by 1970 increased to 50 per cent. Similarly, the *Handbook of the West African Examinations Council* stresses the need to respect 'the familiar collocations which have passed into everyday use in West African speech and writing'. In its note on standards, it also goes on to state that 'in any test of continuous writing, and in objective tests of lexis and structure, the Examiners will be assessing the candidates' mastery of standard English, as currently used by educated African writers and speakers of English in Commonwealth West Africa'. In francophone Africa similar approaches have been recommended at conferences of francophone Ministers of Education, but Kelly concludes that 'in fact it is possible to say that the Africanization of syllabuses . . . has proceeded much further in the English-speaking countries of West Africa than in the French-speaking ones'.

One of the great difficulties in Africa, and in some parts of other developing regions, is the existence of a variety of vernacular languages in the same country, so that instruction does not take place in the mother tongue. In some countries 50 per cent of a child's effort in school consists of mastering a language of instruction which is not his own. A French educational group writes of primary education in francophone Africa as follows:

It is an education which is not imparted in the maternal tongue, but in a foreign language, French, with all that that implies—not only the unrooting and blocking of the concrete and living frames of reference, but also the mental efforts, which no child in the world (no matter how gifted he may be in intelligence and alertness, qualities which African children do not lack) can sustain without provoking a sometimes permanent blockage of his potential resources.

It is an education organized and imparted according to principles, methods and practices which are completely foreign to the social structures within the family life of the child.

Lastly, it is an education which, in the absence of an industrial job market, and due to stagnation in agricultural production destined for comestic markets, offers no other outlet than to seek minor posts in public or military administration. Even if this means having to wait for years for such an occasion to present itself.

The problem of unsuitable curricula has attracted heavy criticism. Unesco undertook for the International Bureau of Education an enquiry of a large number of countries as to the causes of wastage.[7] About half of the countries in their replies to Unesco referred to what the study summarizes as 'overloading, encyclopedic learning, sterile memorizing, and the too abstract content of curricula ... and its irrelevance to local living conditions'.

The report on Asian curricula[8] made by the Japanese National Institute of Education Research, under Unesco sponsorship and with the participation of its Asian member states, points to the need for continuing revision of curricula and for measures to improve the facilities and training of staff for curriculum development and evaluation. Some of the comments made in this study are illuminating as to the causes of poor curricula.

Thus, the Report states for Afghanistan: 'The people engaged in curriculum development and revision are not trained . . ..'; for India: 'The States do not have any regular programme of curriculum evaluation . . .. Curriculum is narrowly conceived and very often important aspects such as teacher orientation, development of a variety of instructional materials for pupils and teachers are excluded from the terms of references of the syllabus committees'.

For Indonesia it states: 'One problem is the coordination between the curricula of the elementary and the secondary schools. Another problem is the need for flexibility and adjustment of the curriculum to local conditions'; for the Republic of Korea: 'Not enough time and funds have been set aside for developing or revising curriculum'; for Malaysia: 'Lack of suitably qualified personnel to construct evaluation instruments and conduct tests on a more refined degree to find out the effectiveness or otherwise of any plan put on trial'; for Nepal: 'There was lack of coordination between curriculum writing, textbook writing, and teacher training activities'.

In the developing countries of other regions the picture is much the same, though somewhat better in Latin America and rather worse in Africa.

The examination system also plays a primordial role in the quality of education and curriculum development is negated unless the examinations are changed *pari passu*. On this point the *Asian Study on Curriculum* already cited states:

Most of the evils attendant on the present examination system have accumulated because of the fact that examinations are isolated from teaching and learning and are considered as an event in the school-life of the pupil distinct from his day-to-day learning programme and announced with authority by the school and accepted with awe by the pupil.

This sombre picture, while not applicable to the whole of primary education in all areas of the less developed regions, is indicative of the basic problem of educational quality. The malaise is deep and possible remedies are discussed in the later chapter on educational reform and innovation; but let us look now at progress on some of the numerically assessable components of quality, starting with the growth in the number of teachers.

The world's primary school teachers in 1970 numbered 11·4 million. Of these just over half were in the less developed countries, and their increase during the sixties as compared with the other levels can be seen from the Table 4.1.

**Table 4.1** Number of teachers by level of education, annual percentage increase for the period 1960—1970

| Major Regions | First level | 2nd level | 3rd level |
|---|---|---|---|
| World total | 3·4 | 6·5 | 7·6 |
| Africa | 5·2 | 7·9 | 11·6 |
| Latin America | 5·4 | 9·5 | 10·1 |
| Asia | 3·5 | 6·4 | 9·0 |
| Arab States | 7·2 | 8·0 | 11·2 |

This increase has to be set against the growth of enrolments in order to show whether the pupil—teacher ratio, as an index of quality, has altered. This is shown in Table 4.2.

**Table 4.2** First level of education: pupil—teacher ratio, 1960, 1965—68 and 1970

| | 1960 | 1968 | 1970 |
|---|---|---|---|
| World | 30 | 31 | 30 |
| Africa | 39 | 40 | 41 |
| Latin America | 34 | 32 | 33 |
| Asia | 30 | 36 | 34 |
| Arab States | 38 | 34 | 31 |

The Arab States show a remarkable decrease in the pupil—teacher ratio and in Asia a decrease is setting in after a sharp rise. In the case of Africa, which is the least favoured educationally of the regions, the ratio is slightly increasing.

In Asia the growth of enrolments had considerably outstripped that of teacher supply. These average figures, as we pointed out in the preceding chapter, concealed very large classes in some areas and double shift working, as well as the numerous cases of single class schools which exist in the rural areas of those countries.

As regards the proportion of trained personnel in the teacher force, while teacher training has been increasing rapidly in the developing countries, the goal of a hundred per cent of trained teachers is still a long way off. In Indonesia, for instance, data for around 1970 show that about 20 per cent of the teachers could be regarded as fully qualified and about 25 per cent are not qualified at all. There are no statistics which show the proportion of trained teachers for the less developed countries as a whole. Some illustrations are, however, given for individual countries in the report, *Main Trends in Education*, prepared by the International Bureau of Education in 1972. They show that the general scarcity of trained teachers results in a tendency for those qualified for primary teaching to move to lower secondary education and those qualified to teach in lower secondary schools to move to upper secondary education, the result being a general lowering of teaching standards.

If we look at the educational objectives for Asia shown in the Unesco Regional Model,[9] we can see the level of qualification of primary school teachers set out as at 1964 their increase projected up to 1980 (see Table 4.3).

Table 4.3    Percentage distribution of new entrants to teaching force at the first level of education, by qualification, 1964, 1970, 1975, and 1980.

| Qualification: 10 (basic schooling) + (professional training) | 1964 (estimated) | | | 1970 | | | 1975 | | | 1980 | | |
|---|---|---|---|---|---|---|---|---|---|---|---|---|
| | Group* | | | Group | | | Group | | | Group | | |
| | A | B | C | A | B | C | A | B | C | A | B | C |
| 10 or less | 60 | 15 | 5 | 37 | 5 | — | 20 | — | — | — | — | — |
| 10 + 2 | 30 | 58 | 30 | 40 | 35 | 5 | 50 | 10 | — | 60 | — | — |
| 10 + 3 | 3 | 20 | 30 | 12 | 35 | 30 | 16 | 53 | 25 | 20 | 60 | 20 |
| 10 + 4 | | | | | | | | | | | | |
| (or 12 + 2) | 5 | 2 | 25 | 8 | 18 | 52 | 10 | 27 | 60 | 15 | 30 | 60 |
| 12 + 3 or more | 2 | 5 | 10 | 3 | 7 | 13 | 4 | 10 | 15 | 5 | 10 | 20 |

*The groups are defined in Chapter 3.

The figures in Table 4.3 reflect the variations in the training of primary teachers between the different groups of countries; similar variations tend to exist within different regions of the same country. In some, qualifications are only 7 or 8 years of basic schooling with 1 or 2 years of teacher training, though as a rule they are at least 10 years of schooling with 2 or 3 years of training. In the case of the least developed countries and areas, a considerable number of teachers may be found to be without any formal training as teachers and possessing no more than primary education themselves.

The Asian Ministers, in setting up the regional objectives in the sixties, took the view that the problems of buildings, equipment or instructional aids would not hinder educational advance as much as lack of suitable teachers and regarded their status and conditions of service as of fundamental importance. They therefore urged that there should be a shift in the educational qualifications of the teaching force, in that the teachers should be prepared in teacher training institutions and not in general institutions of higher learning, and that salary incentives should rise. The practice of training teachers outside of teacher training institutions, often inevitable for reasons of economy, had the disadvantages of isolating teacher training from that for the system as a whole, leading to gaps between the theory adopted for the system as a whole and the actual practice in schools.

Ideally, teacher training has the following six components, which fall into two groups: those more strictly pedagogic and those more general. First, the teacher should be made fully familiar with the curriculum content and the best systematic way of presenting it. Secondly, he should learn how to encourage learning aptitudes in children and to create productive teaching–learning situations. Thirdly, he should have knowledge of the various textbooks and teacher's aids which are in use. Fourthly, he should be given a sense of his social role in the community, so as not to work in an isolated and bookish manner, especially in rural areas. Fifthly, he should be helped to develop the capacity to make children participate with and learn from each other (both in subjects in the curriculum and in games), as well as receive instruction and learn as individuals. Sixthly, he should be encouraged to have an open mind towards innovations and reforms and to contribute to devising and carrying them out within the framework of the national policy and administration.

More attention is usually paid to the first three rather than the last three of these components. The fourth, namely the widening of the interest of the teaching profession in their social role, is becoming ever more important in the developing countries. One of the inheritances of a number of countries from their colonial history is the English system of leaving much autonomy to the local headmaster. This particular aspect is brought out in the Report of the OECD Centre for Educational Research and Innovation in their publication *Styles of Curriculum Development*, the report of a conference organized jointly with the University of Illinois.[10]

The Report contrasts the British and Swedish systems as follows:

For school–society relations it was clear that Sweden saw the school as an instrument of social construction and reconstruction. Thus in the balance between education for social ends and education for individuals, the shift was to the former in Sweden and to the latter in England.

The corollary for the role of the teacher which the Report draws is 'teacher interpretation is maximized in England and minimized in Sweden'. The Report also states:

North American participants were perhaps somewhat more inclined to see some virtue in the English position, while wincing from time to time at the limits it appears to place on the developers' role and the unreasonable hopes it places on the rank and file of the profession.

It would seem that the Swedish model, if an external model has to be used, would be more applicable than the English to many of the developing countries, owing to their need for social change and their development requirements. This is one of the problems of historical heritages discussed in our Chapter 8 dealing with the planning of primary education.

The fifth component, the teacher's initiative in promoting child participation in group learning and team work, calls more for the British decentralized style of approach. The sixth, which is the encouragement of open-mindedness to innovation is most difficult.

A requirement for increasing the teacher's interest in the role of the school in development and in innovation is that the authorities should themselves take steps to involve teachers in consultation before decision making. Unfortunately few efforts of this kind are made either by teachers or by the authorities. Commenting on this point in India, J. P. Naik writes in *Educational Planning in a District*, a discussion paper issued by the Asian Institute of Educational Planning and Administration:[11]

> It is unfortunate that teachers have so far neglected this important subject and not much interest has been evinced by the teachers' organizations in the three Five Year Plans and in the three Annual Plans. They have not even criticized them either in depth or in a comprehensive manner while what is expected of them is not mere criticism but, if necessary, even the formulation of an alternative plan . . ..

A Unesco publication,[12] *Teachers and Educational Policy*, sets out the results of an enquiry carried out through the World Confederation of Organizations of the Teaching Profession, the World Federation of Teachers' Unions, the International Federation of Free Teachers' Unions, and the World Union of Catholic Teachers, embracing thirty countries. This enquiry arose out of the recommendation concerning the status of teachers prepared jointly by Unesco and the International Labour Organization, adopted by a special inter-governmental conference in Paris in 1966, which concluded 'that teachers' organizations can contribute greatly to educational advance and that they should therefore be associated with the determination of educational policy'.

It emerges that there is great variation between countries in the extent and methods of participation, and also considerable differences within countries as to the degree of central or local activity. We read that in West Bengal and Andhra Pradesh and in Thailand, teachers' organizations have prepared novel textbooks and educational films which have received government approval. In Japan, Korea, Thailand and the United States, teachers' organizations have their own educational research centres replacing those of the state, or functioning side by side with them.

The general situation as regards teacher participation, however, in both the formation and execution of education policy may be described as 'patchy'. The situation is affected by the status of primary school teachers and the shortage of them in many countries, which has led to the dilution of their status. All countries covered by the survey, with the exception of Belgium, Hungary, Japan and the Philippines, reported a shortage of qualified primary school teachers. Much of the activity of the unions is accordingly concerned with questions of remuneration and status rather than with educational policy. Some reformers fear teacher participation in policy making on the ground that they are reluctant to change curricula which they are already trained to teach. This would seem a short-sighted view as teachers themselves, in the last resort, have to a great extent the last word as to what is actually taught.

The question of remuneration and incentives for extra productivity are essential factors in raising the quality of the teaching force. A description of Norwegian efforts to motivate teachers to undertake experimental work states: 'The most effective single step is to make the teacher feel that the innovation will help him personally'. J. P. Naik, writing in the paper just mentioned on the proposal for school complexes put forward by the Indian National Commission for Education, also makes the point that extra remuneration must be given to headmasters of better placed schools to visit and encourage those lower down the line.

Thus, we come back to the point made in our first chapter, that the economic and social returns to society due to primary education, which is the only level most people receive, are not reflected in the salaries and career and incentive conditions for primary teachers. In Chapter 12 on finance we discuss later the possibilities of devoting more funds to the first level and incentives in the form of delayed benefits, since educational returns take a number of years to materialize.

Under present conditions of service it is quite frequent for teacher training to be used as a means of attaining a diploma which is later used to undertake better paid jobs elsewhere in the economy. Further, a number of teachers having entered the profession later resign their post to seek employment in other parts of the civil service or the private sector. This points to the importance not only of better career prospects, but also to forms of in-service training and recycling which will create greater interest and competence in teaching and at the same time open avenues of promotion. A number of developing countries (e.g. Algeria) have made much progress with measures such as weekly teachers' meetings, teaching seminars and courses during the school holidays, study by correspondence and regular retraining cycles undertaken once a year.

A difficult element in raising educational quality through teacher training is the interlock of teacher performance not only with curriculum change but with the lack of low income countries of teaching materials, while the limited material available is not suited to the environment.

The lack of teaching and learning materials is also an obstacle to the introduction of new subjects or the change of old ones in the syllabus. If we look at the allocation of time between subjects, while there exists considerable variation between countries (as is shown in Table 4.4 for Asia), we see in general a heavy concentration upon language arts. This subject tends to be taught by old methods and new methods are mainly centred, when they are in use, on the teaching of science and mathematics. Language is an extremely important subject, especially in countries where there are many local languages, but one which could be better handled. The purely language aspects could be dealt with by more modern teaching methods for the use of foreign tongues, while the arts aspect could be more humanized. The Nuffield-Schools Council Humanities Project contains some methods which may be transferable to the developing countries at the upper primary level. Language difficulties are in many countries a contributing cause of drop-out and few cases exist of adequate compensatory courses for children not speaking the national language.

This brings us to the major problem of drop-out, which plays havoc with quality and educational productivity, and repetition of grade, which is usually a poor solution to problems of quality.

Drop-out, as we saw earlier, is the largest single cause of educational deprivation

Table 4.4    Percentage of time alloted to school subjects at first-level education[13]

| Country | Afghanistan | India (Mysore) | Indonesia | Iran | Japan | Korea, Rep. of | Laos | Malaysia | Nepal | Pakistan | Philippines | Sri Lanka | Thailand | Viet-Nam Rep. of |
|---|---|---|---|---|---|---|---|---|---|---|---|---|---|---|
| Language arts First language | 38·5 | 29·0 | 21·5 | 35·7 | 27·5 | 23·1 | 22·4 | 12·8 | 15·0 | 30·1 | 29·4 | 24·3 | 21·1 | 35·0 |
| Second language Regional | 8·6 | — | — | — | — | — | — | — | — | — | — | — | — | — |
| Foreign | — | — | — | — | — | — | 16·6 | 26·9 | 8·9 | — | — | 9·5 | 6·3 | — |
| Maths/arithmetic | 14·9 | 12·1 | 17·4 | 11·4 | 18·0 | 16·3 | 14·8 | 12·4 | 15·0 | 14·6 | 11·3 | 15·3 | 12·6 | 13·8 |
| Science | 3·5 | 10·7 | 9·3 | 7·9 | 10·8 | 12·1 | 7·0 | 7·1 | 15·0 | 7·3 | 11·3 | 2·3 | 11·0 | 10·5 |
| Social studies | 6·9 | 10·7 | 9·3 | 9·3 | 11·4 | 12·6 | 6·6 | 7·7 | 15·0 | 7·6 | 12·1 | 15·0 | 19·0 | 6·7 |
| Health/ physical education | 3·5 | — | 7·3 | 7·9 | 10·8 | 12·4 | 11·2 | 6·4 | 8·4 | 11·4 | 6·0 | 11·1 | 9·5 | 7·7 |
| Music/fine arts | — | — | 10·5 | — | 7·7 | 14·4 | 3·8 | 6·4 | 10·4 | — | 10·4 | 1·6 | 9·5 | 4·3 |
| Practical arts | 8·6 | 25·0 | 11·3 | 18·5 | 10·2 | 5·0 | 7·4 | — | — | 18·4 | 15·6 | 15·8 | 11·0 | 4·0 |
| Moral/ religious education | 15·5 | — | 8·8 | 9·3 | 3·6 | 4·1 | 4·2 | — | — | 10·6 | 3·9 | 5·1 | — | 9·7 |
| Other curriculum areas | — | 12·5 | 4·6 | — | — | — | 6·0 | 20·3 | 12·3 | — | — | — | — | 8·3 |
| Total | 100·0 | 100·0 | 100·0 | 100·0 | 100·0 | 100·0 | 100·0 | 100·0 | 100·0 | 100·0 | 100·0 | 100·0 | 100·0 | 100·0 |

and responsible for the lack of a minimum basic education in some 150 million children, leading to their growing up illiterate.

The most authoritative examination of wastage on a world scale was undertaken by Brimer and Pauli for the International Bureau of Education/Unesco.[14] The causes of drop-out were shown as lack of control of school attendance; remoteness of pupils' homes from schools; unsuitability of the curriculum, overloading of programmes, the verbalism of teaching, excessive severity of teachers, overcrowded classes, lack of qualified staff; fatigue and poor living conditions in the home.

The study showed a close connection between scholastic performance and premature leaving in which lack of promotion plays an important part. Moreover, where the age of the pupils was high owning to their delayed entry into school and to repetitions of grade, they were liable to leave school prematurely.

In addition, more than a quarter of the countries who replied to a questionnaire deplored the pupils' inadequate knowledge of the language of instruction and the lack of teachers trained to carry out their duties among ethnic groups.

The family situation was also the cause of drop-out where parents were reluctant to send their children to school, especially in the case of girls in traditional societies. The external conditions of poverty and child labour and the early marriage of young girls were also cited as important factors.

A survey in 1969[15] of educational wastage by the Office of Statistics at Unesco studied in the form of input/output ratios the relationship of pupils' years actually spent, to the duration of the educational cycle multiplied by the number of successful completers. Under optimum conditions (no repetition, no drop-outs) the ratios would be one, but in practice the situation disclosed was as shown in Table 4.5.

Table 4.5

| Countries in major regions | Range of country (input/output ratios) | Median (input/output ratios) |
|---|---|---|
| Africa | 1·24 — 3·55 | 2·00 |
| Latin America | 1·53 — 2·42 | 1·90 |
| Asia | 1·00 — 2·48 | 1·31 |
| Europe | 1·00 — 1·56 | 1·20 |

The above ratios show that, in Africa for instance, the median 'cost' to the system per successful completer was double the prescribed one. In other words, only half of the cost was effective, since repetition and drop-out were responsible for the other half. It has, however, to be noted that a pupil, even if he may be literate and have had five or six years of education, is defined as a 'drop-out' under the Unesco definition if he does not complete the required primary cycle, which in some countries is overambitiously long. This reduces somewhat, though not greatly, the validity of the ratios.

An example of how drop-out rates increased as enrolment expanded was the situation in Nigeria (Western Region) between 1959 and 1964, as seen from Table 4.6.

In the literature on this subject wastage is usually treated as a purely negative factor, as indeed it is in principle. It is also necessary, however, to note its role as a regulator. When educational systems expand beyond what the local conditions can bear the local facts assert themselves through an increase in drop-out.

It is reasonable that education should move ahead of local facts and, so to speak, drag them along with it as far as possible. But when drop-out rates are as high as those in many of the developing countries it is clear that a readjustment is required between what education can offer and what society can absorb. This subject is dealt with in Chapter 9 where terminal four year courses are discussed followed by guidance cycles for those who stay at school and intermittent or non-formal education for those who leave.

**Table 4.6**   Drop-out figures in the first year of primary school:
Nigeria (Western Region)

| Year | Total Enrolments (1) | Drop-outs (2) | (2)/ (1) |
|------|----------------------|---------------|----------|
| 1959 | 161 255 | 33 463 | 20·7% |
| 1960 | 169 601 | 34 304 | 20·3% |
| 1961 | 179 239 | 42 023 | 23·5% |
| 1962 | 176 684 | 41 178 | 23·3% |
| 1963 | 178 604 | 39 802 | 22·3% |
| 1964 | 186 402 | 47 002 | 25·2% |

There have been many moves on the part of governments over recent years to tackle the problem of quality. Curriculum reform, for instance, appears regularly in educational plans and has been the subject of considerable external aid. Little impact, however, is yet visible in the field of qualitative improvement to match the great quantitative expansion which has taken place.

The findings of the Unesco-NIER study on Asian curricula already cited show that out of thirteen countries, five stated they had flexible curricula and the others that they had not. Problems or difficulties were stated to be 'lack of well planned programmes for curriculum development or revision, the lack of coordination of the organizations or agencies engaged in this task, the insufficiency of the participation of teachers, the shortage of qualified personnel, materials, and finance, etc.'.

While in most countries curriculum development is centralized, a positive factor is that in some the states and provinces and local authorities were allowed to modify the curriculum to meet their own needs. Further many Asian countries 'have taken steps to systematically evaluate the curriculum. However, there is a shortage of trained personnel who may supervise/conduct the programmes of curriculum evaluation'. The study comments that 'mostly social and economic factors have been responsible for curriculum change practically in all countries'.

The reasons why curriculum improvement has not been able to bring about the necessary rise in the quality and relevance of primary education go beyond the lack of trained personnel and of pedagogic skills which the Unesco-NIER report indicates. Even with best intentions, such as those indicated in the revisions shown in Table 4.7, progress is difficult because so many seemingly obdurate factors hold an

**Table 4.7**  Major changes in Asian curricula

| Country | Nature of changes in | | |
| --- | --- | --- | --- |
| | Objectives | Subjects | Other changes |
| Afghanistan | New social values and needs have been emphasized in accordance with new Afghan Constitution promulgated in 1964. | Increased emphasis on Reading; new content in Health Education, Social Studies and Sciences. | Emphasis continued on Second Language, Mathematics and Physical Education. |
| Ceylon | To develop understanding in the basic functions of social life such as production and consumption. To develop a sense of service and a sense of loyalty as a citizen throughout actual experiences of social life. | Agriculture and Work Experience emphasized. Citizenship Education introduced in grades VI and VII. | Work Experience programmes were instituted. |
| India | Greater emphasis on: inculcating democratic values in life; dignity of labour work-experience and productivity; modernization of society; national integration; international understanding. | Provision for work experience. Teaching History, Geography and Civics as separate disciplines from grades V or VI onwards. Teaching Physics, Chemistry, Biology as separate disciplines from grades V or VI onwards. | The curriculum as a whole is tending to be more science oriented. |
| Indonesia | To restore pure Pantja Sila (i.e. belief in God, in humanity, in nationality, in democracy and in social justice). | All the subjects taught at the elementary level are grouped into three categories: (1) Subjects to promote Pantja Sila Spirit (2) Subjects to promote Basic Knowledge (3) Subjects to promote Specific Skills. | |
| Iran | Train and well-inform generation who will be able to live in a free and democratic society. Meet the need for the skilled manpower. Meet the need for implementation of land reforms. | Religious and Moral instruction; Persian Language; stress on Arithmetic and Geometry; Experimental Science Art and Handicrafts; Physical Exercise; Music. | Education Corps Programme in rural areas has been implemented. |

[*continued overleaf*]

**Table 4.7** *contd.*   Major changes in Asian curricula

| Country | Nature of changes in | | |
|---------|------------|----------|---------------|
| | Objectives | Subjects | Other changes |
| Malaysia | Reduce compart-mentalization in elementary school time table. Ensure the freedom to pursue pupil's interests outside the classroom atmosphere. Ensure a greater degree of informal mixing amongst pupils of various races. | In grades I, II, and III Local Studies integrating basic concepts from History, Geography and Civics is introduced. In grades IV, V, and VI those subjects are taught separately. | 'Group activities' has been made mandatory. |
| Pakistan | Reorganize education according to the needs of the country. Challenge of geographical and cultural variations in in the country. Challenge of mass-involvement. | English made compulsory from grade VI, Urdu made compulsory from grade III for pupils of Sindhi and Pushto medium schools. Social Studies introduced as compulsory subject. General Science to be taught from grade III. | Duration of primary education was extended from 4 to 5 years all over the country. East Pakistan already had 5 years duration. |
| Philippines | Emphasize child centred and community centred education to bring child near to community life. National aspirations of the new Republic. | Meanings, concepts and generalizations of various subject areas were fused together to organize content into larger subject areas such as Language, Arts, Social Studies etc. | Conflicting interests with respect to the medium of instruction — use of native language, aspiration for a unifying language, stress upon economic and scientific advancement. |
| Thailand | Place greater emphasis on democratic values of life and dignity of manual work. | Place greater emphasis on Practical Arts and Moral Education. | |

interlocking grip on educational performance, especially in rural areas where most of the population lives. These are mainly: (1) wastage, as we have seen; (2) the consequent low internal efficiency of the system; (3) low external efficiency, since parents and educators continue to prefer academic to more practical studies better related to the environment; (4) lack of trained teachers and in many cases, particularly in Asia, low teacher salaries; (5) poor conditions surrounding the school which reduce the child's learning capacity; (6) inadequate buildings and shortages of textbooks and equipment and transportation to school; (7) shortages of administrative, planning and inspection personnel; (8) inherited structures of the first level cycle which do not cater sufficiently for pupils who will terminate at an earlier age than the last year of the cycle.

Obviously, to manipulate this powerful set of obstacles is a most difficult task. It is not, therefore, surprising that many educators now feel that tinkering with individual items, such as curriculum reform or teacher training, however vital these are, is not the answer, but that major programmes of educational renovation, regeneration and innovation are required.

Before, however, analysing the possibilities of reform, it is necessary first to set out what are the forces—social, political and educational—determining progress in primary education and what are likely to be the financial resources available over the next decade or two. These matters are pursued in the next two chapters, but the key question of educational quality should not be left without putting it in its wider human context, the day-to-day behaviour of teachers, pupils and parents.

Educational quality can be improved by better planning and administration, by curriculum reform, by more teacher training and financial resources. But a mass of individual decisions and changes of attitude on the part of both educators and parents, and in the community at large, is also required.

It is possible to visit schools and hear well delivered teaching on simple measures of cleanliness and to find the school's own facilities lacking in them, to find teacher training colleges instructing their students in new educational methods and using old ones to do so, to find politicians campaigning in favour of the democratization of education but sending their own children to elite schools, to find teachers urging their pupils to reject racial discrimination but practising it themselves outside the schools because of the social pressure, to find well equipped schools with uninspiring teachers and dull classes and, elsewhere, very poor schools with teachers using progressive methods and having eager pupils. While the enrolment and organizational solution could be found in a decade or two, a longer period would be required for a major and widespread change of quality and attitude in primary education. Young teachers have to be trained in new outlooks and skills and have to rise to positions where they are influential enough to change events.

It is important therefore not to neglect the face-to-face and human aspects of education and its socializing and civilizing role. An indication of a type of education which, given the means, could have a major impact both on personality development and on national progress is given in a contribution by Ben Morris, Director of the University of Bristol Institute of Education, to *The New Curriculum*, where he states:[16]

We have to decide whether the school is primarily a place for instruction and intellectual development—as in fact it has been conceived in many countries—or whether the school is a place primarily for young persons to grow up in—a place where intellectual development takes its proper place within a wider perspective. In England there has always been a trend towards this latter conception.

If the former is what we want, then let us try to turn the school into a really efficient streamlined institution for mastering pre-arranged and selected adult skills and ideas, all the while keeping careful records and checks on achievement and rigorously grading our pupils accordingly. If we were wholeheartedly to pursue this objective the price we would pay would, I think be enormous—probably the loss of much of our essential humanity.

If the latter is what we want then the school must be devoted to giving children and young people the opportunities needed to master the essential arts of civilized life.

What are the foundations of the arts of civilized life? I would say: (1) Love, sympathy and respect for others; (2) Enjoyment of the world, of beauty, of shared experience, of the mystery of an unfathomable universe; (3) Cooperation; (4) Aspirations towards personal and community achievement in the whole range of civilized activities; (5) Responsibility for one's own actions with which goes a real measure of independence of mind and heart.

How can one encourage the acquisition of these arts? Let me suggest what my rough prescription would be.

The school must become a much more open community (in the sense in which many people have already spoken, linking up with homes, industry and social affairs). In its organization our current concepts of class, lessons, timetable, subject, would have to be largely transformed. Homework on the present basis would certainly be banned. We might structure the school day into two main sessions—with an additional evening session for those who wanted to pursue their own special interests (group and individual) and which was open to the whole community.

I would give the morning to project work and discovery, discussion, creative activities—thereby putting many of our so-called extracurricular activities in the very heart of the curriculum. The afternoon would be reserved for tutorial work and individual pursuits on the basis of interests. Here gradually many but not necessarily all the children would seek to study and master the traditional techniques and ideas of the great disciplines—the forms of knowledge.

This view will be found an extreme one by many educators both in the developed and the developing countries since there is a great deal of hard learning as well as civilizing which has to take place in school if the economic and social environment is to be changed. It does, however, reflect an important concern which is growing in many different countries in broadening education to create fuller lives for the pupils. The same concept appears in the title of the Report of the International Commission on the Development of Education, which is *Learning to Be*. It is reflected too in Indonesia in the Pantja Sila set of objectives which are described in Chapter 5 on the forces influencing primary education. It is to be found also in the Report of the Indian Education Commission,[17] which states:

> We believe that India should strive to bring science and the values of the spirit together and in harmony, and thereby pave the way for the eventual emergence of a society which would cater to the needs of the whole man and not only to a particular fragment of his personality. India has a unique advantage with her great tradition of duty without self-involvement, unacquisitive

temperament, tolerance, and innate love of peace and reverence for all living things.

The first sentence of the Commission's Report is: 'The destiny of India is now being shaped in her classrooms'.

President Nyerere of Tanzania in his address to the Dag Hammarskjold seminar on education in Dar-es-Salaam in May 1974 drew the distinction between 'a system of education which makes liberated men and women into skilful users of tools, and a system of education which turns men and women into tools. I want to be quite sure that our technical and practical education is an education for creators, not for creatures'.

The question of the impact of education on society and of society on education is one that has undergone a good deal of rethinking in recent years. Studies, nearly all undertaken in the developed countries, have undermined the long-held belief of educators and sociologists, and still accepted in common sense, that education was a major public instrument for the promotion of social mobility and for reducing inequalities in society.

Recent research[18] in the United States, for instance, is claimed by its authors to show that:

Those who see schools as instruments of social reform usually share a series of assumptions that go roughly as follows:

(1) Social and economic difference between blacks and whites and between rich and poor derive in good part from differences in their cognitive skills.

(2) Cognitive skills can be measured with at least moderate precision by standardized tests of 'intelligence', 'verbal ability', 'reading comprehension', 'mathematical skills', and so forth.

(3) Differences in people's performance on cognitive tests can be partly explained by differences in the amount and quality of schooling they get.

(4) Equalizing educational opportunity would therefore be an important step toward equalizing blacks and whites, rich and poor, and people in general.

Our research has convinced us that this line of reasoning is wrong.

They also state:[18]

The amount of schooling an individual gets has some effect on his test performance, but the quality of his schooling makes extraordinarily little difference. We have therefore abandoned our initial belief that equalizing educational opportunity would substantially reduce cognitive inequality among adults. This does not mean that we think cognitive inequality derives entirely from genetic inequality, or that test scores are immune to environmental influence. It simply means that variations in what children learn in school depend largely on variations in what they bring to school, not on variations in what schools offer them.

Nevertheless the authors also state:[18]

The evidence we have reviewed supports three conclusions:

(1) Preschools have little permanent effect on cognitive development.

(2) Elementary schooling is helpful for middle-class children and crucial for lower-class children.

(3) Secondary schools and colleges do less than elementary schools but more than most jobs or housework in developing the skills measured on standardized tests.

They add:[18]

Perhaps the most astonishing feature of this whole inquiry is that virtually no research has been done on these issues, either by defenders of schools or by their critics. As a result, our conclusions are all based on problematic inferences of uncertain validity. The most we can claim is that such evidence is better than nothing.

Obviously this is an area where research is needed which would be specifically related to conditions in the developing countries, which are so different from the United States as to be able to make the above conclusion invalid on their own methodology, quite apart from whether they themselves, as the authors admit, can be justified as more than problematic inferences.

Many educators and sociologists today believe that the impact of educational systems on society has been overrated as compared with the impact of society on education. Torsten Husen, writing in the OECD publication, *Social Background and Educational Career*,[19] states:

Analyses of data from large-scale national and international surveys have made us aware of how closely related certain features of the formal educational systems, such as structural rigidity, diversity of programmes and selectivity, are to the stratification of society at large. Whereas research relevant to the problem of equality of educational opportunity focused until recently mainly on selection for academic secondary or university education, it is now being directed at the conditions during pre-school and primary school that account for differences later in the educational career.

Primary education is certainly in a special position as regards influence on developing societies since not only is it the only education which most people receive but it is the first contact with learning systems and frequently the first initiation to any form of socialized activity. It will have been noticed that the key word 'crucial' was applied to elementary education in the research results quoted above.

In this chapter we have treated quality in terms of teacher training, class size, content, curricula and social impact. Educational methods are also part of quality and are the subject of Chapter 11.

# REFERENCES

1. The statistics in this chapter are taken from the same sources as those in Chapter 3, and in addition:

   *A Statistical Study of Wastage at School*, Unesco: IBE, 1972.
   *Wastage in Education, A World Problem*, M. A. Brimer and L. Pauli, Unesco: IBE, 1971.

2. *Education in Africa, What Next?*, Dragoljub Najman, Deux Mille, Aubenas, France, 1972, p. 17.

3. 'Primary education in Sukumaland (Tanzania), a summary report of a study made by the centre for the study of education in changing societies', The Hague, J. Cameron, in *Teacher Education in New Countries*, Oxford University Press, Vol. 2, No. 3.

4. *Community Schools in Developing Countries*, Harold Houghton and Peter Tregear, Unesco Institute for Education, Hamburg, 1969, p. 13.

5. 'Education and development', Joseph Ki-Zerbo, in *Prospects*, Vol. II, No. 4, Unesco, 1972.

6. 'The Africanization of syllabuses in anglophone and francophone countries of West Africa', *Teacher Education in New Countries*, Vol. 2, No. 3, February 1971, Oxford University Press.

7. See 1 above.

8. *Asian Study on Curriculum*, National Institute for Educational Research, Tokyo, Japan, 1970.

9. *An Asian Model of Educational Development, Perspectives for 1965–80*, Unesco, 1966.

10. *Styles of Curriculum Development*, report by Stuart Maclure on a conference held at Monticello, Illinois, 19–23 September 1971, organized jointly by the Centre for Educational Research and Innovation at OECD, Paris and the University of Illinois, and sponsored by the National Science Foundation, pp. 43 and 64.

11. *Education Planning in a District*, J. P. Naik, Advisor, Ministry of Education and Youth Services, Government of India. Asian Institute of Educational Planning and Administration, New Delhi, 1969, p. 27.

12. 'Teachers and educational policy', *Educational Studies and Documents, No. 3*, Unesco, 1971.

13. *Bulletin of the Unesco Regional Office for Education in Asia*, No. 14, 1973, Table 21.

14. See 1 above.

15. See 1 above.

16. 'The school: how do we see it functioning (past, present, and future)?, Ben Morris, in *The New Curriculum*, a presentation of ideas, experiments and practical developments, selected from Schools Council publications 1964–7, appearing under the title: *Working Paper No. 12—The Educational Implications of Social and Economic Change*, Her Majesty's Stationery Office, 1967, pp. 6–7. (Extract reproduced by permission of the Controller of Her Majesty's Stationery Office.)

17. *Report of the Education Commission*, Government of India, Delhi, 1966, p. 21.

18. Christopher Jenks *et al.*, *Inequality: A Reassessment of the Effect of Family and Schooling in America* (forthcoming, Penguin, 1975) pp. 52, 53, 89. Copyright © 1972 by Basic Books Inc.

19. *Social Background and Educational Career*, Torsten Husen, OECD, p. 9.

## SELECTED FURTHER READING

*Education, Human Resources, and Development in Latin America*, United Nations, 1968.
*Report of the Study of Absenteeism in Selected Primary Schools 1966–67*, Institute of Education, Mysore, India (*Publication No. 42*), 1968.

*Causes of Student Failure in Elementary School*, Ministry of Education, Teheran, Iran, 1966.

*Behind Mud Walls 1930–1960*, with a sequel *The Village in 1970*, William and Charlotte Wiser, University of California Press, 1972.

*The Child's Situation in School*, Jorge Padua, Latin-American School of Sociology, Santiago, Chile.

*Education in the USSR*, Progress Publishers, Moscow, 1972.

*Chinese Communist Education, Record of the First Decade*, Vanderbilt University Press, 1969.

'Antecedents and consequences of early school leaving', *Educational Documentation and Information*, Bulletin of the International Bureau of Education, No. 182, 1972.

*Youth and Literacy*, Arthur Gillette, Unesco/UNCESI, 1972.

*Education for All*, 'Assignment children', June 1973, No. 22; and *Education and Development*, March 1972, No. 17, Unicef.

*Literacy 1969–71*, Unesco.

*Education in a Changing Mexico*, Clark Gill, US Department of Health, Education and Welfare, 1969.

*Education in Brazil, 1971*, Commission for International Affairs, Ministry of Education and Culture, Brasilia, 1971.

'Trends in educational expansion', H. M. Phillips, in *Education Planning*, ed. Geoge F. Beraday, Joseph A. Lauwerys and Mark Blaug, in *The World Yearbook of Education, 1967*, Evans Bros, London, 1967.

'Growth and change: perspectives of education in Asia', *Educational Studies and Documents, No. 7*, Unesco, 1972.

*School Drop-Outs and the Social Background of Students*, Unesco Courier, June 1972.

'Structure and function in education systems: the duration and content of primary education', G. W. Parkyn; in Africa (S. Rajaona); in Latin America (J. Blat Gimeno); in Asia (A. R. Daward); in *Prospects, No. 1*, Unesco, 1969.

*Conférences des Ministres de l'Éducation Nationale des États Africains et Malgache d'Expression Française*, AUDECAM, Études, Paris.

*Education in East Africa, 1971. A Selected Bibliography*, Makerere University, Kampala, 1972.

*Educational Development in Africa*, African Bibliographic Centre, Washington D.C., 1973.

*L'École en Afrique. Quelques Références Bibliographiques Commentées; Conception de l'Enseignement Agricole en Afrique (Bibliographie); Développement Rural en Afrique Noire. Aspects Pédagogiques: Vulgarisation et Animation (Essai Bibliographique)*, Institut Africain pour le Développement Economique et Social, 1973.

# *Part 2*

## THE DYNAMICS OF EDUCATIONAL CHANGE

# CHAPTER 5

# Forces Determining the Development of Basic Education

Obviously, both the quantity and the quality of a country's primary education system are dependent on its economic and social situation. One can hardly expect to find a large number of well trained primary school teachers in a very poor country, or modern curricula and teaching methods in a traditional society which is only just beginning to modernize.

Nevertheless, there is a large area to manoeuvre in and choice even in the least developed countries, as can be seen from the fact that within groups of countries at similar levels of economic development there are remarkable differences in their degree of educational progress. While educational systems are conditioned by society and the economy, they also have an independent dynamic and sociology of their own.

It is convenient, therefore, to try to distinguish two sets of forces influencing the development of primary education, though there is considerable interlock between the two. They are, first, the impact of society on the school; secondly, the forces internal to the educational process and the school system itself. These two sets of forces, or combinations of them, may run parallel or counter to each other at different times.

The most important of the first, or external, set of forces are the political will of the government and the social pressures for education; parents' conceptions of the type of education needed; finance; the general economic and social conditions (overall level of development, living conditions, job opportunities, fiscal system, population distribution etc.); the rate of growth of the child population.

The most important of the second set of forces, those internal to the educational process, are the content and structure of the existing system and its history, educational expenditure and the present supply and distribution of educational resources; the attitude of the educational establishment to universal primary education as a priority goal; the examination system; the extent of centralization or local administration; and the level of primary teachers' salaries.

Predominant among the external forces are the political factors. These influence education in three main ways: first, as regards the objectives; secondly, as to the programmes which are set up and their coverage; thirdly, as to the actual carrying out of the programmes. The position on objectives is well set out in a brochure published by the International Institute for Educational Planning/Unesco.[1] The author, C. D. Rowley, states:

> Only in short periods of history, and in the specially favoured situation of some national systems, has it been possible to imagine that education may be divorced from politics. Obviously, the nation must be rich enough so that individuals can obtain the education they or their families want. For some time in some Western countries the structure of the legislature, the relationships between offices of the civil service, and the slow rate of change in the laws—reflecting the stability of the society—made it possible (though erroneous) to conceive of politics, with its conflicts of interest, as separate from the institutions of administration, including those concerned with the administration of the national system of public education.

The Report of the International Commission on the Development of Education already cited expresses a similar view:[2] 'No socio-political system can forgo securing its foundations by winning over minds and hearts to the principles, ideas, common references and, beyond these, the myths which bind a nation together'.

The issue was put rather more bluntly by Stalin in the famous interview which H. G. Wells had with the Soviet leader around 1922, in which he reports Stalin as saying that education was the most powerful weapon in the hands of the State and that everything depends upon who holds it and who is hit with it. Wells, by contrast, stressed the liberal objective of an education which is innocent and detached. In one of his novels, the hero Mr. Barnstable, who is projected into the future as a result of a motor accident, reflects as follows on the education of the children in the utopic society in which he finds himself: 'They had never developed that defensive suspicion of the teacher, that resistance to instruction, which is the natural response to teaching that is half aggression. They were beautifully unwary in their communications'.

This is very different from a recent statement by Paulo Freire:[3] 'One cannot educate without having a philosophy of man and the world. It is a lie to speak of neutral education'.

The extent to which a country can have a policy of beautiful unwariness depends not only on its politics, but also on the homogeneity or otherwise of its population. Thus, in schools in the United States, as a result of the great wave of immigration, the practice developed of paying particular attention in schools to symbols of nationality such as the flag. The USSR, for its part, exercises a strong central control of educational doctrine for political reasons but permits a considerable delegation of educational techniques and methods. Thus, the Twenty-Second Congress of the Communist Party of the USSR defined in 1961 the principle function of schools as 'to educate and train men and women with a Communist conscience . . .'.[4]

In the developing countries there are also efforts to introduce, through primary education, definite types of political consciousness. In Indonesia, for instance, the State philosophy, known as 'Pantja Sila' is the 'basic doctrine underlying the Government's development programme, and the working of the educational system. It incorporates five principles; belief in God, in humanity, in nationality, in democracy, and in social justice'.

Another type of political motivation is that adopted in Malaysia which has set as top priority, over and above that of economic development, the establishment of greater ethnic equality and harmony. Educational objectives are being geared to help to remedy educational inequalities between the Malay and the Chinese population.

Another case is Tanzania, which has the socialist, but at the same time, self-help political philosophy of Ujaama, which includes the creation of a cooperative education effort in the villages, directed at raising levels of living.

The reforms in Peru, derived from the Report of the Commission set up by the Revolutionary Military Government in 1970 and the Decree of March 1972 (No. 19326), aim to reshape education as a tool for social and economic development and to use it to aid the revolutionary policy of transforming a traditional oligarchic society into one in which all sections of the population participate in a spirit of personal and national self-reliance.

In India, Article 45 of the Constitution provides that the State should strive to provide free and compulsory education for all children up to the age of 14 years, which was to have been achieved by 1960, but which has remained unfulfilled. At the time the Constitution was drawn up education was regarded as a kind of automatic force which promoted progress to a more egalitarian society. However, in 1966 the Indian Education Commission included in its report the following statement:[5]

In a situation of the type we have in India, it is the responsibility of the educational system to bring the different social classes and groups together and thus promote the emergence of an egalitarian and integrated society. But at present instead of doing so, education itself is tending to increase social segregation and to perpetuate and widen class distinctions. At the primary stage, the free schools to which the masses send their children are maintained by the government and local authorities and are generally of poor quality. Some of the private schools are on the whole, definitely better; but since many of them charge high fees, they are availed of only by the middle and the higher classes.

Gunnar Myrdal, dealing with the same issue in his book *The Challenge of World Poverty*, states,[6]

When independence was won, Nehru and leaders in several other countries insisted that the entire system of education must be 'revolutionized'. But this is exactly what did not happen in India or in the other South Asian countries, except perhaps to an extent in Ceylon. The principal reforms of the system as it was inherited from the colonial times remain largely unaccomplished even today.

He goes on to say, 'A revolution of the education system would assume that which of often mistakenly said to be what these countries have been going through: a social and economic revolution'.

In regard to popular education, Myrdal says:

> Monopoly of education is—together with monopoly of ownership of land—the most fundamental basis of inequality, and it retains its hold more strongly in the poorer countries. It does so even when attempts are made to widen the availability of popular education. The mechanism is the class bias in the operation of the wastage, which in the poorer countries also is greater: drop-outs, repetition and failures in examinations.

This type of problem is not restricted to the developing countries and is at the root of the worldwide pressure for more 'democratization' of education. For the developed countries which have long periods of compulsory education, the principal political issue is the point at which general education ceases and selective education, with its occupational and class implications, begins. This is also an issue in the developing countries and comprehensive schools are being established in a number of countries. But the even greater political issue they face is the inequality of distribution of education in its most elementary and minimum form.

Variations in the distribution of educational effort within different countries are commented on in a recent article by William Rich in *The International Development Review*,[7] discussing the position in South Korea and Brazil, and Taiwan and Mexico. He writes:

> The dispersal of public funds in South Korea makes the educational system in that country accessible to a wider segment of the total population than is the case in Brazil. According to government sources, in 1970 two-thirds of Korea's population of children aged 5 to 14 were in primary school, while in Brazil only half of the same age group were in school, despite that country's much higher *per capita* income . . . .. A country that distributes goods and services on an equitable basis can bring about improvements in the welfare of the relatively poor on a wide scale even if its total resource availability is low.
>
> Thus, in Taiwan, average incomes are relatively well distributed, health services have extended throughout rural areas, and effective primary education is accessible to virtually all of the population. In Mexico, although average income is almost double that in Taiwan, the distribution of benefits is very limited, other social services also appear to be poorly shared, and the total welfare of the poorest groups is extremely low. As a result, the income of the poorest 20 per cent of the population is higher in Taiwan than in Mexico, and the 'real income'—which would include measures for health and education—is noticeably higher in Taiwan.

These comments have to be seen against the demographic and physical background of the countries mentioned. Both Taiwan and Korea are small countries with homogeneous populations. The two Latin American countries, however, have ethnically variegated populations and major topographical problems to be faced, with an inheritance of large social and cultural inequalities, causing serious difficulties in the working out and implementation of social policy.

In the matter of primary education, as in other economic and social activities, a distinction has to be made between troubles due to wrong or ill-defined objectives and those due to the ineffective carrying out of sound objectives. Forms of social change decided upon at the political or governmental level inevitably encounter in developing societies a set of hurdles and deviations before the goals can be reached.

The chief instrument for educational change is legislation. In 42 countries and territories education is not yet compulsory in law. In many other countries where education is legally compulsory, the law is far from being fully applied. This parallels the experience in respect of the Conventions on social standards sponsored by the International Labour Organization, the gap between legislation and practice being considerable except in countries with high levels of political and administrative skills. Legislation adopted nationally, as well as standards subscribed to in international bodies, frequently reflects aspirations rather than realities.

The difficulties of implementation of government decisions are illustrated in the case of primary education in Latin America by Andrew Pearse in the FAO journal *Ceres.*[8] He cites the course of Bolivian education in the period following the 1952 Revolution. He states:

> The Bolivian Revolution of 1952 and subsequent land reform broke the archaic social order . . .. From the official point of view, what the new schools aimed at was announced in the Education Code of 1955, and may be said to have had the most fundamental objectives . . .

but,

> . . . the new education became discriminatory in a new manner.

He quotes an account of the system given by Marcelo Sanguines Uriarte's book, *Educacion Rural y Desarrollo en Bolivia* (La Paz, 1968) to show that

> the aim of rural vocational education to foster peasant participation in national economic development—as stated in the 1955 Education Code—was largely substituted in practice by the expansion of secondary education. Unesco had proposed 10 colleges for the rural areas, one for each of the national regions, but in fact 56 became created, 37 of them financed by the Ministry of Peasant Affairs. These colleges had neither workshops nor equipment and operated on the norms of urban colleges, teaching by repetition for learning by rote.

In the case of Columbia, Pearse stated:

> Effective management of rural and small town schools is in the hands of the parish priest, who holds the *ex officio* position of local inspector. Rural teachers are in effect nominated by him, according to his own criteria of suitability . . .. The absence of trained teachers in the rural school implies that the society's cultural content is not transmitted in accordance with the education system's norms, but rather as a kind of folklore.

Pearse's conclusion is that the ineffectiveness of primary education in Latin America 'is not accidental', but is due to a 'deficiency of operative power on the part of the governments and among a large sector of the intended beneficiaries of the system, namely the town and the rural poor, the peasants, the Indians. This relative feebleness opens the way to modification and transformation of the education system ...' through what he calls 'institutional appropriation'. This citation illustrates not only the external influences which have been operating but also the internal dynamics within educational systems themselves which have impeded educational reform.

This type of analysis has led to the view, put out notably by Paulo Freire, that education cannot play its due role in humanizing and liberating the individual unless it takes place within a fundamental transformation of the type of traditional society still preponderant in Latin America.

In one Latin American country, Peru, where a major programme of social transformation is being attempted, the education reforms being introduced are designed to help to bring about irreversible changes in social structure. The law (Decree No. 19326) which brought in the reform in 1972 states that the reform

> must be defined as a movement oriented towards development and structural changes in Peruvian society and consequently the liberation and affirmation of our national being. Only thus can it contribute to the fulfilment of the large national majorities in overcoming their under-privileged conditions and their secular oppression, by leading them towards the collective creation of an equitable society where all participate in the development of an original and fruitful culture which, for the first time, will be authentically national.

Its purpose is described as

> to awaken in the Peruvian people a critical awareness of their condition and to stimulate them into adopting actions, based on acknowledge, which will make them participants in the historic process of removal of the old structures of dependence and domination, and covert them into free men committed to forging the future of the country.

Let us now look at the influence of parents and the home, though they overlap to some extent with the other forces. In rural areas children are often a productive asset, working in the fields or doing various jobs from quite an early age. The ILO has estimated that some 40 million children under the age of 14 are engaged in some form of work in the less developed countries. However, they are also regarded in many cases as a form of insurance against the old age of the parents. This weakens the inclination to use children as workers rather than sending them to school, since schooling is believed to result in better family income in the long run. The interplay of these two motivations has quite a determinant role in school attendance.

Parents' wishes in the developing countries are usually that their children should have the best and most prestigious (according to local standards) existing type of education available. They are not usually attracted by novel forms of education or those which are specifically related to development tasks. This has an important bearing upon the possibilities of introducing innovations and of relating education more closely to development needs. Too often the real development needs consist of education which will raise the productivity of labour in the fields and villages, whereas what the parents would prefer for their children is white-collar employment. The belief in education as a means of escape from manual occupations persists despite the shortage or total absence of clerical jobs.

Thus the popular demand of the mass of parents for primary education for their children is urgent and unabated. It is quite common to see parents waiting in numbers in front of schools and educational offices with their children, hoping to obtain enrolment, even when there are no places; and they are often prepared to make considerable sacrifices for their children's education.

This is well illustrated in a paper[9] which Kyale Mwenda, Chief Education Officer in the Ministry of Education, Kenya, prepared for a conference, on education, employment and rural development, held in Keyna (the Kericho Conference) in 1968. He wrote:

> Kenyans are avid for more education, both for themselves and their children. ... the villagers have more desire for their children's education than for themselves. They believe that literacy brings more benefit (a better life, a better income, and a better job) to their children than to themselves.

The question how much the expansion of primary education should accelerate as a result of such pressures when employment outlets are few and its methods and curricula are inefficient, is a difficult issue for educational planners, which we take up further in Part 3, Measures and Innovations. Gunnar Myrdal in the work cited earlier, although deeply critical, like Andrew Pearse, of the social forces restricting the spread of popular education, urges that there should be a temporary restriction of its extension in some countries in order to improve quality. As soon as quality has been improved and resources shifted from the other educational levels to make primary education really effective, then further expansion should take place.

The parental pressure for more education for their children is stronger for boys than for girls. In rural areas in many countries enrolment ratios are much lower for girls than for boys. The disparity is decreasing gradually over the years, though it is still marked except in Latin America. The trend has been as shown in Table 5.1.[10]

**Table 5.1**  Female as percentage of total primary enrolment

| Region | 1960 | 1965 | 1970 |
|---|---|---|---|
| Africa | 36 | 37 | 37 |
| Asia | 37 | 38 | 37 |
| Latin America | 48 | 48 | 48 |
| Arab States | 32 | 34 | 35 |

The education of girls and young women is particularly important because of their subsequent role as mothers and because of the influence exercised by the home upon the child's capacity to learn. The fact that so many mothers are uneducated is one of the forces inhibiting school attendance and better performance of the children who attend school. Failure to educate girls and mothers in at least literacy, home economics and family planning is a constant drag on the productivity and progress of the developing regions. A third to a half of agricultural workers in Asia and Africa are women and girls who have a major influence, both at work and in the home, on the standards of living of the whole community.

The force of parental opinion, therefore, while positive in its strong motivation to education as a key to betterment, leaves much to be desired, from a development standpoint, in its view of girls' education.

It is also responsible, combined with the present structure of the school system, for the production of large numbers of jobless and dissatisfied primary school leavers, many of whom move from the countryside to the towns only to find that there, too, the employment outlets they need are not available.

In an even worse position, however, are many of the pupils who go on to secondary education in the hope of getting a commensurately better job. The evidence obtained on the relative advantages of employment or unemployment and of better or worse pay for secondary school, as compared with primary, leavers has been examined by the International Labour Office under its World Employment Programme. Results are set out conveniently in a document by Jan Versluis, submitted to the Unesco International Conference on Education, September, 1973. From detailed studies made in Sri Lanka (Ceylon) and Peru, the additional years of schooling are seen to lead neither to employment prospects nor to better pay to justify the investment. Versluis states: 'Investing in the creation of a job for a person with, say, primary education may contribute more to his future well-being than providing him with a secondary education'.

Thus, the labour market should be influencing both educators and pupils in the direction of giving higher priority to primary and lower to secondary education. In fact, however, this is not at present taking place, largely because the information on the relative benefits is not widely known, but also because the secondary level is the necessary step to the third level and a limited number of higher jobs. This, therefore, is a case where outside forces are not sufficiently influencing the internal forces of educational systems to readjust its priorities, leading to much inefficiency and misinvestment. There are, fortunately, new programmes of reform in both Peru and Sri Lanka which aim at remedying this situation in those countries. In world terms, however, the problem is a general one and plans for solving it are few.

Joseph Ki-Zerbo, in his article[11] 'Education and development', puts the matter vividly as follows:

I often say that today's school is an 'insular' school. The school in the underdeveloped countries is generally the school of crude schooling without a predetermined, very precise orientation. To understand that, one must go back to the colonial period when industrialization hardly existed or was totally absent, when we were engaged in extensive, subsistence agriculture, and when the agricultural yield, export agriculture, was produced on the basis of communal labour which was very cheaply paid. At that time the school was made to furnish a handful of assistants for the administration . . .. Today's school has sometimes been compared to a sacred forest into which enter only a certain number of the initiated, charged to perform esoteric rites, escaping from everyone. Even without a fence one senses that there is an invisible enclosure which keeps out the laymen, and often even if the classes are clean, the yard is a sort of waste ground ... that is why I speak of the 'insular' school ... A school also of uprooting. First, social uprooting. A child is elected from among thousands of others. At the reopening of school there are epic squabbles and the teacher must sometimes break through the waiting line which has formed throughout the whole night. People spend the whole night awaiting recruitment. But once chosen, one is considered by one's own parents as a sort of raw material which should leave at the end of the assembly line as types of very clean, very considerate bureaucrats. And the mentality of the student himself also changes. Two years ago, we asked young pupils in the Upper Volta who started the sixth form to tell us a little about their first impressions when they arrived in the capital. These were really exquisite morsels of spontaneity ... many of these children had never seen houses of more than one storey which they described as houses one on top of the other. So all this was a considerable displacement for them; but four or six years later it is routine. This is the point of no return.

We have drawn attention earlier in this chapter to the harmful effects on development resulting from discrimination against the education of girls. Similar considerations, as well as moral factors and obligations to respect human rights, apply to racial and other discrimination. Unesco has adopted a Convention and Recommendations against Discrimination in Education in December 1960. By May 1972, 58 members had deposited instruments of ratification as acceptance of the Convention.

The purpose of the Convention and Recommendations[12] was

not only to eliminate and to prevent all discrimination but also to promote equality of opportunity and of treatment in education. Thus they correspond to two separate but complementary aims proclaimed in Unesco's Constitution. For the injustices to be fought and eliminated include, in addition to forms of discrimination which, resulting from legal provisions or administrative practices, involve a deliberate denial of the right of certain members of the community to education, inequalities which are often the consequence not so much of a conscious intention as of a set of social, geographical, human, economic and historical circumstances which have sometimes been called 'static' forms of discrimination, the better to distinguish them from 'active' and wilful forms.

The results of a study of reports by Member States on the implementation are set out in the Unesco document cited above. The study, while valuable in publishing of frank statements made by certain governments about existing forms of discrimination they were combatting, was handicapped by certain problems of definition, as can be seen from the following extract:

The reports in general call for two remarks. In the first place it appears that a

76

distinction must sometimes be made between the legislation in force and the *de facto* situation. Some forms of discrimination, based on race for example, may in fact subsist although they are not lawful and in spite of the efforts made to eliminate them. They may be the result of social attitudes too widely shared to be easily eradicated, or, on the contrary, of individual prejudices whose very isolation renders them immune to measures of a general character. In the second place, many reports do not distinguish clearly between discrimination proper and inequality of opportunity due to economic and social inequality.

What this indicates is that, although declarations and conventions in respect of the right to education are of fundamental importance, they also require a day-to-day obligation of educators at all levels to help to reduce discrimination within the institutional frameworks in which they work.

The last two of the main external forces which we listed earlier as influencing the spread of basic education are population growth and economic development. We discussed the former in detail in Chapter 3 on quantitative trends. The growth of the child population has been very rapid and the expression 'population explosion' is commonly used. The term 'explosion' is warranted in terms of its seriousness if it continues unchecked, but the simile is not appropriate. An explosion happens at once whereas the child population grows annually at about 3 per cent at present and the process is spread over time. This gives the opportunity for the trend to be corrected and in fact the annual growth is expected to taper off very considerably in the 1980s and 1990s. Population growth is therefore a serious factor affecting the speed of the attainment of universal primary education but not a prohibitive one.

Emphasis has been placed in the present chapter upon the political and social forces because even when the population rates of growth and the state of the economy permits these forces are frequently the determinants. We move now to the financial and economic factors involved.

## REFERENCES

1. *The Politics of Educational Planning in Developing Countries*, C. D. Rowley, Unesco: IIEP, 1971, p. 13.
2. Report of the International Commission on the Development of Education, from *Learning to Be*, Unesco-Harrap, 1972, p. 150.
3. 'Literacy through Conscientization', Paulo Freire, *Literacy Discussion*, Spring 1974.
4. *Reports of Member States on the Implementation of the Convention and Recommendation against Discrimination in Education*, Unesco 17 C/15, p. 70. (This document, in addition to dealing with the problem of discrimination, contains useful summaries of the educational policies of various countries.)
5. *Report of the Education Commission*, Government of India Press, Delhi, 1966, p. 10.
6. *The Challenge of World Poverty*, Gunnar Myrdal, Penguin Books, 1970, p. 179.
7. *International Development Review*, Vol. XIV, No. 3, 1972/3, p. 12. (Extract reproduced by permission of the Society for International Development.)
8. 'Latin America: with good intentions educational systems fail to promote social mobility in rural areas', Andrew Pearse, in *CERES* (FAO Review), Vol. 4, No. 3, 1971, p. 26.

9. *Education, Employment, and Rural Development*, ed. James Sheffield, East African Publishing House, Nairobi, 1967.
10. *A Summary Statistical Review of Education in the World in the Sixties*, Unesco, ED/BIE/CONFINTED 34/Ref. 1, 1973, p. 14.
11. *Prospects*, Vol. II, No. 4, Unesco, 1972, p. 413.
12. *Second Report of the Committee on Conventions and Recommendations in Education*, Reports of Member States on the implementation of the Convention and Recommendation against Discrimination in Education, Unesco 17 C/15, 1972, pp. 3 and 14.

## SELECTED FURTHER READING

'Social background of children and their chance of success at school'. *Educational Documentation and Information*, Bulletin of the International Bureau of Education, Unesco: IBE, 1971.

*Planning the Primary School Curriculum in Developing Countries*, H. W. R. Hawes, Unesco: IIEP, 1972.

*Education and Development*, ed. James S. Coleman, Princeton University Press, 1965.

*Two Worlds of Childhood. U.S. and USSR*, Urie Bronfenbrenner, Russel Sage Foundation, New York, 1970.

'Teachers and educational policy', *Educational Studies and Documents*, No. 3, Unesco, 1971.

*Pedagogy of the Oppressed*, Paulo Freire, Herder and Herder, 1968.

*National Statements on Educational Goals, Aims, and Objectives in the Asian Countries*, Japanese National Commission for Unesco MEEAA/Final Report, Appendix 6, 1969.

*Study on the Equality of Access for Girls and Women to Education in the Context of Rural Development*, United Nations Economic and Social Council E/CN. 6/566, January 1972.

*Assessment of Projects for the Education and Training of Women and Girls for Family and Community Life*, United Nations Economic and Social Council E/ICEF/L. 1275, March 1970.

'Third World woman', *Unicef News*, Issue 76, July 1973.

# CHAPTER 6

# Financial and Economic Factors

Primary education in the developing countries is almost wholly publicly financed, but in some countries parents must make a contribution through the payment of school fees and they often have to make outlays for textbooks and uniforms. Privately financed primary education is a small part of the total and consists usually of schools set up by foreigners or missionary societies.

In most countries the financing of primary education falls on the central national budget, but in some it is devolved to the provincial governments or there are mixtures of provincial with central financing. Sometimes school buildings are provided by the local community, while the salaries of teachers and inspectors are paid for from either provincial or national budgets; but on the whole little use is made of the resources of the local communities which in any event are usually small. In federal countries, finance for primary education usually comes almost entirely from the constituent states.

Public expenditure on education for the year 1971 amounted to 14·0 billion US dollar equivalent for the developing countries, excluding the People's Republic of China, the Democratic Republic of Viet-Nam, and the Democratic People's Republic of Korea. It took up 3·0 per cent of their gross national product. From 1960–1970 it had been rising at current prices on an average of 10·9 per cent. About half of the expenditure which covered all the educational levels, went to primary education. Most of the children were in countries with incomes per head of population of under 120 dollars a year.

The internal sources from which funds may be provided to finance programmes of universalizing primary education are four: (1) an increase in the total educational budget, the share of primary education in the total being kept constant; (2) redistributions of expenditure within the total educational budget which increase the share given to primary; (3) diversifying the sources of finance by obtaining local contributions and shifting some of the burden from the central or state budgets; (4) improving the cost efficiency of the system so that funds are released to aid expansion. There is also an external source in the form of cooperation programmes which seek to reduce the educational gap between the developed and the developing countries.

To increase the first source raises problems of the priority of education compared with other claims on the national budget. In general the possibilities of an increase in the total educational budget depend upon the proportion it already consumes of the national budget as a whole. This varies greatly from country to country, even between countries of roughly the same level of economic development, as can be seen from Table 6.1. The average for the developing countries is about 15 per cent, but there are very great variations on each side of this average. A few countries spend around 30 per cent of their public expenditure on education, and some as little as under 10 per cent. The figures which follow are for around 1970.

**Table 6.1**

| Country (in order of enrolment ratio) | Per capita income (US $) | Enrolment ratios by level | | Percentage of GNP to education all levels | Percentage of budget to education all levels | Pupil teacher ratio |
|---|---|---|---|---|---|---|
| | | 1st | 2nd | | | |
| Ethiopia | under 100 | 11 | 4 | 1·6 | 10·9 | 49 |
| Mauritania | 170 | 12 | 2 | 4·8 | 17·7 | 20 |
| Mali | under 100 | 20 | 2 | 4·7 | 19·5 | 35 |
| Sudan | 120 | 20 | 9 | 4·7 | 19·1 | 49 |
| Sierra Leone | 200 | 29 | 8 | 3·0 | 17·9 | 31 |
| Malawi | under 100 | 37 | 3 | 4·1 | 15·2 | 42 |
| Dahomey | 100 | 40 | 4 | 5·2 | 30·0 | 42 |
| Senegal | 250 | 40 | 7 | 3·9 | 16·1 | 45 |
| Uganda | 130 | 46 | 4 | 4·3 | 17·8 | 34 |
| Central African Republic | 150 | 76 | 4 | 1·6 | 15·4 | 63 |
| Togo | 150 | 76 | 7 | 2·2 | 19·9 | 58 |
| Ivory Coast | 330 | 77 | 10 | 5·5 | 22·5 | 45 |
| Botswana | 160 | 78 | 7 | 4·6 | 13·2 | 36 |
| Cameroon | 200 | 108 | 8 | 3·1 | 19·6 | 47 |
| Congo (People's Republic of | 270 | 145 | 21 | 7·5 | 27·2 | 60 |

These variations are not only due to different appreciations of the utility of education for national development; they also arise from differences in the proportion of national income which different countries raise in taxation and from variations in unit costs. The percentage of the budget allocated to education may be high because the budget itself is small, or because unit costs are heavy. A large percentage allocation of public funds to education does not necessarily mean that enrolments are correspondingly high. The capacity of public budgets to provide the additional educational expenditure needed to create universal education depends on fiscal and cost factors particular to each country, as well as on the rate of growth of the national income or gross national product of the country concerned. Obviously educational expenditure could not grow indefinitely at a rate much faster than that of GNP.

The necessary statistics on growth of educational expenditure and growth of GNP or national income are published in the United Nations and Unesco Statistical Yearbooks, but they are presented each on a different basis. The former are at current prices and the latter at constant prices. Thus to use them to show the burden of educational expenditure it is necessary to place them on the same basis—either of constant or of current prices. This is often overlooked and it is common to see it stated that education has been growing at twice the rate of economic growth.

If both figures are placed on the same basis, educational expenditure is shown to have been growing over recent years at between 1·1 and 1·2 times the growth of GNP if we take the developing countries as a whole. However, their proportion of GNP spent on education, after rising from 2·4 per cent in 1960 to 3·4 per cent in 1970 declined to 3 per cent in 1971, GNP having grown faster than educational expenditure in 1971.

The safest financial index of the national educational effort is thus the proportion of GNP spent on education. The most authoritative attempt to set objectives for the attainment of universal education in the developing countries were the models developed at the Unesco Conferences held in the 1960s of the Ministers of Education and overall planning authorities of the different developing regions. The quantities and the phasing over time of the educational resources required were discussed in Chapter 3 and here we need only recall the financial provision, which were also phased to stay within what were then considered to be the limits of both possible budgetary allocations and of a reasonable proportion of consumption of GNP.

The proportions of gross national product required for both the attainment of universal primary education by 1980, and in some cases 1985 (but in Latin America 1975), and also the growth of second level and higher education to meet national needs, were 6 per cent in Africa, 4·3 per cent in Asia and 4·7 per cent in Latin America.

These figures were based on an average annual economic growth rate of 5 per cent for the developing countries as a whole prevailing up to 1980. For the 1960s it turned out in fact to be 5·5 per cent. However, an average 6 per cent growth rate of GNP is postulated by the United Nations for the 1970s and has been attained for 1970–73. The latest figures are shown in Table 6.2. On this basis the models would indicate that it would be necessary to raise the percentage of GNP devoted to public

Table 6.2  Developing countries: growth of total production, 1971–1973*

| Country group | 1971 | 1972 | 1973 † |
|---|---|---|---|
| | | (percentage) | |
| Developing countries, total | 5·6 | 5·2 | 7·2 |
| Latin America | 6·5 | 6·3 | 7·4 |
| Africa | 3·8 | 5·0 | 4·3 |
| West Asia | 11·9 | 10·4 | 11·4 |
| Southern and south-eastern Asia | 3·9 | 2·5 | 7·1 |

*Measured at constant market prices.
†Preliminary.
Source: United Nations E/5521/Add 3, p. iv—20.

educational expenditure for the developing countries as a whole to 4·68 per cent of GNP by 1980, while the average percentage of educational expenditure in the revenues of the developing countries would have to rise from its average around 18 per cent in 1968 to 20–21 per cent in 1980. This is on the assumption that the proportion of GNP raised in taxes remained constant, though in fact it normally increases as the economy grows.

These proportions of GNP and revenue allocated to education have already been attained and exceeded by a considerable number of the less developed countries and would seem quite feasible as an average, though there would be difficulties in particular cases. Such cases would be where the proportion of national income raised in taxation was small, or where education costs were particularly high, and income per head low.

However, the regional objectives, as we saw in Chapter 3, have now to be reassessed in the light of the bulge in the rate of growth of the school age population estimated to take place between 1970 and 1985, and the threatened decline of economic growth rates in the developing countries adversely affected by the increase in oil prices; and this raises the question whether there is likely to be a further

**Table 6.3**  Selected developing countries: indicated changes in gross domestic product, 1973*

| Countries whose rates of growth were | | | | | | |
|---|---|---|---|---|---|---|
| More than 10 per cent | Between 8·0 and 9·9 per cent | Between 6·0 and 7·9 per cent | Between 5.0 and 5·9 per cent | Between 3·0 and 4·9 per cent | Less than 2.9 per cent | Negative |
| Saudi Arabia | Guinea | Guatemala | Congo | Argentina | Egypt | Niger |
| Republic of | Philippines | Equatorial | Panama | Rwanda | Tunisia | Guyana |
| Korea | Malawi | Guinea | Nigeria | Mozambique | United | Kuwait |
| Qatar | Dominican | Togo | Haiti | Sudan | Republic of | Mali |
| Botswana | Republic | Colombia | Paraguay | Liberia | Cameroon | Nepal |
| Iran | Venezuela | Mexico | Kenya | Namibia | Nicaragua | Chile |
| Iraq | Thailand | Fiji | Bolivia | El Salvador | Chad | Jordan |
| Ecuador | Upper | Indonesia | Peru | Israel | Morocco | Khmer Republic |
| Brazil | Volta | Zaire | Angola | Swaziland | Sri Lanka | Senegal |
| Gabon | Hong | Algeria | Libyan Arab | Costa Rica | Republic of | |
| Mauritius | Kong | Pakistan | Republic | Trinidad and | Viet-Nam | |
| Lesotho | Mauritania | Southern | Ivory Coast | Tobago | Ethiopia | |
| Singapore | Malaysia | Rhodesia | Burma | Somalia | Sierra Leone | |
| | | Bangladesh | Gambia | United | Uganda | |
| | | India | Oman | Republic of | Uruguay | |
| | | | | Tanzania | Madagascar | |
| | | | | Burundi | Dahomey | |
| | | | | Honduras | Bahrain | |
| | | | | Central | | |
| | | | | African | | |
| | | | | Republic | | |
| | | | | Ghana | | |
| | | | | Jamaica | | |

Source: United Nations E/5521/Add 3, p. iv—25.

elasticity of educational expenditure beyond that postulated in the models. This is leaving aside for the moment the fact that regional models of this kind obscure wide differences between individual countries and great disparities between different district within each country.

It would seem that in the case of the nations with the smallest enrolment ratios, the lowest *per capita* incomes and the highest unit costs, or those which are most heavily affected by oil prices, the answer would certainly be negative. The objectives would have to be scaled down and rephased, or innovatory and less costly types of education be developed. In the countries which have already attained higher enrolment ratios and are a step further up the development ladder, it would seem that some period of stagnation may have to be faced, until the bulge in the child population growth rate subsides, if expansion is sought on existing lines.

The fall in the growth rate of the child population of age to enter school which the United Nations foresees for the 1980s and 1990s is obviously of crucial importance for educational finance as it will affect both recurrent and capital expenditure. Economically it will also be important because of the so-called 'hidden bonus' which arises once the growth of gross national product overtakes that of population growth. Thus, if GNP is growing at 5 per cent and population at 3 per cent, an increase of the GNP growth rate to 6 per cent represents an increase of 50 per cent in disposable GNP. The rate for 1973 of growth of GNP was 7·2 per cent for the developing countries as a whole, an overall figure masking considerable variations between countries as illustrated by Table 6.3.

Another bonus to education would be any reduction which could take place in the expenditure of the developing countries on armaments. The developing countries spent slightly more of their gross national product on military expenditure in 1969–70 than they spent on education (3·4 per cent). Historically there have been interesting examples of how educational expansion has been based on reduction of military expenditure (e.g. the rapid increase of the educational budget in France following the end of hostilities in Algeria). A reduction of world tension and of tensions between the developing countries themselves could undoubtedly assist the growth of allocations for education. The proportion of the budgets of the developing countries taken as a whole devoted to military expenditure has been rising, as can be seen from Table 6.4 which gives figures prepared by Unesco's Statistical Office.[1]

Educational expenditure competes not only with armaments but also with the other economic and social development expenditure, such as physical investment, employment creating programmes, the demand for skilled manpower, health, housing and the social services. In strictly economic terms an increase of funds to universalize primary education would have to show greater returns than investment in these alternatives. There is, however, no satisfactory allocation procedure either in theory or still less in practice. On this issue the United Nations Committee for Development Planning wrote in the following terms:[2]

In principle, priority should be given to those elements which are conducive to acceleration in the rate of overall growth. However, there will be cases necessitating a sacrifice in the pace of growth in order to prevent social injustice. There will also be cases where the immediate impact on the rate of growth is uncertain but the long-run necessity is clear; as already mentioned, education is typically such a case. On the other hand, it should be recognized that without an adequate rate of growth the action for transforming the society will be jeopardized.

A good deal of evidence has been collected over recent years on the contribution of education to economic growth through the process of the formation of human capital. The American economist Theodore Schulz, among others, has for many years produced material on the subject. In a paper prepared by the Conference on Education and Development Reconsidered, held in 1972, he retains the view that when account is taken of the benefits conferred on the next generation, and given a

Table 6.4

| Major regions | | Military expenditure | | Public expenditure on education | |
|---|---|---|---|---|---|
| | | Million US $ | Percentage of GNP | Million US $ | Percentage of GNP |
| World * | 1967 | 170 165 | 7·1 | 117 800 | 4·9 |
| | 1970 | 197 495 | 6·4 | 160 750 | 5·2 |
| Africa | 1967 | 1 750 | 3·4 | 2 190 | 4.2 |
| | 1970 | 2 190 | 3·3 | 2 855 | 4.3 |
| Northern | 1967 | 77 265 | 9·1 | 49 950 | 5·9 |
| America | 1970 | 79 735 | 7·5 | 71 780 | 6·8 |
| Latin | 1967 | 2 200 | 2·0 | 3 440 | 3·1 |
| America | 1970 | 2 930 | 2·0 | 4 710 | 3·2 |
| Asia * | 1967 | 7 240 | 2·9 | 8 800 | 3·6 |
| | 1970 | 10 820 | 3·0 | 13 170 | 3·6 |
| Europe and | 1967 | 80 450 | 7·3 | 52 110 | 4·7 |
| USSR | 1970 | 100 385 | 7·0 | 66 290 | 4·6 |
| Oceania | 1967 | 1 260 | 4·1; | 1 310 | 4·2 |
| | 1970 | 1 435 | 3·6 | 1 945 | 4·9 |
| (Arab | 1967 | (1 870) | (7·2) | (1 250) | (4·8) |
| States) | 1970 | (2 480) | (7·3) | (1 750) | (5·2) |
| Developed | 1967 | 161 035 | 7·7 | 109 000 | 5·2 |
| countries | 1970 | 184 815 | 6·7 | 148 520 | 5·4 |
| Developing | 1967 | 9 130 | 3·1 | 8 800 | 3·0 |
| countries | 1970 | 12 680 | 3·5 | 12 230 | 3·4 |

* Not including China (mainland), Democratic People's Republic of Korea and Democratic Republic of Viet-Nam.

successful development process, the rates of return to schooling tend to be fully as high as they are on the better half of the investments in non-human capital. He states that, in terms of rates of return, higher education ranks far below elementary schooling. The rate of return on completing the elementary years is as a rule the highest.

He draws special attention to the benefits of the education of girls, and states:[3]

Most women in the developing countries are poorly equipped in terms of the schooling that is required to manage their households skilfully in taking advantage of new technical information with respect to nutrition, health and child care. Another favourable effect of the schooling of women is the improvement in their ability to decode, interpret and successfully adopt the new superior contraceptive techniques. The most important effect of the schooling of females may well be the social benefit that arises out of the marked advantage that children derive from being reared in homes where the mothers have had schooling. There is a growing body of evidence in support of the inference that the level of schooling of mothers is most important in accounting for the quality of the inputs they provide for their children. It is this particular social benefit that accounts for the relatively high social rates of return to the investment in the education of women.

The results of field studies showing the impact of literacy in improving productivity and reducing family size, argue positively for increased investment in the reduction of illiteracy. A number of these results are set out in the Unesco publication *Literacy and Development*. The impact of literacy on productivity can be seen from the results of a study in Bombay which made a comparison of the productivity of literate and illiterate workers in textile factories. It was found that even when illiterate workers were trained on the job their performance was much below that of literates under a range of criteria including working speeds, good work habits, cooperation with factory requirements, etc. A composite index of performance was found to be as follows:[4]

Composite index of performance

|                  | Low | Average | High | Total |
|------------------|-----|---------|------|-------|
| Illiterate trained | 47  | 137     | 66   | 250   |
| Literate trained   | 15  | 66      | 171  | 250   |

The effect of formal schooling in reducing the average number of births can be seen from the Table 6.5 which shows the result of a case study in a village in Chile.[5]

Table 6.5    The relationship between educational level and fertility in Cauquenes, Chile

| Education level of women interviewed | Average no. of births Per Couple | Percentage of population |
|--------------------------------------|----------------------------------|--------------------------|
| No formal education       | 4·86 | 20·2 |
| Some primary school       | 3·40 | 48·3 |
| Complete primary school   | 1·26 | 13·1 |
| Some secondary school     | 1·21 | 14·4 |
| Complete secondary school | 1·69 | 4·0  |

There is thus a basis for believing that in many cases, especially in countries where educational expenditure is below the world average for their level of development, a judicious increase in the proportion of government funds devoted to education is desirable on economic grounds alone.

Up to this point our concern has been with the question of increasing the proportion of educational expenditure in public budgets, which, it will be recalled, we had listed as the first possible source of financing universal primary education. We turn now to the second source of funds for universalizing primary education, namely switching resources between the educational levels. This course is no less free from difficulties than the first. Apart from constraints and resistencies which may be encountered in the educational system itself, a change in the balance between the different educational levels is a political as well as an educational issue in developing countries. It is also one which has to be considered in the whole context of the educational plan and the country's manpower needs.

A switch of resources could take place in two ways. Either the existing proportions between the levels can be changed, or the rates of future growth can be redistributed. The second involves less difficulty than the first, especially as the rate of growth of the second and higher levels has been much higher—and often double—that of the first level during the last decade. A slackening of the high growth of these levels could release funds for expanding primary education.

Some studies at the macro-educational level of the rate of return on the different educational levels suggest that such a course may be desirable in a number of cases on economic grounds. Nalla Gounden, for instance, writes in a study of education in India:[6]

> The rates of return to different levels of education vary considerably. The highest rate accrues to primary education, whereas the lowest accrues to a non-technical Bachelor's degree. Thus, the rates of return and levels of education are inversely related. This is an economic equivalent of the criticism that Indian education is heavy at the top and weak at the bottom. It is also an economic argument in favour of expediting the implementation of the constitutional directive that free and compulsory education should be provided to all children up to the age of 14.

His tables setting out the rates of return found in his enquiry, show a $15 \cdot 9$ return for schooling which makes children literate as compared with illiteracy, a $17 \cdot 0$ return for full primary education as compared with the simple attainment of literacy, but only an $11 \cdot 8$ return on obtaining middle level education as compared with primary.

At the Conference on Education and Development Reconsidered which we have already mentioned, Mark Blaug, the British economist, stated in the document he submitted:[3]

> We have relevant data for ten developing countries and in most of these (Brazil, Malaysia and the Phillipines are exceptions) primary education yields higher social rates of return (i.e. economic return to the community as a whole) than any other level of education. As between secondary and higher education, however, the situation is more mixed: in half of the developing countries secondary education also ranks above higher education, but in the other half the ranking is reversed. The discrepancies in most cases are so large that even huge shifts of resources over a period of five to ten years would not suffice to close the gap.

Naturally the situation has to be examined in each country, but the existence of possible areas of manoeuvre can be seen from the variations between countries. In Thailand for instance 61 per cent of the educational budget was allocated to

86

**Table 6.5**    Change in percentage of educational budget
allocated to first level
(1969–70 – a few cases a year or two earlier)

The 25 least developed countries

| Down (13)[1] | Up (6)[2] |
|---|---|
| Burundi | Chad |
| Dahomey | Ethiopia |
| Malawi | Mali |
| Niger | Upper Volta |
| Uganda | Haiti |
| Rwanda | Laos |
| Somalia | |
| Sudan | |
| Tanzania | |
| Afghanistan | |
| Bhutan | |
| Guinea | |
| Botswana | |

AFRICA

| Down (23) | Up (7) |
|---|---|
| Algeria | CAF |
| Botswana | Chad |
| Burundi | Ethiopia |
| Cameroon | Mali |
| Congo | Mauritius |
| Dahomey | Togo |
| Gambia | Upper Volta |
| Ghana | |
| Guinea | |
| Ivory Coast | |
| Madagascar | |
| Malawi | |
| Niger | |
| Nigeria | |
| Uganda | |
| Rwanda | |
| Sierra Leone | |
| Somalia | |
| Sudan | |
| Swaziland | |
| Tunisia | |
| Tanzania | |
| Zambia | |

ASIA

| Down (15) | Up (6) |
|---|---|
| Afghanistan | Iran |
| Bahrain | Khmer R. (1965–67) |
| Bhutan | Kuwait |
| Brunei | Laos |
| India (1966–67) | Sabah |
| Iraq | Syria |
| Jordan | |
| Korea | |
| Lebanon | |
| Malaysia (West) | |
| Pakistan | |

**Table 6.5** (continued)

Quatar
Singapore
Thailand
Viet-Nam
(no figures for Indonesia)

LATIN AMERICA

| Down (12) | Up (9) |
| --- | --- |
| Honduras (British) | Costa Rica |
| Cuba | Guatemala |
| El Salvador | Haiti |
| Jamaica | Honduras |
| Nicaragua | Mexico |
| Panama | Bolivia |
| Trinidad and Tobago | Chile |
| Argentina | Brazil |
| Colombia | Guyana |
| Ecuador | |
| Paraguay | |
| Peru | |

primary education in 1969, and in Afghanistan 36·7 per cent. Key factors would appear to be the economic and social objectives which countries set, or can afford to set, at different levels of development.

However, it would seem that despite the over-production in the second and higher levels and the new importance generally being ascribed to the first level, the percentage of the educational budget spent on primary and pre-primary education fell between 1969 and 1970 for most countries. Out of 34 African countries the percentage went down in 24 and up in 7. In Latin America it went down in 12 and up in 10. In Asia the percentage was down in 15 and up in 6. In other countries it was more or less stable. Table 6.5 shows the position. Few countries, it would seem, are undertaking the 'huge shifts of resources' between the educational levels which the rate of return studies quoted show would be required to correct the gap between the higher returns on primary education and the lower returns on secondary and higher.

The third means of raising additional funds for helping to finance the universalizing of primary education is by diversifying sources of finance and obtaining a greater contribution from local communities, either through voluntary contributions or regular or special taxes. This has the effect of taking the pressure off state expenditure where competition with other priorities is high.

It is interesting to note that three of the economically well-developed countries (the United States, the United Kingdom, the USSR) with very different economic systems relied heavily upon breaking down the problem at the central level by drawing upon local resources and initiatives. During the year 1929–30, for instance, only 4·6 per cent of the 53,647 schools in the USSR engaged in the eradication of illiteracy were paid for out of the State budget, whereas 74·4 per cent were supported by local municipal, district and rural budgets, and 21 per cent were financed from extra-budgetary sources (trade unions, cooperatives etc.). During the same financial year the number of schools in the USSR with paid teachers was

50,965, and with unpaid teachers 46,142 (the latter coming from 'anti-illiteracy societies', factories and institutions of various kinds). In the case of the great expansion of the United States in the last century, the building of a school was one of the first charges on the resources of the newly established communities and voluntary teachers were widely used.

As regards special taxes fiscal opinion is usually opposed to them on the ground that they do not increase the amount of funds forthcoming but merely earmark their use in advance and therefore make it difficult to undertake financial planning of resources. However, it is also true that people pay more readily for items they can see such as school buildings and the enrolment of their children than they do for distant expenses of the central government. Also experience has shown that they are willing to go to considerable lengths and sacrifices to get their children to school.

This point was made by Professor Alerko of Nigeria in a paper[7] presented to a Congress of the International Institute of Public Finance, when he stated that the enthusiasm for education was so widespread in Nigeria that while women resent the imposition of income taxes on them they will readily pay a levy devoted exclusively to the education of their children.

Similarly an educational levy on industry, particularly on foreign firms, could be a valuable contribution. In some of the developing countries industry and mining, or other types of private enterprise (national or foreign) often draw large profits without giving much support to the socio-economic infrastructures of the areas where they work. In one African country about one third of its gross national product is exported in the form of returns on foreign investment.

It seems more than reasonable in such cases, and in the interest of the private enterprises involved, since they draw upon local labour, that some kind of levy to raise the educational level of the labour force should be instituted, either by legislation or by voluntary cooperation among the enterprises involved and the state. Some private companies do in fact set up primary schools in which both local and expatriate children are educated. An extension of this practice under state supervision is to be welcomed.

As regards voluntary contributions, this possibility varies from country to country and area to area. Kenya is a particularly interesting example of voluntary local effort. In 1970 enrolments in secondary schools unaided by the government (mainly the Harambee schools) took up 40 per cent of the total secondary enrolment. On the other hand, there are great disparities in educational opportunity between the different parts of the country. These tend to be increased by local voluntary effort in the richer areas and the reduction of inequalities depends on a nationwide effort based on public budgets.

There has also been a tendency for schools to be built by local voluntary effort followed by demands on the government to provide numbers of teachers sometimes in excess of public financial possibilities. Nevertheless well organized voluntary effort can make an important contribution. Fee paying, on the other hand, is to be discouraged since it frequently excludes the underprivileged, as it is in practice usually impossible to apply a 'means test'. The evidence is that even a small rise in fees tends to lead to withdrawals and in low income countries fees are a cause of non-enrolment. In some low income countries, like Indonesia, fee paying exists parallel with the allocation of a relatively low proportion of public expenditure to education.

An account of what has been found possible in the form of self-help in the financing of primary education in Kenya and in the distribution of expenditure to local rather than central sources is to be found in a document[8] of the International Institute of Educational Planning, by J. E. Anderson. He points out that the local community pays, through fees or some form of taxation, for approximately two-thirds of the recurrent cost of primary education. As regards capital expenditure for buildings etc., the proportion is about 93 per cent.

The fourth in our list of sources from which finance can be provided for universalizing primary education, it will be recalled, was the introduction of changes which may give the same output for less cost, or which may accept more modest forms of output. Here too there are difficulties, especially because the present quality of primary education is very low and more rather than less expenditure seems required.

Nevertheless there are a number of measures which could increase output without the input of additional funds. For instance, there is considerable evidence, as we saw in Chapter 4, that the system of grade-by-grade tests which leads to large numbers of pupils having to repeat grades and so become a sort of dam, blocking access to those below, frequently does not justify itself and should be replaced by automatic promotion. Similarly shorter but more efficient cycles of basic education are more economical than longer inefficient cycles afflicted with heavy drop-out.

An interesting example of how a country can improve the efficiency of its primary education is that of Sri Lanka (Ceylon). In a recent publication,[9] J. Hallak states in conclusion:

The raising of the admission age from 5 to 6, the shortening of first level schooling from eight to five grades (with the introduction of automatic promotion in some grades), will be compensated for by the increased participation of children in the age group 6–11, and by quality improvement in grades 1–5.

Thus, on the whole, the mechanical effect of the school reform on educational cost will be: a decrease in the proportion of the budget going to first level; a major increase in the proportion allocated to the second level; and some increase in the proportion devoted to the other sectors of education.

The cost variation between countries is illustrated by a study by Botti.[10] He showed that 'an enrolment rate of 7 per cent for Mauritania would involve as great an effort as total enrolment for Gabon'. This is based on a formula

$$\frac{y}{p \times c}$$

where $y$ is *per capita* income, $p$ the percentage of school-age population (6–13 years) out of total population and $c$ the ratio between the cost of primary education and the population educated to that level. Taking 100 as the index of the cost of total enrolment for Gabon, he finds the same effort would produce only 73 per cent for East Cameroun, 17 per cent for Dahomey, 12 per cent for Mali, 10 per cent for Niger and 7 per cent for Mauritania. These figures show the huge cost differentials between countries.

While it is easy to identify low or excessive costs, it is very difficult to change cost structures, as they are usually a function of the level of teachers' salaries, which are the predominant factor in primary educational expenditure making up 85 to 90 per cent of the total.

Broadly, it will be found that primary school teachers' salaries in Asia are on the low side in comparison with *per capita* income. Asian unit costs permit fairly high enrolment ratios but do not favour quality. In Africa teachers' salaries at the primary level are in many countries on the high side in relation to *per capita* income and unit costs are correspondingly high, without, unfortunately, comparable gains in quality, owing to the number of untrained teachers. In Latin America a better equilibrium between unit costs and *per capita* income exists, a situation affected both by the fact that four fifths of the teachers are women and by the level of economic development being higher.

Where teachers' salaries are relatively low their status tends also to be low, except in areas where modernization is taking place. In traditional areas the teacher in public primary schools is at some disadvantage as regards claims for higher remuneration, since traditionally the teachers in the religious schools have received gifts in kind, partly because the local economy worked that way and partly as a result of value attached in the Islamic and Buddhic traditions to the offer and receipt of alms by imams and monks.

Raising the social status of teachers is less difficult than producing the large sums required to increase their salaries. It is an inducement not to be overlooked in areas where there are not great possibilities of consumer spending and where status is still a major form of satisfaction. The provision of fringe benefits also are important, especially in the form of housing and free education for teachers' children and social service facilities for teachers' families.

Ways of increasing the living levels of the teaching force without throwing an immediate heavy burden on the budget have to be sought. Among these might be the conferring upon village teachers of part-time community tasks which would be a supplementary form of income. Examples would be adult literacy classes in the evenings, community development work and liaison between the school and other social services affecting child development, to which a contribution might be made from those services (e.g. health and nutrition). Such measures might not only give extra remuneration and status to the local teacher but help to break down the isolation of the school and teachers from the rest of the community which has been deplored in earlier chapters.

Within the same type of action it should be possible to improve the security of employment of teachers and to raise their retirement pensions, combined with a better selection for entry into permanent employment. John Vaizey has pointed out that retirement pensions offered now on a non-contributory basis to teachers in their twenties will only fall due for payment in thirty to forty years time when *per capita* national income will have risen very considerably. Because the economic returns on investment (mostly in the form of teachers' salaries) in primary education requires a considerable period of time to mature (i.e. it is necessary to wait until the children become average workers in the labour force), it is not improvident to finance the country's future productivity from the future, rather than the present.

An allied consideration is that the number of children in the age group 6–11 in the developing countries will rise over the next decade, but will fall thereafter according to the United Nations estimates. This will relatively reduce the educational burden falling upon the future, as opposed to the present, working population.

A factor on the other side of the balance is that the rapid expansion of education in the 1960s has brought into education large numbers of young teachers in their twenties. These will steadily rise up the salary scale and considerably increase unit costs as they do so. More funds have to be found, both for teachers' salaries and for teacher training.

It is now necessary to envisage the other side of the problem, namely cases where teachers' salaries are exceptionally high relative to *per capita* income. An example would be an African country where the average salary of a primary school teacher is as much as twenty times or more than of the average national income per head (compared with two or three times in Europe) and where projections of educational costs preclude the attainment of universal primary education for a very long time. In Niger, for instance, in 1961 the midpoint salary for a primary school teacher was 46·2 times *per capita* income, whereas in Ghana it was ten times less, namely 4·2 (see *The World Educational Crisis* by Philip Coombs.[11]

In some cases the cause is often the colonial history of the country, the government on obtaining independence having applied standards previously enjoyed by expatriates. This applies particularly to countries where the colonial power took an active interest in government and in the organization of education. In other cases where the initiative was largely left to missionaries and voluntary agencies, more financially economical systems have been set up, the teachers sometimes receiving gifts in kind to supplement low salaries and being closely integrated with the rest of the community. In such cases the teacher is not regarded so much as the village intellectual but as a general handyman and member of the group charged with the problems of bringing the community into direct relation with the government educational machinery. While this has many social advantages it also has some pedagogic disadvantages. At present, it seems rare for the right balance to be struck between the teacher being seen as an outside intellectual force and his appearing as an active member of the day-to-day community.

In the circumstances of high teacher cost countries, it is very unlikely that it would be possible or desirable to bring about a planned reduction of teachers' salaries. An approach more likely to be feasible would be to have greater use of monitors and even to set up a new grade of village teachers trained differently and paid at a rate more in keeping with the income of the average villager, with perhaps additional sources of income from other social and community functions. There should also be a more discriminating use of one teacher schools in poor localities, and of non-formal education centres linked by ladders and bridges to nuclear schools, which will reduce wastage.

Other measures such as converting rural teachers into more multi-purpose instructors who would be recruited from the rural environment itself are discussed in the chapter on rural education.

Apart from the question of teachers' salaries there are not many economies to be made in cost-efficiency, since the standards of school accommodation and of inspection and administration do not provide much room for manoeuvre. Where there is a large investment in new school buildings, however, economies can be made in their design, cost of construction and location. It is interesting to note, though the lesson is not necessarily transferable, that the cost of a place in a primary school in England and Wales was £195 in 1949, but by 1956 the cost had been reduced to £154, although building costs had risen by 50 per cent over the same period.

In some cases it will be desirable to increase the size of schools in order to achieve economies of scale where there are too many small schools in a populous neighbourhood where transportation to school is available. In other cases benefits in relation to cost will be great if the plan is to increase the number of small or one-teacher schools for scattered populations.

An example of the economies arising from consolidating schools is evident from a study made in Ireland by the OECD whose report[12] states:

> For both the primary and secondary schools, the key school characteristic was discovered to be school size. For the primary schools, the planning team experimentally ran a massive tabulation of school characteristics through a computer analysis which demonstrated a strategy for feasible school consolidation that could result in a saving of 500 classrooms and 1200 teachers in the immediate future of Irish school development.

Before concluding this chapter it is useful to reflect on some important general aspects of educational finance and the nature of the real burden which educational expenditure places upon the country. What happens when the education system is publicly financed is that 90 per cent of the money involved goes from the pockets of the taxpayers into those of the primary school teachers. The economics of the transfer depend not only on what alternative use the government could have made of the money, but also on the extent to which it causes a regression of the country's taxable capacity, or it constitutes a desirable or undesirable form of income redistribution.

On the latter point it is to be noted that schoolteachers have on the whole better than average consumption patterns and propensities to save, though their salaries are small. A further point is that the expansion of primary education provides, through the increase of the teaching force, additional employment outlets for secondary school leavers who would otherwise be unemployed.

This does not mean that educational budgets can grow indefinitely or too fast and each country certainly has its own particular difficulties. Nor does it deny that there is in fact a hard core of least educationally developed countries, and district within countries, where progress is bound to be slow. What is meant is that it is a mistake to consider the rise in educational expenditure at the primary level as merely an addition to consumption expenditure. It is also a form of investment which may be well worth while for economic reasons alone, given the development conjunction of the average developing country, particularly as its consumption of capital in the form of buildings and equipment is relatively small, and the average expenditure on primary education in the developing countries was only between 1·5 and 1·7 of their gross national product.

We have already drawn attention to the erroneous conclusions which arise from comparing educational expenditure over the years at current prices with the figures for the rise in GNP which are given at constant prices. A similar confusion arises in respect of education costs which are frequently described as 'spiralling' and being escalated by inflation.

It is true that recurrent expenditure on education has built into it certain escalatory costs owing to the fact that teachers proceed up a scale of seniority and therefore increase the burden on the budget as they obtain higher increments. Further, it is also true that a substantial proportion of the teachers in the developing countries are untrained and, as they become replaced by trained teachers, higher salaries will have to be paid. These rises, however, have nothing to do with inflation.

Indeed the evidence is that inflation is reducing rather than increasing the real costs of education. This would not be surprising since educational costs are made up primarily of teachers' salaries and since salaries usually lag behind price increases until eventually corrected, by which time prices have further increased. The Unesco Regional Office for Asia points out that in Asia while in all cases the rate of educational expenditure has been ahead of the enrolment increase, a considerable part of the per pupil expenditure is caused by increasing prices.[13] Only for four countries in Asia (Republic of Korea, Laos, Singapore and Thailand) has per pupil expenditure increased faster than prices. For the other countries prices have increased faster than expenditure per pupil. The result of this is either lower salaries in real terms for the teachers or less educational materials and overcrowded school buildings.

This does not mean that inflation is helpful to educational development. On the contrary, it has the result of making public funds harder to get and has notoriously bad effects on the economy as a whole from which education suffers more than it gains from a decline in real costs.

This is illustrated in Table 6.6.[13]

It will have been seen from this chapter that the real financial restraints and possibilities affecting the universalization of primary education are not reflected in simple budgetary percentages. The complexity of the factors involved and the variations between individual countries are illustrated by the Table 6.1 and by the set of indicators shown in Appendix 1 at the end of this book, which includes comparisons of tax effort and rates of growth of the child population of the different countries.

It is, however, of little use for Ministers of Education and Finance to be confronted at the time the yearly financial allocations are being made with the wider considerations we have discussed. Allocations for any given year have to be made with the then existing tax effort and the then existing set of unit costs and prevailing type of organization of the educational system. The confrontation which is needed with these wider considerations has to take place at the level of the medium-term and long-term plan. In Chapter 8 we suggest a model in which the various factors, economic, social and organizational may be confronted, in order to universalize basic education and, at the same time, achieve a well balanced educational development. The sources and problems of educational finance we have been describing so far relate to formal primary education. There is less that can be said about the financing of non-formal education since as we shall see later from Chapter 9 its extent is much more limited, though it is hoped in many quarters that it will increase greatly in the future.

**Table 6.6** Development of per pupil recurring expenditure in first-level education, period 1960–1970 (selected countries)

| Country | Period | Increase in per pupil recurring expenditure (%) | Increase in consumer prices (%) |
|---------|--------|--------------------------------|--------------------|
| Afghanistan | 1960–1970 | 18 | 100* |
| India | 1961–1967 | 39 | 66 |
| Indonesia | 1961–1970 | 619 | 405 000 |
| Iran | 1962–1969 | 6 | 13 |
| Korea, Rep. of | 1962–1971 | 281 | 170† |
| Laos | 1963–1970 | 244 | 198 |
| Malaysia (West) | 1962–1969 | 6 | 7 |
| Nepal | 1963–1969 | 13 | 38 |
| Philippines | 1961–1967 | 23 | 39 |
| Singapore | 1960–1969 | 42 | 13 |
| Sri Lanka | 1960–1969 | 11 | 26 |
| Thailand | 1960–1970 | 92 | 23 |
| Viet-Nam, Rep. of | 1963–1972 | 352 | 725 |

\* Period 1961–1969
† Period 1962–1969

At present non-formal education is not financed from the budget of the Ministry of Education except in a few cases such as special education for the handicapped. The usual source of funds is the ministry which is concerned with the particular field of activity such as the ministries of Agriculture or Health or Industry or those handling community development.

The most authoritative study of non-formal education in the developing countries and of its possibilities and costs is contained in a research report prepared for the World Bank by the International Council for Educational Development.[14] This report, written by Philip Coombs and Manzoor Ahmed, states that the main potential sources of finance other than external aid are the public budgets at the national or provincial level; the use of resources at present devoted to formal education or from the normal expansion of the educational system; local contributions at the local community level; special taxes for the purpose or levies on payrolls of larger employers; funds devoted to improving communications such as mass media facilities; self support and voluntary effort; partial self financing through selling services and articles produced in training centres; fees from participants.

To these sources we might ourselves add the suggestion of an administrative measure which might prove helpful. A country which took as one of its overriding objectives the need to give a minimum basic education to all children and youth before they became adult might usefully establish some central authority linked to the Ministry of Education which would have the specific task of setting up recuperative programmes for children and youth who had missed schooling and were swelling the ranks of adult illiterates.

Such an authority would not necessarily operate in a centralized manner but rather devolve the responsibilities for finding resources both on provincial and local governments and on industry and agriculture itself. This would have the advantage of avoiding difficult clashes between claims for funds for the formal and non-formal educational programmes. While in reality the two should be regarded as interlocking and supplementary to each other and not in competition, difficulties are bound to arise in practice on this score.

Since, as we saw, the growth of expenditure on formal basic education raises in itself serious problems, and as non-formal education has at present little chance of having the preference of the electorate and the administration over formal education, a special effort is required to take it off public budgets. On the other hand, if it is left only to local initiative, self-help, and the marginal interest of the other ministries, its development will continue to be sporadic and limited as at present. Thus the case for a central authority closely linked to the Ministry of Education, but able to promote initiatives in the other ministries concerned and among employers, is a strong one. It may be that as has been experienced in a few countries such as Iran which have made a direct attack on illiteracy as a matter of national priority, this organization should have a special link with the Prime Minister's Office, not because the programme is more important than that of the individual ministries but owing to the difficulties of launching programmes of this kind which cut across various lines of authorities.

Such a central source of effort would inevitably be concerned not only with universalizing basic education for youth before the age of adulthood but also and perhaps more particularly with adult illiteracy. This in turn is likely to mean programmes directed at the sectors of the population where the returns on literacy would be highest and incentives strongest and results most lasting namely the illiterate population already in industry or in areas where economic development is going ahead. This type of reasoning is illustrated by a statement made by Dr. Julius Nyerere, President of the Republic of Tanzania in a declaration to Parliament during the inauguration of the first five-year development plan in 1964, in which he said: 'First we must educate adults. Our children will not have an impact on our economic development for five, ten, or even twenty years'. The Tanzanian programme, however, has not followed this course which runs counter to general sentiment.

However, within the objective of recuperating youth who have missed education we could look as a first step at the same kind of selective and economic approach applied in the case of adults, namely the setting up by employers of literacy classes within factories and large farms and plantations. This would mean that while a full attempt was made to universalize basic education for children up to 15, the programme for those over 15 and under 18 would as a matter of strategy be limited initially to the areas where development was most active, though other areas could be included for pilot projects as opportunities arose. This is hard doctrine but no alternative would seem possible in most developing countries which would be feasible both financially and educationally.

If this view is taken then employers and development authorities benefiting from the universalizing of primary education have a special responsibility to contribute. This point was made in the present author's *Literacy and Development* which concludes with three appeals to sources of funds. He states in regard to the first appeal:[4]

Obviously the sector of society with which the greatest means lie for eliminating illiteracy is employers themselves. If lasting motivations for literacy and its successful acquisition depend upon literacy being functional and work oriented, then it is to those who provide work that we must look for the highest proportion of effort for the eradication of illiteracy. This means that a special responsibility falls primarily on employers, but also on development agencies and financing organizations concerned with the development projects which will create employment.

A second appeal was made to all of the administration and civic activities dealing with people in the home or family life. An increasing number of health, family planning, community and agricultural extension services are being set up and need for their effective operation the advantages which literacy can bring to their clientele. The third appeal was to the group of ordinary people who are concerned with world development and are prepared to contribute with external financial aid or as volunteers to the elimination of illiteracy.

The unit costs of education vary greatly according to the type of project. Those with a strong vocational bias which involve equipment are obviously more expensive, whereas educational clubs for youths and classes which make use of school premises and teachers with the minimum of extra equipment are much cheaper. The range of unit costs is probably between $10 and $15 per pupil to over a $100. However, the type of project with a vocational input is rare for older children and youth and normally involves a minimum of basic education which children who have not attended school do not have.

The question whether non-formal education has a cost advantage over formal is very relevant for the least developed countries and for programmes for pushing out basic education into less favoured areas of individual countries. On this point the research study we quoted above states:

Non-formal education has a number of potential cost advantages over formal education programmes with comparable educational objectives. But it should never ben taken for granted that these advantages will be realized in practice.

There is little that can be said with certainty on this matter without further detailed studies and studies would at present compare existing types of projects in nonformal education.

What is needed is a series of experiments which can be carefully costed and evaluated from the start so that a comparison can be made with well-conceived projects rather than those which exist, many of which have grown up sporadically and not been developed in a scientific manner. The fundamental issue however as the study points out is not so much the comparative costs but how this cost relates to the output achieved under the two alternatives taken not only in terms of minimum learning needs but also the contribution made to national development.

For adult literacy, such an experiment exists in the form of the Unesco/UNDP Experimental Work Orientated Literacy Programme in operation now for some eight years. Under this programme a million persons have entered literacy courses associated with work projects in their environment. The cost including both the national and the international expenditure has been around US $24 million indicating a rough enrolment unit cost of $24. Although intended for adults some adolescents have found their way into the courses.

The unit cost of $24 a pupil covers both recurrent and capital expenditure, the latter being extremely small since the programme is based on using the existing facilities of the work enrivonment. The cost does, however, include a substantial amount, which is of a research and development character, namely the expenditure on the remuneration of experts to design the project, the preparation of manuals and teaching materials, and the scientific control and evaluation of the experiment. Once the research and development expenditure is completed and the projects are running on their own the unit cost it is anticipated will be about the same as that of formal primary education.

On such a unit cost basis 10 million young persons between the ages of 14 and 18 could receive a functional work orientated training for a sum of $240 million. It may be noted that the sum represents only 2 per cent of the total annual educational budgets of the developing countries and could be met by a 4 per cent reduction of the funds going to the second and higher levels; though this comparison is unreal in the sense that each country's case is different. Less expensive projects are also possible.

As regards the extension of the primary school system itself, overall estimates are much more difficult.

For a programme of universalizing minimum basic education with a four-year cycle the task in terms of teacher supply, pupil places and finance would be substantially less onerous and cost efficiency would certainly be improved by the reduction of wastage. Teacher training for the purpose of a four-year course of basic education would similarly be less onerous to supply than the higher qualifications required under the present regional objectives.

On the other hand, additional cost as compared with the original objectives would result from the structures between village and district nuclear schools which would need to be created to make programmes of minimum basic education accep-

98

table to parents and to provide at least minimum educational opportunity. A further additional cost would be the selective recuperative programmes of non-formal education undertaken in areas where development was active for youth who missed a minimum basic education at school.

Provision would also have to be made for increased research and development expenditure and other financial inputs directly related to bringing about educational change.

Financially there would, in the average country, be no absolute impediment to such programmes, provided that, in addition to the increase found possible in educational budgets, some reallocation of resources was made over the period as necessary which increased the share of the growth of expenditure going to the first educational level in the total educational budget and reduced that of the second and higher levels, owing to a new assessment of their relative priorities. A redeployment in the same sense of external assistance, which plays a substantial role in some of the developing countries, could also contribute substantially, especially in providing 'pump priming' inputs of various kinds to which national budgets can usually only respond slowly.

It would seem that a 5 to 10 per cent increase in the allocation to the first level within the educational budget, combined with a 5 per cent annual growth of the educational budget which GNP growth usually permits would provide not only for the required programme of universalizing minimum basic education but also for ongoing and new efforts, within the ordinary first level expenditure, to substantially help improve first level education as a whole including the establishment of guidance courses related to life and work and improving the educational quality of the upper part of the primary cycle.

A strong impression is also justifiable that the gains in terms of educational output and cost efficiency would far exceed the expense of reorganizing the primary cycle and setting up non-formal education for youth on the terms proposed.

## REFERENCES

1. *A Summary Statistical Review of Education in the World in the Sixties*, Unesco: IBE ED/CONFINTED 34/Ref. 1, 1973, p. 34.
2. *Towards Accelerated Development: Proposals for the Second United Nations Development Decade*, Report of the Committee for Development Planning, United Nations, 1970.
3. Background papers for *Conference on Education and Development Reconsidered*, held at Bellagio, sponsored by Rockefeller and Ford Foundations, New York, 1972.
4. *Literacy and Development*, H. M. Phillips, Unesco, 1970, pp. 26, 43, 55.
5. 'Influences affecting fertility in urban and rural Latin America', Carmen Miro and Walter Mertens, *Milbank Memorial Fund Quarterly*, July 1968, p. 105.
6. *Journal of Human Resources*, Vol. II, No. 3, p. 357.
7. 'Public finance and education in Nigeria', S. A. Alerko, in *Public Finance and Education,* International Institute of Public Finance, Paris, 1966.
8. *The Organization and Financing of Self-Help in Kenya*, J. E. Anderson, International Institute of Educational Planning 525/3.

9. *The Financing of Educational Expenditure 1970–1980*, R. Poignant, J. Hallak, Ta Ngoc Chau and C. Tibi, International Commission on the Development of Education, Series B: Opinions, No. 15. Unesco, 1972.
10. *Costs of Primary Education in Madagascar and Eight Other French-Speaking Countries of Africa*, Botti, IIEP Occasional Papers.
11. *The World Educational Crisis*, Philip Coombs, Oxford University Press, London, 1968, p. 58.
12. *Investment in Education: Ireland*, OECD.
13. *Bulletin of the Unesco Regional Office for Education in Asia*, No. 14, 1973, p. xxxi, xxxiii.
14. *Attacking Rural Poverty, How Nonformal Education Can Help*, Philip Coombs with Manzoor Ahmed, Report for the World Bank, 1974, p. 184.

## SELECTED FURTHER READING

*Investment in the National Education System up to 1970 and Sources of Financing*, Carlos Izquierdo Munoz, Centro de Estudios Educativos, Mexico, 1971.
'Expenditure on education', F. Edding, in *The Economics of Education*, MacMillan, London, 1966.
*Efficiency in Resource Utilisation in Education*, OECD, 1969.
'International comparison of educational outlay: problems and approaches', Gunter Palm, in *Internationa International Social Science Journal*, Vol. XX, No. 1, 1968, Unesco.
*Educational Development in Africa, Vol. II, Cost and Financing*, Unesco: IIEP, 1969.
*Cost Benefit Analysis in Education, A Case Study on Kenya*, Hans Thias and Martin Carnoy, Report No. 173, International Bank for Reconstruction and Development, Washington D.C., 1969.
*Financing of Education*, Educational Documentation and Information. Bulletin of the International Bureau of Education, No. 178, 1971, Unesco: IBE.
*Reports of Regional Technical Assistance Seminars on Investment in Education*, held in Bangkok, Santiago and Beirut. 1964, 1967 and 1968, Unesco.
*The Financial Aspects of First-Level Education in Iran*, J. Hallak, M. Cheikhestani and H. Varlet, Unesco: IIEP, 1972.
*Managing Educational Costs*, Philip H. Coombs and J. Hallak, Oxford University Press, London, 1972.
*Public Finance and Education*, Report of Congress of the International Institute of Public Finance, Paris, 1966.
'Some of the main issues in the strategy of educational supply', John Vaizey, in *Education and the Development of Nations*, ed. John Hanson and Cole S. Brembeck, Holt, Rinehart and Winston, 1966, p. 370.
*Readings in the Economics of Education*, eds. Mary Jean Bowman (University of Chicago), Michel Debeauvais (University of Paris), V. E. Komerov (Institute of World Economy, Moscow) and John Vaizey (University of Oxford), Unesco, 1968, Section XI.
*Effectifs, Cout et Rendement des Enseignements Primaire et Secondaire en Afrique Noire Francophone et à Madagascar*, M. Bernard Reysset, Caisse Centrale de Coopération Économique, Paris.
'Historical trends and present patterns in educational expenditure', S. Sachs, in the *World Yearbook of Education*, Evans Bros., London, 1967.
'Rates of return on investment in education: a tool for short term educational planning: illustrated with Uganda data', J. A. Smyth and Nicolas Bennett, in *The World Yearbook of Education*, Evans Bros., London, 1967.
'Criteria for public expenditure on education', John Vaizey; and 'Criteria for public expenditure on education', P. N. C. Okigbo, in *The Economics of Education*, Proceedings of a

Conference held by the International Economic Association, eds., E. A. G. Robinson and John Vaizey, MacMillan, 1960.

*Task Force on Educational Finance*, Indian National Education Commission Monograph, Government of India, New Delhi, 1965.

'Economic approaches to investment decision-making in education', H. N. Pandit, *Indian Educational Review*, Vol. V, No. 1, New Delhi, 1970, p. 1–54.

*Financing Education in the Arab States: A Survey of Recent Trends and Future Prospects*, Mohamed El Ghannan, Unesco: IIEP Occasional Papers, No. 20.

'Costs and confusions in African education', Richard Jolly, in *Education in Africa: Research and Action*, East African Publishing House, Nairobi, 1969, p. 47–62.

*Investment in Education in Latin America*, Benjamin Higgins, Unesco/SS/ED/Inv 6A, Santiago de Chile, 1966.

*The Control of Education*, John Vaizey, Faber and Faber, 1963.

*The Economics of Education*, John Vaizey, MacMillan, 1973.

*The Political Economy of Education*, John Vaizey, Duckworth, London, 1972.

'Main problems of financing of education', H. M. Phillips, in *International Finance and Development Planning in West Africa*, ed. Sune Carlson and O. Olakanpo, University of Uppsala.

*Cost-Benefit Analysis in Educational Planning*, Maureen Woodhall, Unesco: IIEP, 1970.

'Elementary education as a prerequisite for economic growth', Alexander Peaslee, in *International Development Review*, Vol. VII, No. 3, Society for International Development, 1965.

*Education*, Sector Working Paper, published by the World Bank, December 1974.

# CHAPTER 7

# Reform and Innovation; Types of Innovation; INNOTECH and APEID

To discuss innovation in education it is useful first to distinguish two distinct aspects of education. First, there is its organizational aspect. Organizationally, education is undoubtedly a system whose parts interlock. The application in recent years of methods of systems analysis to public education is appropriate in the sense that the educational levels are interdependent and inputs and outputs can be combined in many alternative ways, though the more abstract forms of systems analysis are less helpful.

The second aspect of education is that it consists of a vast day-to-day and face-to-face meeting of teachers and children; the problem is behavioural rather than organizational. In this aspect it is a continuous process of transmission and evocation in which the teacher is an intermediary in a variety of teaching–learning situations. Both aspects require reform and innovation, but the ways of dealing with them and both the constraints and the skills involved in overcoming them are different.

To recognize that education is a system does not take us far in the task of universalizing primary education unless we also ask how the individual child stands in relation to it. The present expression to describe his acquisition of education, which is in wide use, is that of giving him 'access to education'. The education system is envisaged under this expression as a structure which the individual has the opportunity to enter. A major conceptual innovation, which is starting to gain ground, is to regard it not as a structure to which entrance is granted, but as a delivery or distributive service. This conception fits closer with the Declaration of Human Rights, which says that education should be 'free and compulsory'. It clearly cannot be compulsory without the state also having an obligation to deliver it.

Similarly, to recognize that education is a behavioural problem does not take us far unless there is a good idea of what are the most useful teaching–learning patterns and how they can be disseminated.

In the light of these two aspects let us consider first some key policy statements which have been made about the need for reform and innovation.

The theme of educational change runs throughout the Report of the International Commission on the Development of Education set up by Unesco (the 'Faure Commission') under its title *Learning To Be*, which we have already cited. The letter from the Chairman of the Commission, Edgar Faure, to Rene Maheu, the Director General of Unesco, which submits the Report states:

Traditional formulae and partial reforms cannot meet the unprecedented demand for education arising out of the new tasks and functions to be fulfilled. We accordingly rejected timid, half-measures which are, in fact, costly because of their very inefficiency and turned our attention to discoveries and other factors holding promise for the future: recently developed intellectual procedures, conceptual approaches and technological advances—to the extent, of course, that these were set in the context of over-all innovation, corresponding to that broad ultimate aim of education to which I referred earlier: that of educating the complete man.

Maheu had himself in 1971 spoken in the same sense in his opening statement to the Third Regional Conference of Ministers of Education and Those Reponsible for Economic Planning in Asia:

Partial improvements or innovations restricted to a single point or aspect of the educational system useful as they may be, cannot suffice for the future. The reform of education must be all embracing, because education is a system closely interwoven at every point with the whole fabric of the community and is, either naturally or designedly, subjected to a complex body of constraints and purposes. To my mind, it is on the adoption or non-adoption of clearly defined overall policies, and on their soundness or their errors, that, in the last analysis, the future of education in Asia, as in the rest of the world will depend. It is here above all that innovation is required—and precisely here that it is most difficult.

The Asian Ministers in their conclusions stated that the Conference 'welcomes the growing awareness of Member States of the need for a thorough transformation of the educational systems as a prerequisite for their further expansion', and that 'short of a thrust in favor of innovations leading to a regeneration of education in the region, solutions to the quantitative demand will be increasingly difficult to find'.

The rejection of partial approaches in favour of thorough transformation is not, however, the view of all educational experts, as can be seen from some different advice given by Arnold Anderson:[1] 'Given the improbability of early "dramatic discoveries" in education emphasis should be placed on "micro-educational decision" resulting in a "steady flow of tiny improvements" in existing systems.'

It should be noted that the above quotations relate to the education system as a whole. If we look for studies relating specifically to primary education, the literature is small. There is, however, an important study which deals on an international basis with innovation in primary education, namely the work with that title by Bassett.[2] The utility of this for our purposes, however, is somewhat restricted by the fact that it relates only to England and the United States. It deals therefore with changes in practices affecting children in schools and not with reforms and innovations to bring into educational systems large numbers of children who are at present outside them.

Nonetheless, the conclusions of this interesting study should be cited. Bassett concludes:

Innovation in primary education is likely to be unspectacular—in spite of some of the unusual investigations in progress involving modern technology—and to be measured in ordinary human terms such as increased understanding and heightened appreciation. Old objectives, inadequately realized, will come closer to attainment as new knowledge and more effective materials are put at the service of the teacher and administrator . . .. It seems that the innovations we should seek in primary education are familiar enough; but for us to be successful in achieving them revolutionary new approaches are necessary.

It is interesting also to note the comment (quoted by Bassett) of a British school superintendent who wrote in 1967:

A look at the educational changes over the past few decades would not impress one with the significance of many of them. The impression of massive change sweeping the educational world is conveyed by our journals, and by our annual reports, but these aim largely at surface features. Generally our reports to the public emphasize the new gadgets or tools or groupings we are using, rather than the changes in how the student learns, what he knows, or how he acts on his knowledge.

An American educator, Henry J. Otto,[3] comments similarly:

To anyone who is familiar with what went on in elementary schools 40 years ago and with what goes on in such schools today, it seems clear that much change has taken place—but we cannot document the characteristics of those changes. To the writer it also seems evident that the undocumented changes are areas of school operation, pupil services, teacher–pupil relations etc., and not in the basic objectives and subject offerings of the schools.

These various statements will no doubt leave in the reader's mind a number of questions; what, for example, did Edgar Faure mean when he stated that partial reforms cannot meet the demand and that the Commission rejected timid half-measures; and what did he mean when he used the term 'overall innovation'? When Rene Maheu stated that partial improvements cannot suffice for the future, what kind of alternative overall policies did he have in mind? What does Arnold Anderson mean by tiny improvements, and why must they be tiny? How does Faure's statement in the letter of transmission of the Report, which we have quoted, square with the actual recommendations and commentary regarding primary education which says:[4]

Considerable progress towards giving all people in the world a primary education has already been made. This is a long-range effort, and it must, of course, be continued. However, it would also seem possible to find a remedy for many of the harmful effects of this situation on the present generation by judiciously balancing several solutions.

What is the exact difference between 'timid half-measures' and 'judicious balancing'?

To try to answer these and similar questions it seems necessary to analyse the matter inside the following headings: (a) definitions; (b) different schools of thought; (c) different types of reforms or innovations; (d) obstacles to innovation; (e) strengthening innovatory capacity.

## (a) Definitions

The words 'reform', 'renovation' and 'innovation' are frequently used interchangeably, but there are differences of meaning between them which are important for an understanding of the process of change. When we come, as we will do shortly, to examples of change, it will be seen that reality, as so often happens, does not always allow itself to be carved up on analytic lines. We ourselves, therefore, cannot guarantee always to use these terms with precision except at those points of the discussion where the distinction is particularly important.

Strictly, 'reform' would normally mean a substantial change affecting the social and political access of a considerable portion of the population to education, or the improvement of their educational status and opportunities. 'Regeneration' is sometimes used also by those who wish to avoid the criticisms implicit in the word 'reform' and to denote changes which would be a reassertion and improvement of existing educational objectives. 'Renovation' would usually mean improving the existing system with some additions to bring it up to date.

'Innovation', which is the most difficult of the expressions used, is interpreted variously by different authorities, as well as in common speech. Some writers deal with innovation in education as a form of social change, education being predominantly a social activity. Others find it useful for the purpose of analysis to look at education as an input–output system and to apply concepts taken from the productive processes. Under this treatment innovation is not any form of change but one brought into existence as a result of discovery, invention or research and development (R and D), as in industry.

In ordinary speech and in some authors' usage it means any change, but this is not very helpful. Others limit it to the new audio-visual devices. As we proceed we will show that in education, or in other productive processes, know-how, organization and methods may be more important than physical forms of technological change. Whitehead commented aptly on this point in *Science and the Modern World*, when he wrote: 'In order to understand our epoch we can neglect all the details of change, such as railways, telegraphs, radios, spinning machines, synthetic dyes. We must concentrate upon the method of research itself; that is the real novelty, which has broken up the foundations of the old civilization'. This applies to educational change as well as to industry.

## (b) Different schools of thought

Whatever type of analysis is used the range of views put forward in the current discussions of educational change can be divided roughly into three schools of thought: (1) those who question the whole utility of educational systems as they exist today and propose a complete and dramatic transformation; (2) those who reject or consider as quite unfeasible the idea of replacing the present system by another, but who nonetheless believe in profound and fundamental change; (3) those who believe in change at the micro-educational level, i.e. that the system can be made to work efficiently by a series of specific changes and improvements within it.

*In the first school of thought* the most extreme view is that of Illich and Reimers and other members of the CIDOC Centre at Cuernavaca in Mexico, who believe that schools as now known should be abolished and education be de-institutionalized. According to Illich, education now operates as an institution in its own right, which it should not since it represses, alienates and de-humanizes the societies it is supposed to serve. The school as an institution, therefore, should be suppressed so that people can control the learning process themselves through educational activities which they themselves control. While recognizing that some form of schooling may still be necessary for certain limited types of learning, the basic concept is that young persons form their characters and their livelihood possibilities within the community by performing practical work and by having access to self-learning processes including modern teaching machines and centres of information.

Present educational systems are to be replaced by what are called four educational resource networks defined as (1) educational objects, i.e. materials; (2) skill models, i.e. skill demonstrations by teachers or other people; (3) peers, i.e. matching like children in groups; (4) education (stated to be 'the least essential of the major learning resources, consisting of pedagogues and experts).

*The second school of thought*, which believes that the system has to be accepted but must be fundamentally revised, has a much more realistic and established bases and, as we have seen, receives a certain support from the Faure Commission and Unesco.

The discerning reader will, however, in studying the quotations with which we introduced this chapter, have noticed a difference between the rejection of timid half-measures in the Preamble of the International Commission's report and the apparently similar view expressed by Maheu that partial improvements cannot suffice for the future and reform 'must be all-embracing, because education is a system closely interwoven at every point with the fabric of the community, and is, either naturally or designedly subjected to a complex body of constraints and purposes'.

Maheu's statement recognizes that educational reform cannot outstep by any great distance the reform of society itself and that partial changes (e.g. the introduction of new curricula at the primary level) cannot succeed unless there are concurrent changes elsewhere in the system (e.g. the education of teachers and other personnel concerned with primary education at the second and higher levels in the new curricula, the alteration of the inspection and examination criteria etc.).

However, the statement also contains the implication, which we should examine, that because education depends on the fabric of the community it cannot be sufficiently reformed partially. The case in which this would not be true would be that in which the community was also changing partially. It will be one of the main theses of our own thought, as the reader will see, that the fabric of communities is changing not in an all-embracing way, but partially and thread by thread. As in the case of Hume's famous question whether a sock which has been completely redarned remains the same sock, we hope to show that step-by-step change can also be total change.

The difficulty faced by the second school of thought is that few of the developing or the developed countries, are yet in fact adopting this view in practice and that there are few models to guide Ministers of Education of the developing countries who wish to take this course. Peru and Tanzania are engaged in bold changes of this nature, and is also to a lesser extent the case with Sri Lanka and Costa Rica, while Cuba, as part of its social revolution, also completely recast its educational system.

*The third school of thought* is very conscious of the difficulties of bringing about sweeping educational reform, even within the present system. It points to the fact that little large-scale reform, despite the examples given, is in fact taking place, and that the fundamental changes initiated in Peru and Tanzania, for instance, have not yet been put full into operation and evaluated.

The partisans of this school of thought point to the inertia common to most educational establishments, the extra costs involved in large-scale reform and the absence as yet of new educational technologies which can revolutionize education as medicine has been revolutionized over the last hundred years. Piaget, the well known child psychologist has remarked that education today is where medicine was in the last century. But the role of physical aids (chemistry, surgery etc.) is much smaller in education where the basic components of productivity are organizational and psychological (curricula, teaching and learning behaviour).

The scepticism of this school of thought does not mean that they take up themselves an inert position. The difference is that they believe that the main thrust of educational progress should be to improve the present system wherever and whenever possible, rather than to tilt at what they would regard as the windmills of total change.

It is not clear why Arnold Anderson in the passage already cited believes that the steady flow should be of 'tiny' improvements at the micro-decision level, rather than step by step action at the government level.

Looking at these three schools of thought, there is a sense in which the first can be called 'anarchist' since its approach towards schools is similar to that of anarchist philosophers to society; the second could be called a form of state socialism since it urges that society should be completely transformed—society is maintained, but its basic instruments are transformed; the third position could be called constructive conservation.

It is of interest to reflect on the present state of education in the developing countries in terms of the situation as regards social progress in the West at the beginning of the century when all three groups were active. The anarchists never had a chance of succeeding any more than Illich has. They were several hundred years too late or too early. The revolutionary socialists were only able to succeed where the social dilemma was excessively serious, as in Russia. The conservatives would have held the lead throughout but for the appearance of an intermediate school of thought, namely the Fabian or social welfare school.

These comparisons, with all their limitations, point to the need for *a fourth alternative* of what might be called the social engineering or Fabian approach to educational reform, which was in fact the approach which succeeded in setting up the free enterprise or mixed welfare economies of Western Europe.

In the Report of the International Commission on the Development of Education, the question of the methods and framework within which the recommendations are to be implemented is not pursued far, no doubt owing to the variety of politico-social systems to which its members belonged. Thus, the Report states:[6] 'The concept of democracy itself must be developed, for it can no longer be limited to a minimum of juridical guarantees protecting citizens from the arbitrary exercise of power in a subsistence society'. On the other hand, we also read:

> What is known as formal democracy—which it would be wrong to deride, for it marked great progress—has become obsolete. The delegation of authority for a fixed period had and still has the advantage of protecting the citizen from the arbitrary exercise of power and of providing him with the minimum of juridical guarantees. But it is not capable of providing him with an adequate share of the benefits of expansion or with the possibility of influencing his own fate in a world of flux and change; nor does it allow him to develop his own potential to best advantage.

The reader may well question whether this latter statement takes sufficiently into account the important interventions in income distribution for social purposes which have taken place over the last fifty years in a number of 'welfare states' with formal democratic systems.

Few of the developing countries have as yet intervened effectively in income distribution. But it is difficult to see not only how reforms of the kind proposed by the Commission can be obtained in the educational, as in other social spheres, except by the formal action of governments, but also what alternatives there are to the methods of formal democracy.

The weakest part of the Commission's Report is in fact precisely the lack of concrete suggestions as to how the approaches recommended are to be put into operation. This led to criticism when the Report was discussed in the Unesco Executive Board and General Conference. While it was recognized that each socio-political system would have its own solution, it was felt that a discussion of *types of solution* would have been profitable.

Most developing countries are not yet ready for the administrative tasks of large-scale educational reform, even if they were galvanized into them politically. This means that it is necessary to expand and improve their planning and management resources and their research and development effort so as to increase their capacity to innovate. This involves (1) training of planners, administrators and specialists of various kinds (educational technologists, curriculum development and evaluation experts, etc.) as well as teachers; (2) working out norms and designs for innovatory projects; (3) stimulating teacher, parent and public interest in educational change; (4) applied research in new educational approaches at the country and local levels.

It also means utilizing committees of parents, employers, and students, both on a central and a local basis, to work with educators on projects of renovating and extending the educational system and linking it more closely with non-formal education and the country's communications media.

We discussed in Chapter 5 the political forces influencing educational reform and the traditional social and educational structures inhibiting implementation, with illustrations from Latin America and the work of Paulo Freire. Undoubtedly, reform moves very much quicker when it is part of an overall reform of social structure; but it does not follow that educational change does not have to move at all if there is no political change.

The context of Freire's work is adult education in oligarchic societies and his overall criticism of most government sponsored adult literacy programmes that they are usually of a bourgeois paternalist nature and use uncreative curricula is well taken. In his detailed formulation of the need, both social and pedagogic, to replace the 'banking' concept of education (i.e. depositing knowledge in the individual) by the concept of critical awareness he has also rendered a service which educators widely accept as a major contribution to the methodology of literacy teachers as well as to personality development of the pupil during the process.

What is less acceptable to many educators is the intrinsic linkage he makes of pedagogic method to the concept of a revolutionary dialectic which is to transform society. This aspect as well as the fact that he has not drawn upon research by predecessors in this field of methodology has led to criticism. A useful account of the arguments on both sides, in the articles by Freire himself and his critic W. S. Griffith, is contained in the Spring 1974 issue of the review *Literacy Discussion* published by the International Institute for Adult Literacy in Teheran.

The value of his pedagogic writings are sometimes obscured by such polemics as well as by his rhetorical language. Thus when he speaks of the need to 'engage the learners in the constant problematization of their existential situations' he is saying what many good elementary school teachers know very well. More research is also needed on how to increase the number of good teachers in the non-revolutionary societies.

### (c) Types of innovation

The main types of educational innovation may be listed as follows:

(1) Structural and organizational changes in the different cycles (e.g. in promotion rates, in the balance between the academic and the practical streams of pupil flow, in the population coverage, in the distribution of educational opportunity and in the links with the community and with non-formal education).

(2) The introduction of new or rearranged or differently emphasized content.

(3) The introduction of new mechanical teaching aids, e.g. the new audio-visual media and teaching machines. This type of innovation, commonly known as 'hardware', may be purely mechanical and not deal with the fundamental problems; or it may be accompanied by curriculum change.

(4) New methods of organizing the flow of information required in the presenting educational process, e.g. by the use of instructional lesson cards, film strips, new types of textbook, radio and television sequences, tapes, cassettes etc.

(5) Changes in the methods of interaction between teachers and students, e.g. team teaching, learning in small groups, ungraded classes etc.

(6) Changes in examination systems designed to evaluate progress.

(7) The reduction of unit costs and new methods of financing education.

(8) Changes in the planning and promotion of innovation itself, in project identification methods, in the training of planners and specialist staff and in research and development activities.

There is overlap between the impact of these different categories of innovation because changes in methods are seldom entirely mechanical or neutral and frequently throw up the need for changes in content, in assessment procedures and in teacher training.

The test of successful innovation is its effect on output and coverage over a given period. In the case of the Ivory Coast Television Project, for instance, which is perhaps the largest single innovatory form involving new teaching aids (discussed further in Chapter 11), the final test will be whether by 1986 it will result, as it aims to, in bringing the whole of the school age population to an educational level superior to that which would have been achieved otherwise, earlier than would otherwise have been possible and with less cost in relation to benefit.

In pursuit of progressive educational objectives, of the kind set out in the International Commission's Report, it would seem that the innovations which would have the greatest leverage on primary education would be: (1) those which both increase the population coverage of at least minimum basic education by structural and organizational changes; (2) those which improve the quality of the cycle as a whole and its relevance to development needs; (3) those which introduce new methods and aids for teaching and learning which will increase both quality and coverage.

This applies to large-scale reform and innovation and should not obscure the value of efforts of all kinds, whether by educational administrators or by teachers in the class, to bring about educational renovation and adaptation, however and whenever possible. While important innovation usually means structural changes and new content, minor innovatory action can be taken to improve ongoing systems, e.g. rearranging hours of school attendance, local fabrication of teaching aids, the introduction of learning games etc.

Moreover, not all types of innovation have necessarily to be preceded by prolonged studies. Where clear and tested methods and patterns exist, the problem is one of imitation and adaptation rather than of research. Imitation and rediscovery may be important innovatory influences.

The most dynamic potential single factor in the development of primary education, provided the content and structure are suitable, is the well-trained teacher and how he organizes his time. This need will be increased rather than diminished by innovations, since new types of projects require new types of teaching skill. Bassett has described in *Innovation in Primary Education* the experimentation taking place in the United Kingdom and the United States on new methods of teaching the primary school child. The United Kingdom has stressed the diversifying and intensifying of the role of the teacher; the United States has concentrated on problems of organization and on teacher aids. The new methods may be found to be valuable if adjusted to the different conditions of the developing countries.

However, teaching and better teacher-training cannot give their full benefit if the child's learning capacity is impaired by tiredness and malnutrition. The child's learning capacity depends heavily upon his health, nutrition, distance from school, and the educational and welfare background in the home and community. Therefore, large-scale innovations should be accompanied by action in favour of the overall development of the child and, to use the words of the International Commission's Report, there has to be a 'judicious balancing' of various solutions. Unicef is playing an important catalytic role in the developing countries in the promotion of the concept of the overall development of the child and the link between the educational and other services available which are essential to child welfare. Innovation in education is seldom purely technical since primary education is so closely linked with the child's place in his environment.

Nevertheless, some analogies from industry have a certain relevance since education systems are big organizations employing large resources of manpower and finance. In industry, innovation is usually the result of the following sequence: (1) invention, which may be spontaneous or the result of scientific research; (2) studies of the feasibility of adopting the invention or new methods; (3) development of the new methods by trial and error to the point at which they are ready for application; (4) production based on the new methods. Innovation is only achieved when the last stage is reached, the previous stages being efforts to achieve innovation. Only a small proportion, around 2 or 3 per cent, of invention and research results in actual innovation, and only rarely is innovation achieved without a good deal of research and development activity having followed the invention.

This sequence is a useful frame of reference, *mutatis mutandis*, for considering educational change. It is not enough to have new ideas or to produce valuable research in individual schools, though these processes have also to be encouraged. The most significant stage is the passage from ideas to the required inputs and thence to the production of new educational output. This involves identifying key areas of change, testing possible new designs, giving them 'trial runs' and following through with a process of adjustment, adaptation and development. In the process of educational change, adaptation may be as important as invention.

The time normally required to bring about a really important innovation in education, even in the best circumstances, is probably about eight to ten years. This period starts with the diagnosis by the educational authorities of the problems needing solution and the recognition that there are new methods that could be adopted. This period, which may last two years or more, is one of promotion of the idea, study of its feasibility, and acceptance by the leaders of the teaching profession. It is followed by another period of two years or more during which the specific programmes or pilot projects required are prepared in detail, costed and budgeted for, and the ancillary and complementary means explored. The latter include the possibilities of foreign aid, provision for the production or import of the new materials and equipment, textbooks etc. required. The process of receiving the foreign aid itself will take two or three years within this second phase.

Thus, after a period of four or five years the supplies of materials, textbooks and trained teachers may begin to arrive and the new outlooks and educational patterns start to be applied in the schools. At this stage there begins a process similar to that in the motor industry know as 'taking the bugs out of a new model'. It does not involve the high-level designers but, as in engineering, is the work of the foreman, or in education of the headmaster or inspector. In education, this step, which may last two or three years, consists of securing the acceptance by the teacher of the new methods, by conviction as well as on paper, and his adjustment to them to local conditions. It is at this stage, which may take two or three years, that the activity starts to be really innovatory—i.e., things are actually done differently over a large part of the educational system and output starts to improve. In industry and agriculture it takes, on the average, ten to twelve years for important innovations to affect 50 per cent of the producers, followed by a further period of imitation by most of the remainder. In education, this period is shorter because most of education is under the control of central or local authorities.

An important difference between education and industry is that, whereas the most complicated pieces of machinery take a few months to move over the assembly line, four years or more are usually required before pupils leave the educational system with the necessary benefit from the new methods, i.e. the production cycle is much longer.

### (d) Obstacles to innovation

In addition to the inevitable delays for purely technical reasons, which take place before large-scale educational change can mature (time to test new curricula, to produce new textbooks, teaching aids etc.), there are obstacles of a psychological and social nature, as we saw in the preceding chapter dealing with the forces conditioning educational reform.

As regards the 'hardware' type of mechanical innovation, although there are sometimes hesitations on the part of traditionally minded educators and parents, there is normally little opposition; though there will be, no doubt, when the time comes to consider replacing the school by 'town brains' to which children are electronically connected through shoulder carrels.

Difficulty usually arises only when new 'hardware' is accompanied by organizational and content changes that are not acceptable. Since most 'hardware' involves supplementing the teachers' efforts and not replacing them, and since the new media have their own 'magic', little opposition exists apart from cost, which frequently is prohibitive. Lowering of costs involves breaking the vicious circle of limited supply based on small demand. Efforts are already being made by research groups associated with industry to produce chaper and more long-wearing products needing less maintenance, but greatly intensified cooperation is needed between educational authorities and industry.

In the case of innovations which involve major changes in content and structure, there is frequently involved a difficult process of changing attitudes both among parents and in the education profession itself. Little educational innovation materialized in developing countries in the 1960s (although some useful changes in educational structure and curriculum have taken place in a few countries), for this reason as well as because of sheer pressure of expansion. However, the limit to which educational policy can move ahead of the accepted educational values of given societies is tending to advance. Since the young absorb innovatory ideas more quickly than the older generation, progress depends greatly on securing the participation of youth as well as interesting young parents in educational change.

Parents as well as teachers are frequently opposed to innovation. Changes in the streaming of pupils as between different fields of study, and alterations in the content and length of the educational cycle, often encounter serious opposition. Parents do not agree readily with the idea that the educational system should be arranged on a functional basis serving development plans. The experience of the 1960s has shown that educational plans based on development allocations have rarely been implemented, but that parental pressures, usually from the more well-to-do sections of the population, have been the dominant force.

In Chapter 5 on the forces determining progress in primary education we drew attention to the power of the educational 'establishment' in problems of reform, and their capacity to interpret legislative decisions differently in practice to what was intended. In the case quoted of a Bolivian reform it was shown that resources as well as practices were deviated from the Government's intention.

Differences of view between the teaching force and that of the government and of the population at large are not confined to developing countries. In Torsten Husen's paper for the International Commission on the Development of Education,[7] called *Strategies of Educational Innovation*, we read:

In 1958, when about one-fourth of the school districts in Sweden had introduced the nine-year comprehensive school on a trial basis, the Swedish Radio Corporation sponsored a public opinion poll pertaining to the changing school situation. The poll showed that between one-half and two-thirds of the public preferred the comprehensive system, about one-fourth was against it and the rest were undecided. Thus, at a period when the overwhelming majority of the secondary school teachers, who were accustomed to an elitest system with pronounced selective features, rejected the blueprint for the educational system which was laid down in the 1950 Education Act, the majority of the electorate was in favour of it. In the Riksdag the backing of the Reform was even more overwhelming. No votes had to be taken on major points in the education bills.

Husen goes on to develop the point of view that much of the difficulty arises from the fact that too often the innovatory process has been attempted without sufficient regard to securing the cooperation of the teachers. He states: 'We need among other things proper positive reinforcement agents which will reward innovative behaviour. So far innovative behaviour has been negatively reinforced. The teachers who try new practices have been punished by increased work load and disapproval on the part of their colleagues'.

He lists some of the forces which 'keep the system in equilibrium' as follows: 'Learning is supposed to occur only when the teacher gives something to the children. Work is regulated by a fixed timetable. The learning tasks are chopped up into standard assignments. Extra assignments are often given as punishments. Administrative procedures within and outside the classroom are authoritarian'.

If these difficulties occur in Sweden, how much more so are they operative in the traditional societies of the developing countries. Husen's basic thesis of the need to work with the teaching force is clearly right and we have already taken this position in Chapter 4 on quality, when discussing the teacher's role.

In his brief paper Husen does not develop the means of doing so, though he does mention the need to improve the status of teachers. Our own view is that progress in this has to be tied to progress in teachers' salaries and in providing incentives within the profession for innovative suggestions and practices which have the necessary support from research results and social legislation. Also, more effort should be made by teachers' unions to bring their organizational power to bear on educational reform as well as on teachers' conditions and status. This is further developed in the chapter on financial measures.

A similar point was made by John Stuart Mill in his inaugural address to the University of Saint Andrew in 1864, when he said: 'Reform even of government and churches is not so slow as that of schools, for there is the great preliminary difficulty of fashioning the instruments of teaching the teacher'. Time is needed in educational reform to have the new objectives accepted by the teaching force, and by parents and the community, and to improve the planning, management and administrative services.

Nor are educators the only conservative people in societies, even societies which have experienced revolution. Thus, we note Mr. Nikita Kruschev saying in a picturesque outburst: 'Production of steel is, so to speak, a well-worn road with deep tracks, and here even a blind horse will not swerve because the wheels will break. A material has appeared which is superior to steel and cheaper, but they still shout: Steel! Steel!'. The 'they' he is referring to are not headmasters or teachers but the officials of his country's planning organization and heads of industry during the time of which he was speaking, the early 1960s.

Thus, we come back again to Maheu's remark about the interlock between education and society. Only by much patient work of political progress accompanied by social engineering can reformed patterns of teaching and learning and new structures be created.

A classic case of the delays and obstacles in implementing educational innovation, even when sponsored by the highest authorities, is that of the People's Republic of China.

Although Mao had long taken a close personal interest in reorganizing the

Chinese educational system as part of the Great Leap Forward, and since his period in 1942 in Yenan, some 25 years elapsed before the Cultural Revolution of the 1960s implemented these ideas effectively.

In 1960 Mr. Yang Yiu-Feng, his Minister of Education, was making the statement at the Second National People's Congress, to which we have already referred in Chapter 4: 'the problems in our school system and pedagogical methods which cause our general education programme to achieve smaller, slower, poorer aid and uneconomical results'.

In 1963 a set of regulations and guidelines to improve educational quality were issued by the Chinese Ministry of Education under the heading *1963 Temporary Work Regulations for Full-time Middle and Primary Schools*. These held the field for four years until 1967 when they were circulated during the Cultural Revolution to serve as examples of how not to draw up educational instructions.

These regulations are translated and analysed by Susan Shirk in *The China Quarterly* of July/September 1973. Susan Shirk writes:[8]

> The Liuist educational policies put forward in the 1963 regulations are, then, no aberration; they simply represent a modernizing elite's acceptance of the customary western view of how schools should promote development. Mao is the innovator; it is his conception of a popularized practical work-study education which is new and different. The policy-makers in power during the 1961–66 period, reacting to what they saw as the failure of the Great Leap Forward experiments, rejected Mao's radical conception and tried to find the safest, most risk-free strategy to guarantee that schools channelled expertise into the economy. No wonder they fell back on the usual academic 'quality' approach.

She goes on to say:

> The professional bias of the policy-makers for the conventional western educational model, their bureaucratic interest in centralizing and monopolizing educational decision-making, and the preference of ordinary citizens for full-time academic schooling, all came together in the dismantling of the Maoist experiments of the Great Leap Forward and the promotion of 'quality' education which was expressed in the 1963 regulations. Because the failure of the Great Leap had diminished his credibility and power, Mao was unable to resist this decision.

She adds:

> The Maoist approaches which fascinate western ververs—work-study schools, decentralized administration, open admissions, near student–teacher equality, etc.—have been tried in Chinese schools only at Yenan, during the Great Leap Forward, and since the Cultural Revolution. The frustration of Mao and his allies at being unable to implement these innovations was one important motivating factor in the launching of the Cultural Revolution.

An educator may well marvel at the obstinacy or the resilience, according to how you look at it, of his profession. Susan Shirk writes:

And yet today foreign visitors to China report that although the number of rural schools has multiplied and the practical component has increased for all students, schools are once again 'experimenting' with examinations and grades and attempting to raise academic standards. Opponents of radical educational change both within the bureaucratic elite and at the mass level may be dragging their heels and impeding the implementation of the educational reforms .... Readers of these 1963 regulations for primary and middle schools should keep in mind not only that these rules represent the orientation towards 'quality' education which has characterized most of the 23 years since Liberation, but also that this orientation may have survived the Cultural Revolution.

The latter speculation would appear somewhat dubious since after the Cultural Revolution only two years of lower middle school, plus two years experience as a worker, peasant or soldier, is now required before entry to higher education, together with approval of the local Communist party and a satisfactory assessment of the work experience. Moreover the length of the educational cycle as a whole has been reduced.

Belief in the possibility of a Great Leap Forward is food and drink to many reformists. In the International Commission's Report we read (page 206) in regard to adult education: 'Step by step progress is not enough; what is required is a giant leap forward' (an unconscious improvement of Mao's famous phrase). We also read (page 181): 'we must innovate and envisage fundamental alternatives to the very concepts and structures of education'. At the same time we read on the preceding page: 'The capacity to effect partial reforms is a sign of vitality in an educational system and proof that it may be able to undergo even more sweeping changes'.

Thus the International Commission itself, as it proceeded, did not in fact reject partial solutions and what it called 'timid half measures', despite the bold language of the letter of presentation.

These considerations are mentioned not to minimize in any way the importance of the Commission's Report, which will long have an immense inspirational value, but to indicate the further need now for Ministers of Education and international agencies to turn their attention to practical measures of implementation, most of which are likely to require painstaking pieces of educational engineering.

Some of the more interesting specific innovations and reforms, a number of which are described in more detail in the two chapters which follow, are:

(1) *Developing countries*

(i)    the fundamental reorganization of objectives and methods of primary education taking place in Tanzania and Peru;

(ii)    the recycling of primary education (e.g. in Iran, Ceylon, Peru, Costa Rica and Mexico);

116

(iii) new syllabuses reducing the time required for the first part of the primary cycle (e.g. reducing it from 4 to 3 years as in some of the Asian republics of the Soviet Union and in Nepal);

(iv) complexes of schools of different lengths of cycle with ladders and bridges between them as in the 'godfather' system of Madras, the Peruvian 'nuclear' school or the Mexican 'consolidated' school;

(v) sharing of facilities among schools as in experiments in the Punjab and Mysore;

(vi) community schools in urban centres attended by both adults and children as in the Philippines, and the use of community and social services for educational purposes as in the Senegalese rural service and rural community schools and community centres in the Sudan;

(vii) reduction of wastage through rearrangement of the school schedule as in Rajasthan, India;

(viii) introduction of functional work-oriented literacy for adolescents into the Unesco Experimental Literacy Projects, e.g. in Iran;

(ix) the use of television for the formal system on a massive scale as in the Ivory Coast or for non-formal education also addressed to parents as well as children in El Salvador;

(x) the trying out of new learning methods in experimental areas as in Tanzania and India;

(xi) schemes to use the spare time of grandparents for kindergartens as in China;

(xii) district planning to mobilize local resources as in the Punjab and Tanzania;

(xiii) self-help schools as in Kenya, rural cooperatives in the Congo, the 4K movement in Kenya, and the young farmers movement in Uganda;

(xiv) national service corps for education as in Iran (The Army of Knowledge);

(xv) reduction of school hours to morning only and spreading of the cycle over a greater number of years in order to increase retention rates;

(xvi) education modules including parent education, covering health and nutrition; centres for village girls and women as in Kenya;

(xvii) introduction of a system by which older pupils can move in and out of primary education and non-formal education and into and out of employment;

(xviii) experiments in non-formal education in Brazil, Ecuador, Nigeria and Ghana;

(xix) Unesco's Experimental Project for Programmed Instruction in Asia;

(2) *Developed countries*

(i) substitution of class learning as a whole by individualized teaching in small groups and the use of the monitor system as in experiments in the United Kingdom; team teaching;

(ii) recurrent education—see results of the studies made by the OECD Centre for Educational Innovation and Research;

(iii)  the use of television to give disadvantaged children a head start as in the United States *Sesame Street* programme;

(iv)  its use combined with correspondence courses as in the Quebec TEVEC Programme;

(v)  the family hostel cum school system in rural areas of France and Italy combining school with family education;

(vi)  self-service learning with language laboratories, programmed instruction, testing devices, feedback processes, computer-assisted learning;

(vii)  the new mathematics.

### (e) Strengthening innovatory capacity

To strengthen the base of innovation, more funds are needed for research; it is also necessary to overcome shortages of research staff and the lack of opportunity to undertake pilot projects. Few of the governments of the developing countries have sufficient facilities of this kind. Internationally, as well as in the developing countries themselves, there is a shortage of the relevant skills. Efforts are required to increase the present supply of these skills for use at all levels. The International Institute of Educational Planning, for instance, has at present few resources for this task. Its resources should be increased to enable it to train the necessary experts to design and advise on the carrying out of innovatory projects.

A most serious obstacle is the absence of funds for innovatory experiments in the budgets of the Ministers of Education. The average educational budget is so heavily pressed with meeting the expansion of the educational system, the expenses of which are predominantly made up of teachers' salaries and administrative expenses (and in the educationally least-developed countries and disadvantaged areas, the capital needs of school construction) that only rarely is it possible to allocate funds to research and development and to 'trial runs' of new educational patterns. To achieve lasting results, the developing countries must themselves allocate resources for innovation, but external aid can have a particularly useful role. It could sponsor projects involving more 'risks' than national administrations may be able to take.

At present it is probable that no more than 10 per cent of all projects assisted by external aid, whether multilateral or bilateral, are innovatory in the institutional sense described above. Most add to or make small improvements in existing educational patterns. The latter is an important activity for the purpose of raising productivity in the short term. Nevertheless, particularly when the subject is children and the innovatory process is a long one, regard has to be paid also to the longer term, which would indicate redeploying educational assistance so as to make an effective contribution to increasing the capacities of the less developed countries for educational innovation.

In deciding how to promote innovation there is a recurrent dilemma. The one horn of it is to consider innovation as a subject in itself; the other is to regard innovation as a pervasive force in other subjects and a factor in their treatment.

The danger of the first course is visible throughout the less developed countries. A subject called 'new (or innovatory) methods of teaching' is introduced into teachers training colleges. But the old methods of instruction are used to teach about the new methods.

The danger of the second course is that innovation is treated so pervasively that it becomes in effect educational development, and nothing more, and becomes absorbed in, rather than catalysing, existing practices.

Unesco encountered this dilemma when its Executive Board debated a proposal to establish an international voluntary fund for educational development. The Secretariat had advised against an overall fund on the ground that it would not lead to an addition of resources, but raised the possibility of a fund limited to the promotion of educational innovation—a possibility the Board did not follow up. In the meantime the Organization for Economic Cooperation and Development (OECD) had established a Centre for Educational Research on Innovation (CERI) to work on problems of its member states, mostly the educationally developed countries.

When the International Commission on the Development of Education[7] studied this question it fell into a duality of view. Some members felt that it was

> not necessary to create new programmes, centres, or special funds in order to introduce innovations—the importance of which we recognize and welcome—into education. Those in question believe that a reasonable balance must be reached between innovation in education and the tried and tested present-day educational models, and that this requires proposals aimed at reorganizing and redistributing programmes, centres, and existing means in a new way . . . . Others among us have devised a method which would appear to deserve attention. It would involve launching an international programme aimed solely at providing scientific, technical and financial aid for States wishing to explore new educational paths . . . .

The Report goes on to state:

> 'International Programme' should be understood to mean here an organism attached to an existing international institution. Its mission would be to mobilize funds from various sources for specific and limited goals, and to assist countries at their request for specific activities engaging both governmental and non-governmental sectors. The World Food Programme is a precedent demonstrating the validity of this type of action.

No steps have as yet been taken by Unesco to establish any central programme of this kind following the Commission's proposal—there was not sufficient support in the General Conference for the proposal when its Report was debated. Two related developments, however, had already been set in motion in the Asian Region, arising from action by Ministers of Education, acting first in the South East Asian Ministers of Education Organization (SEAMEO) and then in Unesco's Asian Regional Conference.

In 1967 SEAMEO decided to establish a Regional Centre for Educational Innovation and Technology (INNOTECH) first located in Singapore and now in Saigon. The functions of the Centre are described by SEAMEO as follows:[9]

The centre offers at present a three-month course three times a year for key educators from the region who share with their fellow participants and the Centre staff the experience gained in their respective countries while at the same time acquiring the latest skills and knowledge necessary for educational planning, decision-making and application of realistic change strategies.

In the field of research and development, INNOTECH is engaged in two of the four projects of the SEAMEO Educational Development Programmes for the 1970s, namely:

(1) Development of Instructional Objectives by SEAMEO Member Countries; and

(2) Development of an Effective and Economical Delivery System for Mass Primary Education.

The latter is a long-term project upon which the Centre will concentrate its efforts in the coming years.

The second project, which deals with mass primary education is beginning with case studies in selected areas in the Philippines and in Indonesia. The Canadian International Development Research Centre (IDRC) and the Canadian International Development Agency (CIDA) are supporting this project, which may well make an important contribution to the development of primary education. The official description of the study is:[9]

This Study addresses itself to existing or proposed educational systems with a view to assisting member countries in their efforts to find an effective and economical delivery system for mass primary education which can lead to eventual implementation on a wide scale. The Study will be followed by the construction and try-out of one or more systems.

The action taken by the Unesco Conference of Asian Ministers of Education, and suggested by Unesco's General Conference in 1972, was the decision to establish an Asian Programme of Educational Innovation for Development (APEID) attached to the Unesco Regional Office for Education in Asia at Bangkok, which became operational at the beginning of 1973.

The Programme of APEID[10] has as its main objective to increase each Member State's *capacity to find new solutions*, rather than to try to present 'instant' remedies. Its institutional framework will be a regional centre for cooperation (ACEID) and associated centres in Member States.

The functions of the regional centre are:

(1) to provide consultative and technical services to participating cooperating associated centres;

(2) to coordinate and support pilot experiments, studies and programmes of regional interest in the Member States, such as those which are of direct relevance to the management of innovation;

(3) to encourage and facilitate exchange of persons and experiences among the Member States;

(4) to assemble and diffuse documentation and information on new techniques and educational innovation;

(5) to serve as the secretariat to the Regional Experts Committee and to assemble data for periodic review and evaluation.

The functions of the Associated Centres are:

(1) carrying out problem-oriented action programmes and R and D work on new methods and techniques, in cooperation with ACEID and other agents in Member States;

(2) organizing regional or sub-regional training courses and seminars to prepare key personnel in the Member States in the development, adaptation and use of innovative approaches and products;

(3) cooperating in the design, implementation or evaluation of pilot experiments and innovative schemes and projects, with the regional centre (ACEID) and institutions in other Member States;

(4) facilitating dissemination and exchange of experience and information on new developments in its programme area.

The methods of work will be the use of technical and consulting sessions, seminars, workshops and meetings, training courses, pilot projects, technical working groups, national development groups in educational innovation, and an innovation information network. The criteria for the selection of innovative projects are that they should have direct relevance or great sensitivity to socio-economic development, that the experience should be transferable and accessible and that they should improve both quality and efficiency.

Six main areas of programme activity were selected: (1) new orientations and structures in education (e.g. democratization, non-formal education, recurrent education); (2) educational management (e.g. planning, administrative implementation and control, evaluation, staff training); (3) curriculum development (e.g. great relevance to development, production and trial of new curricula); (4) educational technology (e.g. television, radio, programmed learning); (5) teacher training (e.g. new structures and methods in teacher training institutions, teachers as change agents, experimental projects); (6) science education (e.g. production of instructional materials and equipment, pilot projects).

This Programme will clearly be of great interest not only to Asia, but also to other regions. Its modest approach of aiming to improve the capacity to innovate rather than to suggest specific remedies, will command general support. It remains to be seen how far it will be possible for the programme to separate out the capacity for innovation from the capacity for educational development as such, since the two are interlocked, but a rose is sweet by any other name.

Two other international initiatives in the field of innovation are those which arose from the Ford-Rockefeller meetings at Ballagio, Italy in 1972 and 1973 of heads of agencies concerned with educational assistance. One is a project for a million dollar fund for educational innovation in Indonesia, and the other for a reporting service to exchange information on innovations and their progress, being set up in the Unesco/International Bureau of Education at Geneva. Both are being funded from a number of sources, bilateral, multilateral, and by the Ford Foundation.

## REFERENCES

1. *Fostering Educational Research in the Third World*, background paper by C. Arnold Anderson for Conference on Education and Development, Bellagio, 1972, sponsored by the Rockefeller and Ford Foundations.
2. *Innovation in Primary Education*, G. W. Bassett, Wiley-Interscience, London, 1970.
3. 'Innovations in the elementary school curriculum', Henry J. Otto, in *Curriculum Design in a Changing Society*, ed. Richard W. Burns and Gary D. Brooks, Educational Technology Publications, Englewood Cliffs, New Jersey, p. 187.
4. *Learning To Be*, Unesco-Harrap, 1972, pp. 192, 261, 262.
5. 'Unusual ideas in education', Everett Reimer, International Commission on the Development of Education, Series B: *Opinions, No. 39*, Unesco; and 'On the necessity to de-school society', Ivan Illich, International Commission on the Development of Education, Series B: *Opinions, No. 38*, Unesco.
6. *Learning To Be*, Unesco-Harrap, 1972, pp. xxiv–xxvi.
7. International Commission on the Development of Education, Series B: *Opinion, No. 28*, Unesco, pp. 4.
8. '1963 Temporary work regulations for full-time middle and primary schools', Susan Shirk, in *The China Quarterly*, July/September 1972. (Extract reproduced by permission of *The China Quarterly*.)
9. Brochure of the South East Asian Ministers of Education Organization (SEAMEO), Bangkok.
10. *APEID. Programme Development Meeting*, November 1973, Unesco Regional Office for Education in Asia, Bangkok.

## SELECTED FURTHER READINGS

'Resistance to the adoption of audio-visual aids by elementary school teachers', G. Eicholz and E. Rogers, in *Innovation in Education*, ed. M. Miles, Teachers College Press, New York, 1964, p. 299–316.
'Educational innovation: the nature of the problem', M. Miles, in *Innovation in Education*, ed. M. Miles, Teachers College Press, New York, 1964, p. 1–48.
*The Management of Innovation in Education*, Report of a Workshop held at St. John's College, Cambridge, OECD(CERI), 1969.
*Understanding Change in Education: An Introduction*, A. M. Huberman, Unesco: IBE, 1973.
*The School Readiness Project*, Wincenty Okon and Barbara Wilgocka-Okon, Institute for Education, Warsaw, Unesco: IBE, 1973.
'Resistance to change', G. Watson, in *Concepts for Social Change*, ed. G. Watson, NTL Institute for Applied Behavioral Science, Washington, D.C., 1967, pp. 11–25.
'Appraising the effects of innovation in local schooling', in *Educational Evaluation, New Roles, New Means*, National Society for the Study of Education, Rand McNally, Chicago, 1968, pp. 284–304.

122

*Adoption of Educational Innovations*, R. Carlson, University of Oregon, Eugene, Oregon, 1965.

*L'Éducation Rurale et la Diffusion des Nouvelles Techniques Agricoles en Haute-Volta*, ICED-IEDES, University of Paris, 1973.

*Television and Educational Reform in El Salvador. Final Report*, published by the Institute of Communications Research, Stanford University.

'The teacher as innovator, seeker and sharer of new practices', R. Lippitt, in *Perspectives of Educational Change*, ed. R. Miller, Appleton-Century-Crofts, New York, 1967.

*Report of the Missions for the Evaluation of Educational Television in Niger, El Salvador and American Samoa*, Publications on the Educational Television Programme, Vol III, Ministry of Education of the Republic of the Ivory Coast.

*Deschooling Society*, Ivan Illich, Harper and Row, New York, 1970.

*The School Without Walls*, John Bremer and Michael von Moschzisker, Holt, Rinehart and Winston, New York, 1971.

*The Evolution of Tanzanian Rural Development*, John Connell, Institute of Development Studies, Occasional Papers, University of Sussex, 1973.

# Part 3

## MEASURES AND INNOVATIONS

# CHAPTER 8

# Planning Basic Education

To turn to measures is to turn first to planning and this involves introducing the awkward word 'priorities'. Awkward because everything cannot be done at once and difficult choices have to be made.

The main options in the planning of primary education itself are (1) to give priority to special measures to increase the quantitative population coverage of primary education and close the drop-out gap or (2) to apply the strongest effort to improving the quality of primary education. The taking up of either option would not mean the neglect of the other, but would affect the distribution of effort between the two.

In practice the two options overlap because, as we saw in Chapters 3 and 4, quantity and quality are interlocked at a number of points. This overlap and the points of interlock (e.g. number of years of education, pupil–teacher ratio, size of schools) provide leverage for redesigning the primary level to better fit the needs for both quantity and quality.

The above options relate to planning within the primary level. But there are also two further sets of options affecting the attainment of universal primary education. First, the choice of priority between the primary level and the other educational levels and, secondly, between education and the other sectors of the country's overall development plan.

The actual options can, of course, only be made in each country in the light of the national facts. These are not always known in the necessary detail and the first step in a world programme for universal primary education would be for each country to establish the number and location of its children below the educational poverty line and diagnose their conditions and prospects.

At the same time it is desirable for planning purposes to establish at the international level some general principles and definitions as to what is meant by such terms as 'basic education', 'minimum basic education' and 'below the educational poverty line', and to be clear as to what is entailed in the United Nations Declaration of Human Rights in which education is included.

There are two meanings of basic education as applied to children and adolescents. *The first* is predominantly educational, namely that there should be provided at the national level an adequate preparation for life and for further education which is suited to the average citizen of the country. Its amount and content vary widely among countries according to their state of educational development, their economic, social and cultural background, and the job possibilities.

Basic education in this sense means the first level of formal education at the base of the educational pyramid, i.e. the whole of the primary cycle, or in countries where primary and lower secondary are grouped into a unitary compulsory cycle it means the whole of the unitary cycle. For older children it may mean, in addition, some preparation for employment in non-formal education at the senior primary or junior secondary level.

The second meaning is predominantly social and arises from the fact that a mass of children have never been to school or have dropped out too soon to become literate. Under this meaning basic education is regarded as a minimum social requirement, like the number of calories needed to secure freedom from hunger, or the need to have so many doctors per hundred thousand population. It arises because full basic education in the first sense is not yet feasible in a number of developing countries.

In this sense basic education equates with only the first part of the primary cycle, often called 'elementary education', usually of four years, but recently, as we saw earlier, reduced to three years in the USSR. In the case of older children it equates with functional literacy and pre-employment preparation of an elementary nature.

Overlap between the two senses occurs in some of the educationally well developed countries because, in addition to retaining an 'elementary' cycle within the first level, they have compulsory first level cycles of 8 to 10 years, thus making basic education in the first sense a social minimum. Further, it must not be supposed that the 'minimum' sense is only a social concept. In many environments existing in the developing countries it can be the right economic and educational solution as well as a social aim.

While basic education in both senses varies from country to country, the range of variation is narrower in the second sense than in the first, because the minimum cannot normally be reduced beyond the core of literacy and numeracy—except in areas untouched by modern processes.

Minimum needs in developing countries would normally be literacy, numeracy, adequate verbal expression and some knowledge of citizenship and of the physical and social environment, of health and nutrition, learned by methods which rouse curiosity, develop self-reliance and encourage physical and mental adaptability. In the case of older children, some knowledge of family planning and some orientation for local employment, or in the subsistence sector for raising productivity, would be included. In addition there is the need from a national development standpoint for opportunity to move to fuller and higher forms of education, based on talent.

The idea of minimum needs, whether in education or in wages or health or similar fields, has to be applied with great care, so as not to be used to fossilize lower standards for one section of the population and higher ones for the rest. For this reason Education Ministers and parents usually and justifiably oppose having two education systems in the same country, except for limited types of remedial education.

It follows that programmes of minimum basic education (unless they are purely remedial) have either to be incorporated in the overall system (which may involve its structural reform) or they must, if conducted outside through non-formal education, be linked to it by at least a minimum set of ladders and bridges to create educational opportunity.

Let us now look at the statement that education is a human right. Although this proposition is seldom defined, what must be meant is that everyone has a right to at least a minimum basic education in the sense above. It can scarcely be maintained that everyone has a right to a university degree. This is so impracticable that it would be merely a wish and in no sense a right.

Nevertheless there is a sense of the words 'human right' which equates not with obligations but with desires and exhortations that are thought to be implementable without too much delay. These are often referred to as conditional rights and this is the sense in which many authorities use the expression 'right to education'. Thus, in the brochure *Unesco and Human Rights*,[1] we read:

> Although education is a right, like other rights it is conditional and not absolute: its exercise depends on the practical possibilities of applying it. This concept indicates the line of action followed by Unesco which is to strive for an ideal by proposing the means for making it a reality.
>
> Too many countries still face too many difficulties of all kinds—economic, social and cultural, scientific and technical—which, despite the enormous efforts they are making, prevent them from providing schooling for all their children. In many cases, there are just not enough teachers, schools or books. For this reason, Unesco has repeatedly emphasized the importance of educational planning which offers the means of harmonizing resources and needs. It also co-ordinates problems such as the training of teachers, the financing and administration of education, school building programmes and the improvement of teaching methods, techniques and structures.
>
> Action has also been taken to make the public aware of a form of discrimination which, more than any other, divides mankind: the problem of illiteracy which today affects over 780 million adults, or almost one man in three.

This concept of education being a conditional right certainly reflects current usage and is to be found also in the allied phrase 'access to education' in general use in resolutions of Unesco's General Conference and among educators. The image is of a system to which the child has access or entry which should not be withheld.

There are, however, a number of difficulties about this point of view. If rights are conditional on the efforts to provide schools, who is to say whether they are adequate? What attitude has to be taken to educational systems which heavily overspend on the second and higher levels and for this reason leave large sections of the population growing up illiterate? If the right is conditional is the obligation to meet it also conditional, or is there an absolute obligation to make it no longer conditional as soon as possible?

Clearly some limitation should be placed on the 'conditionality', otherwise the concept of right may disappear. A better expression, though clumsy, might be to describe minimum basic education as an absolute right which is subject to a supply problem. Since it competes with other rights for resources, the real issue becomes the place it occupies in the allocation of resources.

When the matter becomes a supply problem, the image of 'access to education' also changes. Instead the emphasis shifts to those who are responsible for the supply, namely the state, and we have a delivery and not an access problem. Rights create obligations and the obligation falls on the Educational Ministry to deliver at least basic minimum education to all as soon as it can amass the resources. The terms 'conditional right' and 'access to education' may well be valid for the educational system as a whole, but minimum basic education has a different conceptual base.

A similar difficulty arises over the concept of discrimination. Discrimination normally means that action is taken by authorities or by individuals to exclude certain persons from their rights (conditional or absolute) without reason other than race, sex, religion or other group attachments. Is illiteracy due to discrimination in this sense? In some cases it undoubtedly is. But in the overwhelming number of cases illiteracy is due to a supply problem, i.e. the absence for a large section of the population, whatever their group affiliations, of the requisite delivery service or of the necessary economic and social conditions to sustain it.

Unesco's General Conference of 1960, which adopted the *Convention and Recommendation against Discrimination in Education*, ran into difficulty on this matter. The problem of discrimination became entangled with the separate problem of equality of opportunity. In fact, they are complementary but the treatment required is different.

The Executive Board of Unesco established a Special Committee in 1965 to report on the carrying out of the Recommendation by questionnaires to governments, and the work of this committee is conveniently set out in the *Report of the Unesco General Conference*.[2] In its conclusions and recommendations, as we mentioned earlier in Chapter 5, it drew attention to this difficulty and stated: 'Many reports (from Member States) do not distinguish clearly between discrimination proper and inequality'. The importance of this distinction is that discrimination can usually be prevented by legislation and behavioural changes, whereas inequality due to the lack of supply of resources on the part of the state is in the first place a planning problem and, in implementation of the plans, a problem of the creation and distribution of the necessary inputs and outputs required.

These concepts are important for education planning and in particular for the planning of the primary level. A method for doing this, based on the line of thought adopted above, is suggested by the author in the first chapter of a publication by Unesco, *Economic and Social Aspects of Educational Planning*,[3] in the form of a thirteen point model for the planning of education integrated with the planning of overall development. Development is defined in the model as the process of maximizing, in harmony with each other, the nine components of the index of standards of living[4] set out by the United Nations Statistical Commission, of which education is one. But since living standards depend to a substantial degree (though not entirely, because income distribution is also important) on the size of national product per head, their cost in economic as well as social terms has to be evaluated.

In the model the postulation of a minimum level of universal education, required on social grounds and as a human right, is the immediate step to be taken after the completion of the first point of analysis, namely the size and growth of the population. It is postulated as an absolute obligation. This postulate is then tested against the economic and fiscal possibilities and the claims of the other educational levels as contributors to development, and the allocation necessary for the purpose.

The speed of attainment of universal basic or primary education would depend not only on the feedback from economic growth and restraint in uneconomic expansion of the other educational levels but also on how soon the primary level can be made ready to absorb additional finance and the time lags for teacher training and school building. In Unesco's Asian Model adopted by Ministers of Education in 1965 it was found that the governing factor in the time required for universal primary education was not finance so much as the inevitable time lags in the creation of the 'real' resources (teachers, buildings etc.).

Further, since forces of conservation are likely to hold on to and want to increase progress attained at other levels rather than feed resources back into minimum basic education, there are likely to be delays and distortions in resources actually coming available, as was shown in the Bolivian case in Chapter 5. This points to the need for a regular review of progress by a standing 'watchdog' committee of high officials or Ministers and by the legislature.

It may be the case that in the newer and least developed countries, where the gaps in coverage are largest and the national income is lowest, the initial priority for resource allocation should be the second and higher levels of education in order to produce the middle and higher level personnel necessary for the country to step forward into nationhood and build its economy. This was the doctrine underlying the recommendation giving priority to secondary education adopted at the Unesco Regional Conference of Ministers of Education at Addis Ababa which set regional objectives for Africa in 1961. This conception is consistent with the delivery of minimum basic education being an absolute right if the process of feedback and checking is followed as above.

This priority for second level and higher education, while valid at the time, became largely obsolete as it became clear towards the end of the 1960s that the overall pace of the second and higher levels of education was exceeding employment outlet, though there were shortages of specialist grades, and that the priority was shifting back to primary. A dangerous course has to be taken between the Scylla of concentrating on minimum basic education for all before the economy can afford it and the Charybdis of over-investing in the higher levels and neglecting the educational gap.

In addition to changes in employment outlet, priorities may be upset by variations in the rate of growth of the child population. As was shown in Chapter 3 on quantitative trends, the situation over the next ten or so years is that the universalizing of primary education in the sense of everyone going through the full cycle which each country provides is likely to be held up by a population bulge which is travelling up the age scale. This will mean a heavy increase for a number of years of children of entering school age, followed by a relief when the effects of the reduced fertility which is forecast in turn affects the number of children of school age. If the concept of the absolute obligation to provide education is maintained, this will mean holding the concept of universal primary education in abeyance in low enrolment countries and replacing it temporarily by universal basic education (UBE instead of UPE). This is clearly one of the options which has to be faced on demographic grounds alone over most of the populations of the developing countries for a decade or two, in others for longer periods, having regard to their present unit costs and likely economic future.

A further point of possible danger is that switches of priority towards minimum basic education may weaken the capacity of the other levels to meet the need for more teachers and other types of educational personnel, both expert and administrative, as well as the occupational needs of the country.

Finally, if minimum basic education for all, accompanied as it should be by new interpretations of content, relevance and methods, is given first priority it is necessary to grapple with a number of questions for which there are at present few ready answers and which will involve additional research and development, more pilot projects and experimentation, the re-cycling of teachers and changes in their training. The necessary educational research and development activities have, therefore, also to be planned and allocations provided, as well as increases in and improvements of present statistical and administrative resources.

The exercise of delineating the objectives and constraints, and interpreting them quantitatively wherever possible, is salutary even when data is thin. The process involved may be summarized as follows.

*Objectives*

(1) Aim at a delivery service which could ensure that at some point between 5 and 14 each child should have at least 4 or 6 years continuous education. Create that number of places. Find out, by localities, the suitable minimum basic 'learning package' and the optimum years of attendance, including perhaps intermittent courses and combination of formal and non-formal education.

(2) Add a degree of access to the full primary cycle and to the second level, geared to the demands of the economy and the availability of resources. Construct opportunity bridges and ladders, and compensatory cycles, rationed at first but extending gradually to provide for all, as resources can be fed back to basic education from the other levels.

(3) Add also services for youth 15 to 17 without basic education by providing non-formal education, at first in areas of rapid development and then extending outward on a scale of feasibility.

(1) Examine the enrolment percentages for each year of age between 5 and 14 and extract the highest continuous peak for (a) four years, (b) six years continuous education, and (c) for the length of the prescribed national primary cycle. This will show the current attendance cycles produced by environmental conditions.

(2) Show the extent of the gap by region or district by pupil's age and by type of primary school (incomplete, lower or full primary) and make broad allocation of

causes to (a) incompleteness of school (insufficient number of grades), (b) other educational reasons, (c) economic and social and family reasons, (d) drop-out.

(3) Do this both in terms of the standard definition of drop-out (which is failure to complete the declared national cycle—even if it is a long one) and also in attainment terms (e.g. drop-out before attainment of minimum basic education, drop-out after a completed 7 years of education if the national cycle happens to be 8 years).

(4) Show needs for non-formal basic education for youth 15–17 who missed primary education.

(5) Use these findings as the initial basis of a plan to increase enrolment and reduce drop-out, and develop non-formal education for illiterate youth.

Step Two

(1) Apply population projections for 1970–85 for the age groups 0–4 and 5–14, and other age combinations as may be indicated by the national cycle, to existing enrolment, drop-out and pupil–teacher ratios and see what the school and non-formal output would be in 1985.

(2) Make similar projections on different hypotheses of school building, teacher supply and reduction of drop-out and repetition.

Step Three

(1) Place the projections in a financial context by extrapolating (a) proportion of the national budget spent on education; (b) proportion of gross national product spent on education; (c) proportion of the educational budget devoted to primary education.

(2) Distribute expenditure required for projections between current and capital.

(3) Show proportion of GNP raised in taxes, extent of distribution of educational expenditure between public and private, and central and local sources.

(4) Show unit cost per pupil and its main components. Add trends in rising unit costs to the financial projection. Adjust for inflation and estimate real costs.

(5) Set alongside (1) to (4) similar data for comparable countries and reasons for differences.

Step Four

(1) Consider means of reducing the unit cost in relation to output and increasing the overall productivity of the existing system through such means as (a) better location of schools, (b) the amalgamation of small urban schools into larger groups and (c) introducing automatic promotion and eliminating repetition.

(2) Plan use of local building materials and set up where possible production centres for teacher aids.

132

(3) Increase class size and shift working where necessary in overcrowded areas.

(4) Provide for training and use monitors to supplement teachers.

(5) Make cost benefit studies of the use of television and radio on a national scale as a major educational aid.

(6) Stimulate local voluntary effort for school buildings, school transport, measures to reduce avoidable drop-out etc.

(7) Examine possibilities of eliminating fees and making textbooks and uniforms free.

(8) Study with the other government departments concerned with child development, and with local and voluntary agencies, measures outside of the educational system which affect school attendance, attainment at school and drop-out. Among these items will figure notably health, nutrition, family life and improvement of welfare conditions in the home, transportation to school and attitudes towards girls' education.

(9) The measures in (8) should be considered both from the angle of quantity, since help in these directions can bring many children over into school attendance in low income countries, and also from the quality standpoint, since they can increase the productivity of the purely educational inputs and raise standards of school performance.

*Structure and quality*

Step One

(1) Review the structure of the system in relation to national, local and district needs.

(2) Consider alternative designs of structure to provide maximum population coverage and improve relevance and quality.

(3) Study new types of linkages between incomplete and lower primary schools and complete schools with the whole cycle to provide avenues to secondary education and seek to optimize opportunity.

(4) Review possibilities of additional non-formal education facilities for older children and adolescents who missed schooling, and of bridges between formal and non-formal education.

Step Two

(1) Examine the arrangements for teacher training in the light of Step One and consider a new network of improved teacher training institutions with candidates recruited from districts.

(2) Provide links with these institutions to the nationwide service but establish promotion avenues within the districts so as not to lose talent.

Step Three

(1) Collect data on deficiencies of relevance of content to needs seen by overall and local development authorities, educational experts and parents. Specify local needs.

(2) Analyse teaching and learning deficiencies, e.g. curricula, syllabuses, methods of teaching, lack of equipment etc., to meet those needs.

(3) Review the supply of curriculum development personnel and study the cost and feasibility of additional curriculum development centres with experimental facilities and links with both teachers, examination authorities and parents.

Step Four

(1) Redesign curricula, methods and teacher training, as necessary, and follow through into examination system and teacher training.

(2) Overhaul examination system to make it less bookish for early leavers and consider establishing a certificate of basic education indicating aptitudes.

(3) Overhaul examination system to make it less bookish for likely early leavers and consider establishing a certificate of basic education.

*Relation to education plan and overall national development plan*

(1) Add implication for the other educational levels, e.g. teacher training colleges, supply of specialist personnel etc.

(2) Bring the results together in a design costed and projected over two or three alternative time series.

(3) Submit to overall planning authorities the case of primary and basic education as an economic and social need, using rate of return studies and other data.

If minimum basic education for the whole of the population is considered to be an overriding objective of national policy in the sense that it is a human right, then it has to be treated in the same way as the proposition that the country's defence effective should not fall below a certain level, or that a country must have at least one university or such a proportion of doctors in the population. If this approach is applied to the process of integrating education with the overall economic plan, the options will be limited, as far as primary education is concerned, to the choice of alternative time paths in relation to the taxable capacity, population growth and the speed at which the real effectives of education (trained teachers and school buildings) can be produced.

Few countries other than socialist people's republics have already given top priority to minimum basic education. Their experience, notably that of the USSR, shows that where there is a big lag in minimum basic education to be made up, the granting of a top priority resulting in a very rapid expansion of enrolments does in fact mean a reduction of progress in other vital spheres. The statistics for Uzbekistan, for example, show that during the period when rapid progress was being made in mass education, the indices for the expansion of health and housing were practically stationary. Substantial progress in these indices only started once the educational problem had been solved. There was, therefore, a real problem of resource allocation.

Choices have, therefore, to be made not only between levels of education to be supported (except that universal *minimum* educational attainment may be considered an overriding objective) but also between education and other objectives which may also be regarded as overriding.

Moreover, since some of the evidence on rates of return shows that it is in the higher levels of the primary cycle that the return is greatest, it may be necessary in certain countries to concentrate initially on the upper years of primary education, both as a terminal cycle and as the basis for the quality required for the priority needs of the second and higher levels.

Many of the considerations we have mentioned applying to the planning of primary education within the educational system as a whole also applies to planning minimum basic education within the full primary cycle.

Educational systems, however, as we have already seen earlier, are not easily manoeuvred from one trend to another, and the challenge is how to do this within a ferment of a number of different tendencies. For this reason a strong political decision at the highest level is required if successful attainment of minimum basic education for all is to be realized.

The planning of primary education both within total education and as part of overall development will be assisted by the concept of vector planning, which is now being developed to replace the target planning of the 1960s. William Platt, in a paper presented at the symposium on Science and Man in the Americas, organized by AAAS and CONACYT in Mexico City in June 1973 developed this concept, though to go into it in depth would take us beyond the scope of this book. A brief explanation of the concept of vector planning from his paper can, however, be usefully quoted.[5]

Perhaps a useful analogy to help explain vector planning is the art of aerial navigation. In a flight plan one knows the general orientation—the vector—for his destination, but will depend upon subsequent positional fixes and the changing conditions of wind and weather aloft and *en route* air traffic in order to correct one's progress along the way. So, too, in education we need vectors for getting started in the right direction and *en route* feedback for making course corrections. But this analogy is too simple in that the educational navigator must simultaneously give attention to many vectors at once to make sure, for example, that progress toward diversifying educational offerings doesn't bring with it an unfavourable effect upon student mobility, or upon unit cost. And the analogy is too simple also in that ultimate destinations of educational progress are less known than the general direction in which we want to move.

Platt supplies illustrations of 'vectors' and their 'planning implications', some of which follow:

| Vector | Planning Implications |
|---|---|
| (a) Toward lifelong education | —redefine education's system boundaries in time and space, ultimately to include the learning society |
| (b) Towards diversification of learning opportunities | —revise admission arrangements to encourage multiple entry and re-entry into educational activities |
| (c) Toward education as an integral part of other development efforts | —identify education and training dimensions of development programmes and projects in other sectors |
| | —plan mutual adjustments so that education and other efforts reinforce each other |
| | —stress through education the preparation for performance in the world outside the classroom, not just preparation for more schooling |
| (d) Toward equality of educational opportunity | —prepare school maps with view to equalizing spatially the access to relevant education |
| | —organize 'second chance' arrangements to serve drop-outs and push-outs |
| | —remove obstacles to full participation in education by girls and women |
| | —identify causes of educational inequality |
| (e) Toward relating the world of work to education | —organize work-study programmes, school-connected apprenticeships, simulations which introduce world of work problems and materials into the curricula |
| | —co-opt employing establishments, farming cooperatives etc. to offer education and training activities |
| (f) Toward mobilizing resources not now employed in education | —inventory skills and facilities in the community having learning potential |
| | —enlist volunteers as aides, animateurs |
| | —institute systems of student fees and loans so that beneficiary shares in the cost of his education |

It is necessary to turn these vectors and their implications into actual mechanisms of change. Anticipating now the various measures and innovations set out in detail in the chapters which follow, we can list some of them for illustrative purposes as follows:

(1) The adaptation of the content of primary education to the special needs of the rural population has to be hinged to opportunities to move in and out of the full nationwide system of both formal and non-formal education. (Little adaptation and little non-formal education at present exist; accordingly the hinges are equally absent.)

(2) A streaming system or a guidance cycle has to be instituted throughout the country to cover the period of the full primary cycle which continues after the elementary course. (Models for guidance cycles, as we shall see later, exist in the reforms introduced in Iran and Sri Lanka.) Otherwise recruitment to the second level and opportunity to climb up the educational system will suffer.

(3) The streaming system or the guidance cycle has to be supported by new types of ability testing and by scholarships, free places and other support measures which will serve as bridges for talented rural pupils to move into the full system.

(4) 'Nuclear' or 'godfather' schools with longer cycles have to be planned (with facilities for boarding or extended travel) which will serve clusters of schools with short cycles and so provide ladders of educational opportunity.

(5) The examination system has to be recast to optimize successes rather than select by designating failures.

(6) District planning and local consultations are required for the difficult (but feasible) task of delineating the clusters and catchment areas which the nuclear schools will cover and to secure the cooperation and support of both the nuclear and cluster villages to contribute to the nucleus as a whole in cash or in kind.

The main obstacle to implementing plans based on new vectors and programmes is the shortage of tested examples of the new organizational patterns involved affecting both the structure of the system and the teaching and learning patterns. An increasing amount of effort for reform and innovation is taking place as we saw in the previous chapter, but it falls far below requirements. Much work is still required to convert new aims into actual operations. And here is the real current challenge, since acceptance of new aims is now widespread but knowledge is lacking of how to carry them out.

This means that an essential requirement for the planning of primary education is the promotion of research and development and of experimentation and trial runs of new structures, learning systems and organizational mechanisms to make the changes acceptable.

The final recommendation of the International Commission on the Development of Education underlines this need when it states:[6]

We propose that agencies assisting education, national and international, private and public, review the present state of 'research and development' in education with a view to strengthening the capacities of individual countries to improve their present educational systems and to invent, design and test new educational experiments appropriate to their cultures and resources. We believe that if nations, regional bodies, and assisting agencies make the strengthening of these capacities their first order of business over the next ten years, they will enable a number of countries to begin becoming true 'learning societies'.

In short, it is not sufficient to plan primary education; it is also important to plan improvements in the implementation system. This will usually mean considerably

Table 8.1 Instances of perceived problems and constraints in growth of educational R and D presented per country, in terms of nine categories of problems (October 1972)

|  | Problems and constraints | | | | | | | | |
|---|---|---|---|---|---|---|---|---|---|
|  | Trained personnel | Facilities and equipment | Funds | Concepts: libraries and documentation | Co-ordination and guidance | Publication and translation | Access to primary data | Feedback | Lack of incentives from civil service |
| Afghanistan | ** | * | ** | * | * | * | * | * |  |
| India | ** | * |  | ** |  |  |  |  |  |
| Indonesia | ** |  |  | ** |  | * |  |  |  |
| Iran | * | * |  |  | * | * |  |  |  |
| Japan | * | * | * | * | * | ** |  |  | ** |
| Korea, Republic of | ** | * | ** | * | * | ** |  |  | ** |
| Laos | ** | ** | ** | ** | * | ** | * |  |  |
| Malaysia | * | * |  | * | * |  | * |  |  |
| Nepal | ** | * |  | * | * | * |  |  |  |
| Pakistan | * | ** | ** | * | * | * |  |  |  |
| Philippines | * | * | ** | * | * | * |  |  | * |
| Singapore | ** |  |  |  | * |  |  |  |  |
| Sri Lanka | * | * | * | * |  |  |  | * |  |
| Thailand | * | * | ** |  | * |  |  |  |  |
| Viet-Nam, Republic of | ** | ** | ** | ** | * | ** | * |  | * |

Source: Country reports, MEERADA (Tokyo, 1972) and verbal communication.

Note: * indicates that the problem was mentioned as existing in a country.
 ** indicates the most severe of the problems thus mentioned.

increasing the existing allocation of resources for administrative and managerial improvements and for research, development, and experimentation, and the training of staff for the purpose, which are at present insufficient in almost all countries. An indication of the needs of developing countries for such activities is contained in the report of a regional meeting held on this subject under the Unesco-NIER Regional Programme, which was convened by the National Institute for Educational Research of Japan and published by the Unesco Regional Office for Education in Asia.[7] The results of an enquiry as to the obstacles encountered by Asian countries are set out in Table 8.1.

The Report states that this enquiry

> reveals clearly that the most severe handicap for the growth of education R and D in Asia is the lack of trained personnel. In many countries the problem is directly related to lack of financial resources, but not in all countries. A far greater problem is the absence of adequate training opportunities in most Asian countries. The only countries which mention opportunities for local training of good quality are India (Centre for Advanced Studies in Education, University of Baroda) and Japan.

Some interesting examples of research and development activities recently completed or in process of completion in India are set out as shown in Table 8.2 in the Unesco-NIER Report, *Educational Research and Development in Asia*.[7]

This is an area where external assistance can be particularly helpful. It may take the form of training research workers, of sponsoring experimentation and so taking financial risks the developing countries may not be able to afford, or assisting the setting up of research and development centres in the developing countries.

In educational research and development, as in the rest of educational planning, consultation is needed with the world of education, both directly with teachers and social scientists and also through consultation committees representing parents and the community at large.

The importance of maintaining, in the construction of the educational plan, a dialogue with outside advisory bodies and with the Ministries concerned with national and economic aspects is illustrated by two recent reports issued by the Indian Ministry of Education and Social Welfare, *Education in the Fifth Five Year Plan*—1974–1979 (New Delhi, 1972) and *Education in the Fifth Plan* (New Delhi, 1973). An interesting review is made of these publications in *Education in Asia, Reviews, Reports and Notes*.[8]

The Regional Office review draws attention to the differences between the two documents which reflect the results of the intervening consultations. The review remarks: 'What is significant is that, while both booklets cover exactly the same ground, the change of emphasis and the reallocation of priorities which have taken place during a brief period of six months are substantial'.

It appears, not unexpectedly, that the first of the documents was a good civil service paper, conventional in tone, depending heavily on previous policies and excellent in its analysis of the situation. The second contained a variety of proposals for change and reform which had been introduced during the consultations, in-

**Table 8.2**   Major educational research and development projects recently completed or in the process of completion in India

A. Research projects

1. Development of a comprehensive curriculum for the school stage (NCERT*) — in progress.
2. A comprehensive reading project in Hindi for the first five classes of the primary stage. The project involved the preparation of a comprehensive package consisting of reading, writing tests, flash cards, textbooks, teacher's editions, work books, copy books for students and general handbook for teachers (NCERT) — completed.
3. International survey of educational achievements — achievements in reading, comprehension in the mother tongue and in science. This was sponsored by the International Association for the Evaluation of Educational Achievements (NCERT) — completed.
4. Development of the first mental measurement handbook for India. This book has been published (NCERT) — completed.
5. Pilot Project on the concept of 'work experience' in 1000 upper primary schools (NCERT) — in progress.
6. A pilot project on integrated school system (NCERT).
7. Aspirations and motives of tribal youth (NCERT).
8. Impact of education on tribal institutions (NCERT).
9. Development of science and mathematics curricula for the whole school stage (NCERT) — nearing completion.
10. A survey of school textbooks in India (NCERT) — completed for 12 States; the rest in progress.
11. A study of the patterns of teacher classroom behaviour in Indian schools (CASEt).
12. Inquiry into variables affecting teacher behaviour (CASE).
13. Improving student practice programme using Interaction Analysis Approach (CASE).
14. Effectiveness of Four Response Modes in Programmed Learning (CASE).
15. Pupils' achievement on programmed learning material in relation to some personality variables (CASE).
16. Factors affecting adaptability of schools to take up new ideas (CASE).
17. Characteristics of innovative schools (CASE) — in progress.

B. Development schools

1. Preparation of science kits for primary school classes in India. This is a part of a scheme assisted by Unesco and UNICEF. A large-scale pilot project is now going on involving 1100 primary schools in India. The kits developed by the NCERT as well as the instructional material including textbooks, teachers' guides etc. are being tested.
2. Improvement of teacher training syllabus for primary school teachers. A two year course has been finalized in preparation for introducing the new syllabus. The teacher training schools in India are being equipped with science equipment and audio-visual aids with the assistance of UNICEF.
3. Revision of school textbooks. The first phase of the programme was confined to textbooks in languages and social studies. During the course of the review, norms were developed for evaluation of school textbooks.
4. The Intensive Education District Development Project is a major development scheme launched by the Ministry of Education in 1970. The scheme covers four districts in India. The aim is to launch an integrated educational development programme using all known techniques likely to succeed in the area. The surveys are completed. The actual development schemes are to be started shortly.
5. A scheme for an integrated use of mass media and modern educational technology has been started in 1972 with UNDP assistance. A new institution called Educational Technology Centre is being established in Delhi. This will be a training cum software development centre. There will be close coordination with other schemes of the Government of India such as radio and television broadcasting, satellite broadcasting, film production etc.

* National Council of Educational Research and Training.
† Centre for Advanced Studies in Education.

140

cluding one for 'an over-riding priority to elementary education . . . .' It also proposed 'to radically alter the strategy for its development by emphasizing universal provision of facilities, creating a fairly homogeneous cohort in class I, reduction in wastage and stagnation, multi-point entry, a large programme of part-time education, enrolment of children from the weaker sections of the community (especially scheduled castes and scheduled tribes) and improvement of quality'. At the same time a small reduction was made in the amount of the allocation as a result of economies which it was estimated could be made.

## REFERENCES

1. *Unesco and Human Rights.* Unesco.
2. *Second Report of Committee on Conventions and Recommendations in Education,* Unesco 17 C/15, September 15, 1972, p. 14.
3. 'Education and development', H. M. Phillips in *Economic and Social Aspects of Educational Planning,* Unesco, p. 26.
4. United Nations E/CN.3/179, New York, 1954.
5. *The Faure Report—A Turning Point in Educational Planning,* William J. Platt, presented at Science and Man in the Americas, Technical Symposium, No. 15, AASS and CONACYT, Mexico City, June 1973.
6. *Learning To Be,* Unesco-Harrap, 1972, p. 263.
7. *Educational Research and Development in Asia. Report of a Regional Meeting,* Unesco-Nier Regional Programme for Educational Research in Asia, Unesco Regional Office for Education in Asia, Bangkok, 1973, pp. 63–4 and 76.
8. 'Changing priorities for education in India', in *Education in Asia: Reviews, Reports and Notes,* No. 4, September 1973, Unesco Regional Office for Education in Asia, Bangkok, p. 13.

## SELECTED FURTHER READING

*Educational Planning: A World Survey of Problems and Prospects,* Unesco, 1970.
*Economic and Social Aspects of Educational Planning,* Unesco.
*National Educational Plans* of the main developing countries (obtainable from their Ministries of Education).
*Cost Benefit Analysis in Educational Planning,* Maureen Woodhall, Unesco: HEP.
'Economic and social aspects of the planning of education', H. M. Phillips, in *Readings in the Economics of Education,* Unesco.
'Vector planning for the development of education', William J. Platt, in *Education and Development Reconsidered,* The Bellagio Conference Papers, Ford Foundation/Rockefeller Foundation edited by F. Champion Ward, Praeger, 1974.
'Educational policy and the economics of education: some practical lessons for educational planners in developing countries', Mark Blaug, in *Education and Development Reconsidered,* The Bellagio Conference Papers, Praeger, 1974.

*Research for Educational Planning: Notes on Emergent Needs*, William J. Platt, Unesco: IIEP, 1970.

*The Level of Living Index*, Jan Drewnowski and Wolf Scott, United Nations Research Institute for Social Development, Report No. 4, Geneva, 1966.

*Planning Education for African Development*, R. Jolly, East African Publishing House, Nairobi.

*Policy-Making and International Studies in Educational Evaluation*, William J. Platt, presented at Conference on Educational Achievement, Harvard University, November 1973.

# CHAPTER 9

# Population Coverage and the Structure and Content of the Primary Cycle; Non-Formal Education

The main measures to extend population coverage for basic education for children are the reduction of drop-out and repetition and the increase of school places. It will be remembered from chapters 1 and 3 that the gap as at 1970 of some 269 million children aged 5–14 growing up without at least 4 years of basic education is caused both by drop-out and lack of school places. The greatest single quantitative contribution to be made would be to eliminate drop-out.

Ways in which drop-out can be reduced are:

(1) Material means: provision of school buses or subsidies to other forms of transport to school; free or subsidized midday meals; free or subsidized supply of books and school clothes; reduction or elimination of fees.

(2) Pedagogic means: special language instruction for pupils whose language in the home is different from that used in school; improvement of teaching methods and content to stimulate the interest of pupils and parents; adjustment of examinations to reduce their discouragement; use of criteria of 'mastery' of what is learned, rather than that of competitive attainment.

(3) Action in the community: counselling of parents where children are not sent to school for reasons of prejudice (e.g. in the case of girls) or for reasons of child labour; use of other social services, health and welfare centres etc., and visits to homes by social workers for this purpose; parent education in home economics, family planning; use of the communications media (radio etc.) to show ill effects of drop-out.

(4) Organizational means: shorten the cycle in cases where drop-out is over-long and unlikely to be substantially reduced; variations in school hours to meet local needs; reduction of class size and improvement of premises; eliminate small incomplete primary schools which are unable to offer a minimum teaching and learning cycle.

Although these measures undoubtedly make a substantial contribution, the basic cause of drop-out which is the nature of the social environment surrounding the school will always assert itself. Drop-out acts as an automatic regulator of over-ambitiously long primary cycles which do not have provision for earlier terminal points. One of the fundamental ways of tackling drop-out is, therefore, the reorganization of the structure of the cycle to fit local conditions.

The reduction of repetition works in a different way. In many countries there are blocks of children repeating classes who prevent others coming in. When this is due to over-rigorous conditions for pupils to move from grade to grade the solution is automatic promotion as has been adopted by a number of the developing countries. Where it is due to certain pupils being genuinely backward compared special classes are required for them rather than leaving them out of their element.

Useful experience is available in the Eastern European countries on special action to reduce the problem of repetition through collective efforts of pupils, teachers and parents, the systems in those countries, unlike most of those in the West, not practising automatic promotion.

The case for automatic promotion was strengthened by the results of a survey made by the Bangkok Institute for Child Study,[1] however, in a survey in 1966 of 25,000 children in sample schools which came to some interesting conclusions. It found that

the reported differences in children's achievements largely reflected economic and social variables, that the prescribed standards in grades 1 to 4 were over-optimistic and generally not being attained, that children who were older or younger than the appropriate grade age did less well than the others, that differences between the language at home and at school was a serious disadvantage, and that there was a positive correlation between children's achievements and the educational qualification of the teachers and the size of the school.

The overall conclusion of the Bangkok study was that the repetition of grades appeared to hold no advantage in raising achievement levels. This conclusion would give encouragement to automatic promotion, provided it was combined with raising the efficiency of the teaching staff which appears in the study to be the main factor in achievement.

A chart, useful for reference purposes, in handling problems of drop-out and repetition taken from a pilot simulation study[2] made by the Max-Planck Institute, Berlin, in collaboration with Unesco's Statistical Office, is shown in Figure 9.1.

Additional means of extending the population coverage are better use of existing schools and the creation of new ones. Temporary measures to meet the pressure of the increased demand for enrolment are devices such as larger classes, double shifts and night school for older children who missed full basic education by going into employment too soon. In Burma, for instance, some 200 primary night schools have been set up for drop-out and children who cannot attend school during the day. (The alternative approach is non-formal education.)

The creation of additional schools is required in areas where population is expanding rapidly through the birth rate or migration or where areas previously without schools are on the margin of development.

In the greater part of the development regions, the school map has been completed up to some three quarters of the population coverage and measures required

144

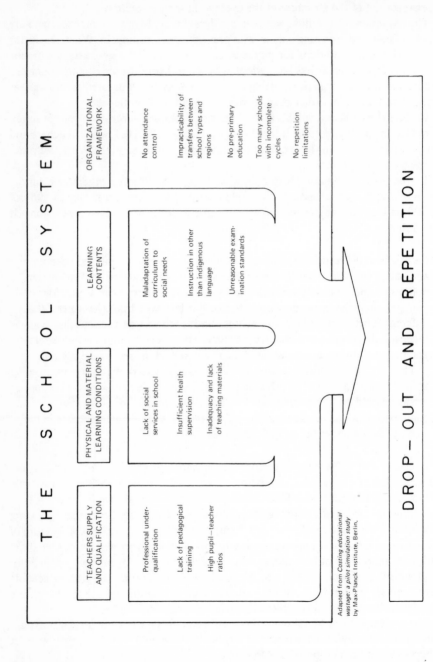

THE SCHOOL SYSTEM

| TEACHERS SUPPLY AND QUALIFICATION | PHYSICAL AND MATERIAL LEARNING CONDITIONS | LEARNING CONTENTS | ORGANIZATIONAL FRAMEWORK |
|---|---|---|---|
| Professional under-qualification | Lack of social services in school | Maladaptation of curriculum to social needs | No attendance control |
| Lack of pedagogical training | Insufficient health supervision | Instruction in other than indigenous language | Impracticability of transfers between school types and regions |
| High pupil—teacher ratios | Inadequacy and lack of teaching materials | Unreasonable exam-ination standards | No pre-primary education |
| | | | Too many schools with incomplete cycles |
| | | | No repetition limitations |

DROP–OUT AND REPETITION

Adapted from *Costing educational wastage: a pilot simulation study* by Max-Planck Institute, Berlin.

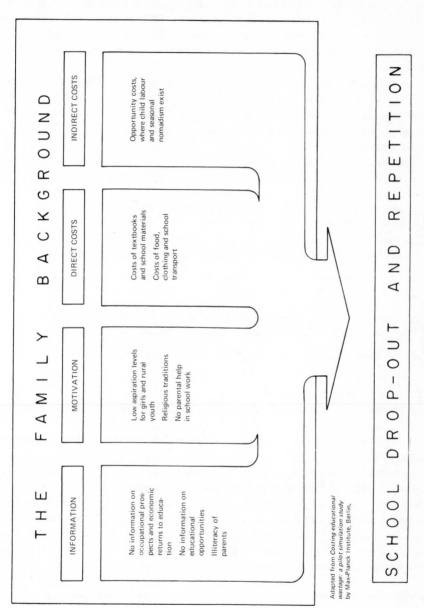

THE FAMILY BACKGROUND

INFORMATION

No information on occupational prospects and economic returns to education

No information on educational opportunities

Illiteracy of parents

MOTIVATION

Low aspiration levels for girls and rural youth

Religious traditions

No parental help in school work

DIRECT COSTS

Costs of textbooks and school materials

Costs of food, clothing and school transport

INDIRECT COSTS

Opportunity costs, where child labour and seasonal nomadism exist

SCHOOL DROP-OUT AND REPETITION

Adapted from *Costing educational wastage: a pilot simulation study* by Max-Planck Institute, Berlin.

**Figure 9.1**

are in some cases adding to the size of schools and in others pushing out into rural areas and shanty towns where new schools are needed.

There are, however, a number of developing countries which have blank places on their school maps, particularly in the case of the 25 least developed countries. In their case there is the problem of locating schools efficiently in relation to the 'catchment area' from which pupils need to be drawn, as well as the question of the size of schools.

The approach required in such countries is one of pushing out schools progressively as areas become capable of supporting and using them to the full and, in the meantime, of undertaking 'first aid projects'. 'First aid projects' may consist of new simplified varieties of education or new schools designed to combat particular weaknesses.

Thus, what is required is a plan for the distribution of additional schools according to the specific location and needs of the deprived population groups to be covered. The plan has to have regard especially to possibilities of transport and the provision of midday meals as well as to the socio-economic conditions of the 'catchment area' and to the development possibilities.

The Indian Education Commission already cited[3] has recommended the following criteria for the location of primary and secondary schools:

(a) A lower primary school teaching classes 1 to 4 should be available within one mile from the home of every child.

(b) A higher primary school, teaching classes 1 to 7 should be available within three miles of the walking distance from the home of every child.

(c) A secondary school teaching classes 8 to 10 should be available within five to seven miles from the home of every child.

As primary education pushes out into the least developed rural areas the well tried solution of one-teacher schools may be particularly applicable, and innovatory school buildings in which the teacher can be housed as well as the school itself. Interesting examples exist in Mexico of small prefabricated schools including the teacher's home.

It is interesting to note that the survey[4] of one-teacher schools made by the International Bureau of Education in 1961 showed a widespread use of this system beyond what had been supposed, its existence having 'no bearing on the level of cultural or economic development of the country concerned'. (Canada, for instance had 10,000 at the time, the United States around 24,000. In France, 17 per cent of primary pupils were in one-teacher schools in 1959.) The survey states: '... in seven-tenths of the countries concerned, the one-teacher school ... covers as many years of schooling as a primary school with several teachers of the same category. By means of these complete one-teacher schools children may proceed without difficulty to secondary schools, teacher-training schools and vocational schools'.

The survey further states:

The replies are unanimous in admitting that it is possible to obtain good results by simultaneous teaching, in spite of the complexity of this method. Contrary to a very widely held opinion, this inquiry shows that in the majority of cases teachers in one-teacher schools have to accomplish their task without any special theoretical training; a few allusions, at most, are made in the course of ordinary lectures on education to the problems involved in running this type of school, and student teachers are sometimes given an opportunity for teaching practice in one-teacher schools.

It seems clear that the further use of one-teacher schools may be an economical way of pushing primary education out into the more remote areas of the less developed countries where at present there is a lack of school places. In addition to being economical and giving increased geographical coverage, this system is consistent with the increasing tendency to allow pupils to work more on their own (provided they have textbooks and educational materials) under the general direction of the teacher and helps to break down the bad effects of a whole class learning by rote, which is the practice still in rural schools in most developing countries.

Another advantage of the one-teacher school is that it can encourage experimentation. The Report of the Indian Educational Commission in 1966 stated:[5]

One of the essential conditions for making an educational system elastic and dynamic, therefore, is for the administrator to develop this competence, to discriminate between school and school, between teacher and teacher, and to adopt a flexible mode of treatment for individuals or institutions at different levels of development. This alone can help to promote initiative, creativity and experimentation on the part of the teachers.

The Commission stated that about 40 per cent of Indian schools were single teacher schools and, even in the other schools, the proportion where the teacher has a single class is very small. Multiple class teaching, which is one of the innovatory trends in developed countries, is therefore usual, to some degree or other, in many developing countries and is a challenge to the teachers and teacher educators concerned.

Against this has to be measured in urban areas the advantage of amalgamating small schools into larger to secure economies and efficiencies of larger-scale educational facilities.

We come now to measures for changing the structure and content of the cycle. Under the standard international classification of education agreed at a Unesco meeting in 1958 and still in use, the term 'first level' is preferred to the expression 'Primary' and the definition reads: 'Education at the first level refers to education "of which the main function is to provide basic instruction in the tools of learning (e.g. at elementary school, primary school)" '.

This definition of function which is under revision, but has not yet been replaced, is unsatisfactory for use for the child population as a whole in the developing countries, since for the vast majority of them the primary level is not a tool for further learning but is terminal, except in the sense of further out-of-school education, or the use of literacy in self-education. Also missing from the definition is any reference to the knowledge needed by school leavers to cope with their socio-economic environment and their working life.

The mechanics of the restructuring of the cycle to attain a minimum and relevant basic education for all may be clear, but as we saw in Chapter 5 on the forces involved, the process is difficult.

The mechanics may be to set up a curriculum which is terminal at the period (from between 3 to 5 years) at which minimum basic education is obtainable, and to follow it, for those who stay on at school, by a guidance cycle. The guidance cycle will select those who will eventually continue into the second level, and give further relevant primary basic education to those who stay on only for another two or three years of school before leaving. It will also be related to work needs and experiences.

Let us look at some examples which, although not numerous, are important, starting with that of Peru. The previous system in Peru suffered from many of the weaknesses, both quantitative and qualitative, which are typical of the developing countries and which were discussed in Chapters 3 and 4. A major reform is now under way to put the system as a whole on a new basis.

The educational system has been divided into three cycles, each conceived as a unit in itself, permitting the child to acquire a 'minimal knowledge of fundamental attitudes and abilities to orient himself to his environment'. The movement of pupils up through the programme is not tied by year to year promotion by grades, but according to individual ability. Parallel to the system is another programme designed for the special needs of youth and adults who dropped out in earlier years, and for them too an entirely new curriculum has been evolved including community and cultural activities.

The nature of the reform is described by a leading Peruvian educator as follows:[6]

Within a period of ten years it is hoped, under the Peruvian reform to eradicate illiteracy; contribute to the social development of the country's most depressed areas; change the old system into a new one more in keeping with the needs of the population; make the initial fundamental education course, and subsequently the complete nine-grade system universally applicable; foster the development of a new culture which will express its historical identity and quicken the creative potentialities of the Peruvian; and, lastly, guide the national education movement along lines similar to those followed by the other Latin American countries.

The idea of direct participation by the community in the educational movement was bound to have its place in the reorganization of Peruvian education. Concrete form is given to this idea in the 'nucleation' of education, consisting in the establishment of communal educational units (nucleos educativos comunales); these basic units of educational administration are the points of convergence for action by the local community, State authorities, parents and teachers. The result is a self-governing communal entity which is to constitute the basis of the whole national educational system. One consequence of action by these educational units will be, moreover, the effective rationalization of the use of the financial and material resources directly or indirectly allocated to education . . . . Fundamental ('basic') education consists of nine grades and is divided into stages. The normal type of instruction provided at this level (instruction for children aged from 6 to approximately 15 years) consists of three stages—comprising respectively four, two and three grades—in that order.

The reform in structure which is involved can be seen from Figure 9.2.

Another type of reform of both structure and content which is of a less radical nature, but of major importance, is that which has been approved in Sri Lanka a country which has had an impressive educational expansion under a system which has not included fee paying and has had a useful scholarship system. Nonetheless, considerable dissatisfaction with the system had developed because, although educational expenditure was high, over a third of the country's children failed to complete the first four grades of a unitary eight year first level cycle, the orientation of which was too bookish and geared to the second level rather than to the needs of those who terminate with primary education.

An important change of both structure and content was introduced with effect from January 1972, the major changes being that the minimum age of admission is raised from 5 to 6 years, automatic promotion will be introduced across certain grades, grades 6 to 9 will be used for an integrated terminal programme or guidance cycle of general education, emphasizing preparation for actual life.

Commenting on the new system in Sri Lanka, the ILO report,[7] states:

There is a good case for dividing level one into five years for basic intellectual skills and three years for training as a citizen and productive worker through the introduction of pre-vocational courses. During the latter period schools should be transformed into centres of rural development, community workshops, centres of craft training, and places where the farmer can come to repair his cart or the home handyman can make himself a kitchen cupboard. The schools would thus be open to all age groups which in itself would go a long way in keeping the early school leavers in touch with education and training. The latter part of this suggestion, which is similar to proposals made for the establishment of community schools where both adults and parents participate, is discussed when we come to alternatives to the present primary education system. These views, however, are those of the ILO expert mission which prepared the report, and have had, so far as community schools are concerned for both adults and children, no official acceptance yet by the government.

A somewhat similar plan of reorganization has been adopted for Iran which, instead of a total period of 12 years divided into six years of primary and six of second level, is moving towards a system of five years of primary education followed by a guidance or orientation cycle of three years. The pace of this reorganization is limited by the problems of the supply of teachers and buildings and of working out suitable curricula and methods of implementing the new policy.

An earlier major innovation in Iran was the setting up of an Education Corps in 1962 to provide graduate and high school students to teach in rural areas as an alternative to military service. The Education Corps schools are set up where ordinary primary schools are lacking owing to poor conditions or inaccessibility. The

150

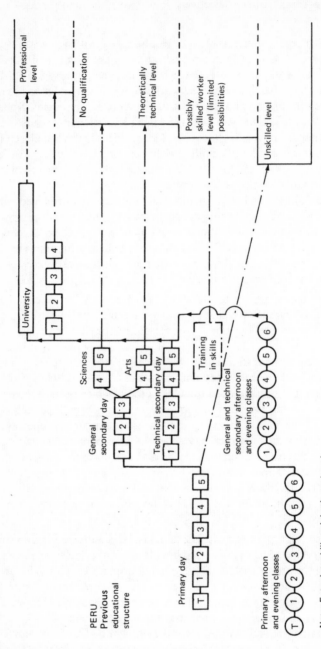

PERU
**Previous**
educational
structure

Primary day

Sciences

General
secondary day

Arts

Technical secondary day

Training
in skills

General and technical
secondary afternoon
and evening classes

University

Professional
level

No qualification

Theoretically
technical level

Possibly
skilled worker
level (limited
possibilities)

Unskilled level

Primary afternoon
and evening classes

Note: Entry into skills training is not based
on educational level.

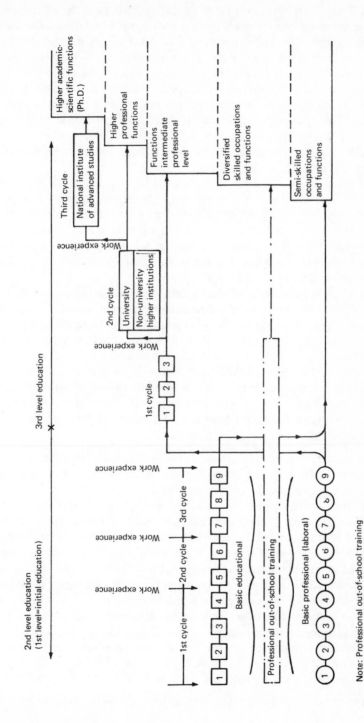

Figure 9.2

national budget bears the cost of the pay and the training of the Education Corps personnel (at lower rates, since it is a form of compulsory national service, than those of the ordinary school teachers). The local community has to lodge the teacher and provide the funds or the labour and materials to build the school.

The original intention had been to cover only grades one and two of the primary cycle, but the whole six years of the primary cycle are now covered. Since 1962, 321,239 (or about 22 per cent) of all rural enrolments in Iran have been in the Education Corps schools. In addition another 57,393 children in rural areas, and another 8,139 in urban, were taught by Education Corps teachers in ordinary schools. Further, a substantial number of children started in Education Corps schools and went on to ordinary schools.

The training period for the teachers is six months and their length of service in the villages is a year and a half. Young university graduates of military service age act as supervisors. Female as well as male teachers have been recruited to the Corps since 1969 and cover 20 per cent of the total, reflecting in some measure the lower ratio of enrolment of girls in Iran (35 per cent girls and 65 per cent boys). The objective is to help to break down the resistance of parents who hesitate to send their girls to school for religious and traditional reasons.

There is some interchange of staff as well as pupils between the two types of schools and it seems clear that the Education Corps programme is integrated into the overall school system to which it provides substantial supplementary resource.

A study has been made[8] of the relative efficiency of the Education Corps and ordinary schools by the International Institute of Educational Planning. The conclusion reached is that although the efficiency level is lower for the Education Corps schools (partly explained by the fact that they are operating in the most difficult areas) the gain from lower cost and from the impulsion they give to rural education (e.g. 23,000 former Corpsmen have stayed on as rural teachers) has made the programme a valuable one. The study states:

> To sum up, the experience of Iran seems to have demonstrated that the Education Corps, subject to its socio-political implications (1) can be introduced in any country, provided that it has a law on military service or other forms of compulsory civilian service, by means of which a sufficient pool of teaching staff can be recruited; (2) stimulates, as a transitional measure, the development of schooling in rural areas by allowing appreciable economies of cost and facilitating the recruitment of teaching staff; (3) does not lead to a permanent and unlimited increase in the financial participation of families and local authorities; (4) to some extent encounters the same sociological obstacles to the development of schooling as the ordinary system . . . . In conclusion, it seems to us that in countries with a low enrolment ratio and a large rural population scattered in small units, which have difficulties in financing educational development and in finding schoolteachers, an experiment modelled on the spirit, structure and working methods of the Iran Education Corps would probably open up encouraging prospects and is therefore worth trying.

Another example of reform of both structure and content is that of Nepal where the primary cycle is being re-examined to introduce a three year elementary course of minimum basic education.

The Nepalese Five Year Plan for Education (1971–76)[9] states that

the educational objective will be to produce citizens who, with full faith in the country and the Crown, will conduct themselves in accordance with the Panchayat system and to meet the manpower requirements of development through the spread of scientific and technical education. Primary education will extend from class one to three and will aim at literacy .... At this level boys and girls will be taught reading, writing, and arithmetic, some rudimentary knowledge of Nepalese and general information regarding the King and the country. It will lay emphasis on development of general knowledge. In the next five years 64 per cent of boys and girls in the age group between 6 and 8 will be given primary education facilities. Individuals with School Leaving Certificates or its equivalent, and trained, will be enrolled as primary school teachers .... Textbooks of good standard will be made available free of cost to children of remote areas and at fair prices to others. District-level examination will be held at the end of the primary school terms. His Majesty's Government will make financial grants to cover the full salary of primary school teachers.

In the adoption of a three year elementary course, Nepal will be acting similarly to proposals adopted by the USSR recently, including the Asian Republics of the Union.[10]

A different strategy of restructuring, which shows a contrary tendency, is apparent in the case of the Sudan. The previous system of four years each for elementary, intermediate and secondary schooling is replaced by six years of primary, three of general secondary and three of higher secondary. At the same time the sub-grade schools giving 2–3 year courses have been abandoned and integrated in the new six-year primary schools.

A reform of a more radical nature than those already described, because the educational situation to be remedied is more severe, is that adopted in Tanzania. It is linked to the overall national policy of self-reliance combined with cooperation (Ujamaa) which was promulgated in 1969.

The policy in the matter of education is set out conveniently (though there are also later statements) in a paper by M. J. Kinunda, Director in Charge of Planning and Development, Ministry of Education.[11]

He states:

The basic elements which constitute the 'Ujamaa' idea (people, hard work, intelligence, modern technology, modern knowledge) mean that education has an important role to play in the new Tanzanian society.

.... This education for self-reliance includes: A review of the curriculum of schools in rural as well as in urban areas, in order to adapt it to the needs of the environment; an attempt to make every level terminal, with a view not only to preparing pupils for the next level but also to preparing them for life in society, should they not be able to go back to school. This concerns primary and secondary, as well as higher education; the introduction of a new system of examination and thus the development of new criteria (such as taking into consideration to what extent a student has contributed to society); integration of school activities in the economic activities of the community; 'schools must learn what they produce and produce what they learn', i.e. work on the farm becomes part of the school curriculum—not a subject added to it. Other new items are: helping in community work, building bridges, cleaning, etc.

A further interesting example of improvement of content and elimination of a non-relevant curriculum is the programme of Mexico.[12] The new curriculum, put into effect in 1960 and still in operation aims to coordinate the schools' activities, teaching content, methods and objectives, with life in the home and in the local, national and world communities. It is organized not by subjects but by six major functions of elementary education, namely (a) to protect health and improve physical fitness; (b) to promote study of the physical environment and of the conservation of natural resources; (c) to create understanding of and to improve social life; (d) to teach creative activities; (e) to teach practical activities; and (f) to develop the elements of culture.

The cycle is for six years, but an intensive programme is given during the first four years, in view of the heavy drop-out rate, thereafter, in order to give the pupil who cannot last for the full cycle better preparation for work and usefulness in the community. In the fifth and sixth year teaching is given especially in manual and occupational activities related to the pupil's aptitudes and the national economic and technical needs. The programme is supported by boarding and social assistance schools, schools for minority groups and schools for the handicapped, as far as resources permit.

Of a somewhat different kind, illustrating the measure recommended by the International Commission[13] of 'special teaching programmes for young people aged between 12 and 16, especially for those who have not attended school', is an interesting programme in India, consisting of 60 pilot centres, set up to integrate back into the education process children from 11 to 14 years of age who have dropped out. In a typical centre, half of the day is spent in workshops while the other half is given to general education; a vocational guidance counsellor is available and there is constant contact with the community.

Moving in the same direction are suggestions that the organization of the cycle would be improved if the school entry age in the less developed countries were raised. In Mr. Najman's recent book, *Education in Africa, What Next?*,[14] which I have already quoted, is the following statement:

It is absolutely indispensable that the entry age in African primary schools be raised in a decisive way. This should be done rather sooner than later and for a very simple reason. Although the 5, 10, or 15 per cent of those who continue education are undoubtedly very important for the future of Africa because they will probably become leaders in the field of economics, politics and development in general, today's African leaders and educators will have to look at the problem of the majority of children who remain in the rural community but who have neither received the preparation nor attained the age to be able to play an active role in that community. Some countries have already tried the new approach. Zambia, for instance, has decided to raise shortly the age of entry to primary education from 5 to 7 years.

Another example is Tanzania where children regularly enter education at the age of 8, sometimes 9, in order to leave at 15 or 16 years of age. The Indonesian cycle starts at 8.

Mr. Najman's argument is that while

psychology has taught us and pedagogy has proved that the younger children are the more easily they learn and it is very important for them to start school at a relatively early age. On the other hand, how can one expect those leaving primary school to be useful young citizens and productive in their community if they are only still between 10 and 13 years of age?

A more extreme version of raising the age of entry was put forward in a paper submitted by Naik to the Bellagio Conference organized in 1972 by the Rockefeller and Ford Foundations.[15] It put forward as an alternative to the present system the proposal to defer the age of entry into State-funded national schools until age 11 or 12. Before age 11–12, all forms of informal and locally supported education would be used, such as tribal elders, Koranic schools, locally financed village schools, radio and/or television, tutoring by older children and literate parents, covering children aged 1–11. It would follow that at age 11 or 12 pupils would enter the national schools differently prepared (some more than literate, some literate, some illiterate). For this reason it would extend the scope of the national schools over ten years of possible educational achievement and place entering students at appropriate entry levels in terms of their previous learning and expect them to attain different terminal levels of achievement in six years. The national schools would not be called either 'primary' or 'secondary', and some opportunity scholarships would be provided for particularly able pupils from poor families who enter illiterate but move rapidly forward during their six-year period of free schooling, to enable them to complete the work offered by the national schools. Higher education would be geared to the competence level to be expected of pupils who attain the tenth achievement level in the national schools.

There is much to be said for Najman's proposal, with the proviso, which he himself inserts, that the local conditions would be the determining factor, but the extreme proposal of Naik's encounters serious difficulties. It is at about the age of 6 or 7 that the child really begins to understand causality and his relation with his environment, and the period between 6 or 7 and 10 or 11 is a decisive one determining the individual's future attitudes to learning, to society and to his own development. These are the ages, therefore, at which the resource of the state should provide at least a minimum of education.

Further, if a choice has to be made between leaving children without formal education, on the one hand when they are between 6 and 10, and on the other between 10 and 14, it is clear that it is much easier to use non-formal out-of-school means of education for older children than for younger. Educative group activities of a community character can be organized for children approaching adolescence, which would be impossible in the case of much younger children. Moreover, the children who go to school at a late age would clearly be at a disadvantage as regards equality of opportunity compared with those in the more prosperous areas for whom public education is provided earlier. It also runs contrary to the concept of spreading the educative process over the individual's whole lifetime.

The most convincing argument in favour of any particular age of entry might seem to be what actually happens in real life. As indicated by the table of enrolment by years in Chapter 3, enrolment is at its maximum in the six countries cited at around 8 or 9 years of age, indicating that this is the natural age of entry in their environment. A glance at the figures for other countries in the Unesco Statistical Yearbook tables of enrolment by age indicates that the six countries are not exceptional in this.

However, real life conditions also often involve children having to work at 12 years of age, and poor conditions exist in the homes during the key learning years of 6 to 8. This may be often a decisive reason for keeping to the present age of the commencement of primary education with only minor adjustments to meet local needs.

The question of the age of entry is linked to the question of pre-primary education, in which a number of the developing countries are showing concern. The situation, however, is that few countries are prepared to invest public funds in pre-primary education (which is largely in private hands and restricted to the parents who are more fortunately placed) so long as their primary education enrolment is incomplete.

A further factor, as we saw in Chapter 3 on quantitative trends, is that a population bulge is moving up the age scale. This would point to universalizing education facilities at the age levels where action is most feasible quantitatively, i.e. in the youngest school age years, as the numbers to be covered are smaller.

An important approach, stressed by the International Commission, which would, if it became operative, offer also a solution to the age of entry problem, is 'recurrent' education. It is based on two main principles—that of intermittent periods of education and work, and that of individualized learning. While the former concerns mostly people of working age, a beginning may be made at the primary level by introducing in the later years of the cycle optional part-time attendance at school with the rest of the time used in practical non-formal instruction. In addition, individualized learning can be encouraged by greater use of team learning in smaller groups than the class.

Some educators believe that from age 7 onwards the percentage of individual work could occupy somewhat more than half of the learning time and could be progressively increased. Individual work or work in small groups of 2 to 4 would gradually be given a progressively greater importance in order to prepare the pupils for the later methods of lifelong education.

These proposals have at present more chance of success in the educationally advanced countries (as, for instance, has already happened to some degree in Sweden) rather than in the less developed. However, recurrent education in the later years of the primary cycle might in the less developed countries be an important means of adjusting the friction between the educational system and the environment, which produces wastage. This would usually mean varying ages of entry (multiple entry) and different ages grouped in the same class, and would call for considerable organizing skills by headmasters and local educational authorities.

In countries at all stages of educational development, there is room and the need for non-formal education. This type of education caters in its own right for many of the practical forms of training and education of people outside school age which the educational system does not normally supply. Up to the present it has, however, played a relatively small part in a country's total educational services and hardly any non-formal education is concerned with minimum or basic education for children and adolescents who missed school. One of the reasons for the paucity of non-formal educational projects for children is the difficulty of developing education projects outside of, or parallel to, the school system. Both parents and pupils are liable to feel that they are acquiring 'second best' education; and certainly unless non-formal education is carefully related to the formal system, pupils in the former will have fewer opportunities than pupils in the latter. Thus ideally, the educational system itself should be broadened and made more practical rather than parallel programmes be set up.

A number of educators believe today, however, that more opportunities lie with developing non-formal educational services than have been properly exploited. If we group under non-formal education all educational activities which take place outside the formal school system it is clear that there is a large possible source to be tapped provided suitable projects can be devised. The movement towards non-formal education springs mainly from the inability of many educational systems in the developing countries to render adequate services for adolescents and children suitably related to their future work environment. Moreover, the difficulties in some of the educationally least developed countries of successfully adapting the formal system in its present form to real educational needs raises the question whether non-formal education could be the principal means of educational expansion.

It is scarcely possible to see in non-formal education an alternative to the formal school system as regards younger children except in the least developed areas of countries, where tribal initiation may be the present main education facility in the society. Carefully devised non-formal education which supplements the initiation instruction may be a useful means of establishing a preliminary bridge with the advancement of the formal educational system into such areas. The value of the traditional tribal initiation instruction may remain until later stages of educational development, even when the formal system has advanced into the areas. Cases are not uncommon where the local acceptance of the new forms of education introduced by the state is dependent on willingness of the authorities to allow them to take place side by side without the replacement of the tribal instruction.

However, the main case for non-formal education rests on the fact that despite the maximum efforts made for the introduction of primary or minimum basic education programmes for the whole of the population, it will be a decade or two before most of the programme can be achieved. What is to happen meantime to the children who cannot get entry into the formal system or who inevitably drop out?

The author put forward some proposals on this subject in an article, which appeared in the Unicef *Carnet* for January 1969.[16] Discussing the alternative or complementary roles of formal primary education and non-formal education in the form of crash programmes for the period before school education is universalized, he wrote:

The argument runs as follows: it is true that universal compulsory primary education for every child is a human right and therefore a national and international goal. It is true that good primary schooling requires a six or seven year course. But achieving universal primary education by expanding present education systems in the developing countries on such a basis also means that large numbers of children have to wait until 1980 or 1985 to obtain what is their right, and meantime are left entirely unschooled. Is there not some means in the interim of giving them some simple functional form of education rather than leaving them untouched by educational processes? Especially since, as we have seen above, employment outlets requiring standard primary education are unlikely to be available in sufficient quantity.

Are there alternative approaches? One approach might be as follows. As a first step, to establish a sound minimum primary education system of the conventional kind, limited to the coverage necessary to provide the base of the school pyramid for entry into secondary and higher education, and also the literate artisans, clerical workers and other types of labour needed. The extent of the resources deployed for this effort should not, however, be so great as to leave no funds over for the second step—a measure which is at present lacking. This second measure is to allocate resources to give partial education to a proportion of the children outside the conventional educational system. The objective of such measures would be to provide a minimum form of functional literacy, similar to that which is given in adult functional literacy programmes. Thus the children in the normal primary classes would have an efficient 4–6 year course with low waste rates. The children outside, instead of being entirely neglected, would have a two year course in literacy and elementary civics and home economics. The existence of such a dual system may be regarded as discriminatory but surely it is less discriminatory than the unconscious present discrimination of giving children no education at all. New opportunities for the adoption of such a change in educational policies and objectives are provided by the developments in the use of new technologies in education, particularly the mass media.

One type of strategy might be the following: a survey might be made in a country with a high unenrolment in those areas where economic development calling for a literate labour force was foreseeable over the next 10 years. The young adults, the youth, and the older children would be given in these areas special intensive two-year courses. The resources for such an effort should be drawn not only from the ordinary sources of education budgets but also from the development projects themselves and from the industries which would profit from the greater productivity of their enterprises through the increased literacy of their workers. In many cases the existence of such forms of functional education and training might make all the difference as to whether capital, both national and foreign, moved into the countries and areas concerned in order to set up the necessary industrial and agricultural enterprises needed to start the progress of economic and social development.

Visiting the developing countries, one frequently notices expensive labour-saving mechanical devices such as bulldozers being used for work which could be undertaken by idle labour, perhaps less quickly but at less cost. The great earthworks that were undertaken in the countries which are at present industrialized did not utilize such machinery. The transformation of the American continent, for instance by the building of railways, canals and roads, was done with human labour and the two-horse drag.

What is needed is that Governments should systematically review their use of capital and their forms of technology in close relation to their educational output and labour supply. Otherwise increased poverty and frustration can result.

The specific measures to be adopted would vary from country to country, but some principles of action might be as follows:

(1) Acceptance of such experimental programmes by Governments and national and international aid agencies as a possible alternative to present policies;

(2) The setting up of a small, high level group of educators, industrial and agricultural employers, economists and technologists, to review the country's policy on the matters discussed above;

(3) Most countries would need to adopt a selective and experimental approach. They should try on such a basis to use part of the future resources, otherwise to be earmarked for primary education, for use instead for short courses in functional literacy for older children and youth. A basis of action might be that adopted in the Unesco/UNDP Functional Literacy Programme for Adults;

(4) In particular, they should set up a system for keeping track of development projects with which such functional literacy and civic education programmes for youth and older children can be assisted. A unit should be set up in the central planning office for this purpose which would keep in touch not only with national industrial and development agencies and firms, but also with foreign enterprises;

(5) The financing of such educational projects should come partly, as indicated, from funds which would otherwise have been allotted to the future development of orthodox primary education, but also partly from the development projects themselves. In some cases, it would be possible to obtain funds from savings, from better educational management, reduction of unit cost, etc. in the primary system;

(6) At the same time orthodox primary education should be subject to a long-term overhaul to create higher retention rates and reduce repeating by relating the system better to the local environment and employment possibilities;

(7) A unit of technologists, education and manpower experts should also be established to keep track of cases of choices of technology for use in development projects and education. Their task would also include the application to development projects of forms of cost benefit appraisal, which include the gains and losses to employment and education of alternative technologies and forms of organization.

A study made for Unicef and presented to its Executive Board in 1972 by the International Council for Educational Development,[17] took up this same subject in the wider context of the extent to which non-formal education for children and adolescents might become a standard educational means parallel with formal education and bridged to it. The study stated:

> Existing forms of non-formal education, which are mostly at the adult level, should be examined from the standpoint of their adaptability to children and adolescents who have no adequate formal education. It is to be noted, for instance, that at present work-orientated literacy programmes are limited in intention and curriculum to adults. However, the fact that a number of adolescents are seeking and often obtain entry into these projects indicates the demand for and the possibility of adapting these projects to provide for adolescents as well as for adults . . . . At the primary age group level also, the need is to incorporate some form of orientation to local conditions which include preparation for making a livelihood. Projects for minimum or basic education for this age group should include a measure of non-formal instruction for this purpose (visits to development projects, health centres, etc.).

An obstacle to the extension of present non-formal education to which the study directs attention is that it is geared to pupils who have already had primary education and is a substitute for formal secondary education rather than primary. Moreover, frequently its cost is too high to enable it to be generalized.

In his paper for the Bellagio Conference[18] Coombs states:

> There are some bright spots, however, in this otherwise bleak picture. Numerous African nations have taken imaginative steps to create national youth services, village polytechnics and other programmes for out-of-school youths; Jamaica has a network of youth camps and centres; South Korea has an impressive 4-H programme; Unicef, in company with ILO, has promoted experimental pre-vocational programmes; a number of private groups in the Philippines are taking fresh initiatives in this field. Many other examples could be cited. However, these programmes, all added together, affect but a tiny fraction of needy young people, especially in the rural areas, and many of the most successful ones are too unique or too expensive to replicate on a larger scale. Nonetheless, some of them offer important clues for a frontal attack on this much neglected set of needs.

... This raises the provocative question of whether it really makes the best sense for the poorest nations to allocate the bulk of their meagre educational resources to the quest for full universal primary schooling—a goal they can only fractionally achieve, at best, in this century. The matter deserves closer scrutiny and experimentation, but possibly a better alternative would be to devote these same scarce resources to eradicating illiteracy among adolescents and giving them other practically useful skills, knowledge and understanding, at an age when many are more mature and motivated, likely to learn more rapidly, and to retain more of what they learn. Meanwhile, younger children might be brought together in a new kind of 'social school' (perhaps presided over by selected teenagers), not to be drilled in the three Rs but to play together, to work on simple projects, to listen to stories and music, and pursue their natural curiosity.

Coomb's recommendations are that there must be a combination of flexible programmes dealing with the different needs of groups of individuals rather than nationwide approaches; that the objective should be a minimum 'package' of fundamental 'learning objectives' which will serve them well in later life; that the teaching method should be tied to practical projects in the surrounding environment including a substantial measure of 'self-instruction'; and that the 'minimum learning package' should include not only functional literacy but also basic preparation for the world of work and managing a home and family and participating in community life.

He recommends 'youth development service centres' to provide learning materials and staff training for local areas wanting help, and simple equipment and programme evaluation and consultant services. These centres would use predominantly local staff but could also be supported by outside and foreign experts. Special attention should be given to involving the manpower and facilities of non-governmental activities such as major religious groups, the students and research facilities of higher educational institutions and extension services. The education of girls in this context will have particular importance.

Important suggestions have also been made by Naik for crash programmes for out-of-school adolescents and youth in the age group 14 to 21. He points out that the costs are less and returns greater than for formal schooling and proposes a massive programme for the education of this group during the 1970s. He proposes a mix of educational objectives having a strong vocational core including family life and family planning education and participation in social services and development and recreational pursuits.

Like Coombs, Naik believes that this 'package' has to vary considerably from group to group. The programme would be supported by part-time classroom instruction as its major instrument. But education by correspondence, through the mass media, and full-time intensive instruction in residential camps should also be arranged. The focal point would be the premises and facilities of the educational system itself used on a part-time basis and expanded as necessary to deal with this form of part-time instruction giving special remuneration to teachers for the extra work involved. The institutions of vocational education attached to other Departments of Government have facilities which could also be harnessed to this purpose, e.g. agricultural universities, demonstration farms, industrial training institutes, institutions of medical education, hospitals and dispensaries. Private industry should also assist and participate. If national service is required from university graduates, as in some countries, the development of such programmes can provide volunteer experience and leadership.

The form of organization required for programmes of this kind is a unit covering a district. The officer in charge should normally belong to the Ministry of Education but would have to coordinate the resources of all Government departments. The physical centre should be some educational institution, either a college or a secondary school, or even a primary middle school. There might be some 50 to 100 centres in a district.

The length of the programme of part-time education envisaged is one or two hours a day for five days a week, which will be an equivalent of three months' full-time education per year. In addition, there would be at least two weeks in full-time residential instruction. The objectives would be at least one year's equivalent of training spread over a number of years.

A survey of non-formal education in Africa has recently been issued by the African–American Institute.[19] Concerned mostly with adult education it reflects the fact that non-formal education for youth usually is for primary school leavers, rather than children who have missed schooling, and tends to be job-oriented.

The ways and means described so far relate mostly to the quantitative expansion of education to cover children at present deprived of basic or minimum levels. But though we have also shown some of the changes in quality and content which are crucial to educational development. The more efficient the educational system, the more damage is done if the content is bad. It is therefore important to define minimum or basic education in terms of local conditions and resources, though there have also to be national educational standards for the purpose of citizenship and language.

There is a clear difference between the content required for a course which is terminal at the level of minimum or basic education and that needed for advancement into secondary and higher education. In educationally advanced countries it is not easy to discern in advance which children will go on to the second level. It is also politically difficult since there is an ever increasing pressure to give secondary education to all. Yet in most developing countries for the great majority of children basic or minimum education will be terminal.

This does not mean that there is no political difficulty in having a two stream system (one terminal and one to higher). On the contrary, the parents of children who are better off and likely to go on to secondary, exercise pressure for curricula leading to secondary education, while the parents of children who will terminate early do not want their children to be put in advance in what they consider the inferior stream. The latter misconception tends to favour and not to diminish present inequalities since it leads to high drop-out rates and the acquisition of education of little use to the majority of children in their environment.

Naik's proposals, in so far as they are a means of supplementing the existing formal primary education given to young children by recuperating at a later age those who drop out before receiving a minimum measure of education, are very valuable. In so far, however, as they replace access to the full primary educational cycle, they restrict opportunity. He argues that the costs are less and returns greater than for formal schooling, but this unlikely to influence the views of parents and of governments except in the very least developed areas and countries. More influential would be the link with the formal system of part-time instruction, as this would link the formal and the non-formal aspects and increase opportunities.

If Coombs' proposals like those of Naik are viewed as action parallel to progress in the effective coverage of children of primary school age by relevant and economical education in the formal system, they are of high priority since they deal with one of the most serious of the problems of the developing countries, i.e. the mass of uneducated and unemployed youth who have missed adequate primary schooling.

The idea that they can replace primary education does not seem feasible. There may be cases in the very least developed countries and areas where such a substitute may be the best solution, but even so it is unlikely that parents would accept the virtual elimination of the primary school.

At the same time, modern research shows that a little less than half of a child's education is acquired in school, the rest being derived from the home, the surrounding stimuli and informal means of communication, and from contact with other children. It is therefore necessary to take a wider view of education than is limited to the formal education system and the greatest single innovation would be steps to improve and harmonize the various complementary educational agents, taken as a whole. Organizational facilities for this are, however, lacking.

The opposition of parents to systems of non-formal education parallel to the formal system, which is apparent in most of the developing countries, does not seem to operate in the case of the socialist societies.

The case of Cuba is set out in some detail in a document prepared for the International Commission on the Development of Education by Raul Perez.[20] Perez states:

Among the essentials of the parallel system are elimination of the constant rise in the cost of education, revision of the implied objectives of school education and their integration within ways of preparing the individual to face the world that awaits him outside the classroom, plus an understanding that educational systems are only one of the means whereby a student acquires the training needed to discharge his various functions in society. This last premise logically implies an appreciation of other factors forming part of the individual's training. Such are the family environment, social groups, community associations and institutions, mass communication media, political and mass organizations, industrial, agricultural and service enterprises, and the cultural agencies of the community (museums, libraries, theatres, cultural groups, etc.).

It was in the light of these ideas and with its objectives that this solution was adopted, training being suitably linked and co-ordinated with that of the regular system of education and associated closely with production.

These objectives began to develop in Cuba gradually as early as 1965, when the first night youth centres were opened for backward pupils and drop-outs who, although too 'adult' for the primary schools of the regular system, were also too much like 'children' to attend classes for workers.

... Awareness of these problems has led the Revolutionary Government to confer upon schools of the parallel system the same degree of social prestige as that of other teaching establishments in the country, placing at their disposal similar resources for their basic studies.

An interesting structural development in the Cuban educational system is the setting up of 'intra-school institutions' whereby 'youth people are trained to adopt forms of behaviour and the habits of a useful social life devoid of contradiction'; this indicates the use of the school for ideological purposes.

The greatest single reform of our times has been that which has taken place in the Chinese People's Republic where 95 per cent enrolment has been achieved with the remaining 5 per cent in outlying areas being covered by mobile instructors and correspondence courses. The resistance and problems of quality which arose and the impact of the Cultural Revolution was discussed in Chapter 7. The changes in the structure of the educational system introduced after the Cultural Revolution can be seen as follows:

|  | Before Cultural Revolution | After Cultural Revolution |
| --- | --- | --- |
| Primary | 6 | 5 |
| Secondary | 6 | 4 to 5 |
| Higher | 4 to 7 | 3 to 4 |

The primary level leads either into work combined with factory classes (in a minority of cases) or evening classes (for most) or to second level education followed by a two-year work experience before higher. The Chinese case is not pursued in detail because, despite its interest, it depends on political conditions and educational objectives not accepted by the rest of the developing countries. Nevertheless the linkages it has, as in the case of the other reforms discussed, with the world of work and life out of school confirms a universal need.

Thus, having started out to discuss the challenge *of* primary education, we are now led to face the challenge *to* primary education. Granted that formal primary education must continue to function under its own right, and not be absorbed into crash programmes or replaced by non-forhal education; it has, to a considerable extent, reshape itself to interact with out-of-school education.

We may sum up and add to this chapter as follows. The quantitative gap in minimum basic education for children is caused by drop-out and by lack of school places. The former is the largest single cause and the most difficult to remedy as it involves both the provision of extra places (since those left free by drop-outs are rapidly filled) and a set of special measures to reduce drop-out itself. But to meet the problem of areas which lack schools and school places is also difficult because, although school enrolment has been on the average brought to three-quarters of the children, the task becomes harder as the school system pushes out into the least developed areas and tries to deal with conditions for which it is not adjusted.

A list of suggestions as to measures to reduce drop-out and repetition were given. For the extension of the system to the least developed areas, suggestions were also made dealing with district planning, one-teacher schools and non-formal education. Changes in the length and content of the primary cycle were also discussed. The steps involved would include working out minimum learning 'packages' while also providing at least minimum opportunity to have access to the full system. These matters will be taken up further in Chapter 11 on rural education.

Measures adopted should deal with both causes of children being below the educational poverty line (and also be interlocked, as we shall see from the next chapter, with measures to improve educational methods and technologies), and they should as far as possible sit astride the two causes because the system has to be seen as a whole.

Chief among the various interlocking measures is the reform of educational structures to bring the primary cycle closer to the actual or natural cycle, as indicated by drop-out rates, and to relate content closer to the needs of those who leave the system early rather than those who stay for the second level. Examples were given of reforms in Sri Lanka, Iran, Tanzania and Peru, which had this objective.

Three cautionary remarks have to be made. First, the programmes of fundamental change of structure and content discussed cover only a few of the countries in the developing world and not those with large populations. Secondly, these programmes are only in their initial stages and are subject to further evaluation. Thus, the reform in Peru will no doubt encounter and, it is to be hoped, overcome some of the problems set out in Chapter 5, concerning the difficulty which some Latin American governments have had of carrying out their good intentions owing to local social, economic and cultural structures. Similarly, the cooperative socialism in Tanzania may risk, as experiences elsewhere show, declines of motivation to productivity. Many circumstances will determine how the educational changes will work out in the long term.

Thirdly, there is always the danger of producing an educational output that conforms neither to academic nor to strictly practical standards, the programme falling between two schools—the educational and the socio-economic. We mentioned this aspect earlier in Chapter 7 in our comments on educational innovation in China.

Other measures which were also discussed in this chapter may be summed up as follows:

(1) recasting of time schedules, age of entry, duration of school term, hours of attendance, to meet local economic and social conditions;

(2) non-formal education facilities to be developed so that older children can,

during a guidance cycle, spread their education between formal and non-formal sources;

(3) structural improvements in the form of ladders and bridges and compensatory courses as discussed in the following chapter on educational opportunity;

(4) closer attention to the influence on education of child welfare services (health, nutrition, home economics, social services, visits to parents, education in the home etc.). Such measures reduce drop-out and should be regarded as a part of measures for the expansion of education no less important than the setting up of additional schools.

Structure, which has been the main preoccupation of this chapter, is a means to an end, the end being educational output. Structural changes alone will not produce the required output unless the necessary changes in the knowledge content and the methods of education are also made. The question is not only: What changes in the organization of primary education are required in order to provide the whole of the child population with four years of schooling? It is also: Can it be done in four years? Which four years of the child's life? By what methods?

In terms of content, the education 'package' should vary by countries and regions, since it would need to contain knowledge appropriate to the child's actual and foreseeable living conditions. While this content would be biased to the local environment in rural areas, though less so in cities, the wider horizon of the nation and beyond has to be seen, especially by talented children and increasingly in the case of all pupils. The output has also to include the capacity to think and understand, as well as the acquisition of knowledge and the development of personal, moral and civic qualities.

The question of the number of years required for such a minimum basic education often causes controversy. The figure of four years is given from time to time in this book, but the more accurate, though clumsy, expression would be the period, having regard to local conditions, teacher training, methods, and whether pre-primary education is prevalent, which tends in many countries to be around four years. We revert to this in Chapter 11 on methods and technologies of teaching and learning, especially in relation to the introduction in the Soviet Union of a three year elementary course.

It is useful to visualize the minimum in terms of a sliding scale, the number on which rises as more weight in the form of educational resources is added and as methods and technologies improve, but which cannot move downwards below the amount of time needed to acquire literacy and numeracy. The movement up the scale, in addition to being dependent on resources and technologies, is also governed from a development standpoint by the necessary demand for entrants to the other educational levels, and politically by the seemingly ineluctable pressure of parents of the more fortunate children who complete primary to proceed to secondary education.

Can new methods and technologies and the mobilization of additional finance provide measures to satisfy all of these requirements? We turn in the next chapters to the problem of opportunity and then to methods and technologies to possible measures for increased financing of primary education, though in the final analysis we have to refer back to the suggested mechanism for planning primary education which we set out in Chapter 8, which is an effort to reconcile the competing claims.

## REFERENCES

1. *A Study of the Primary School Curriculum in Thailand*, Institute for Child Study, Bangkok, 1966. Summary in *Bulletin of the Unesco Regional Office for Education in Asia*, Vol I, No. 2, Bangkok, 1967, pp. 62–63.
2. *Costing Educational Wastage: A Pilot Simulation Study*, D. Berstecher, Max-Planck Institute for Educational Research and Unesco Statistics Division, Unesco, 1970.
3. See Chapter 4, References No. 17.
4. *The One-Teacher School*, International Bureau of Education, Geneva, Publication No. 228, 1961, p. 8.
5. As in 3 above.
6. 'On educational reform in Peru', Augusto Salazar Bondy, in *Prospects*, Vol. II, No. 4, Unesco, 1972, p. 386.
7. *A Programme of Action for Ceylon*, International Labour Office, Geneva, 1971, p. 137.
8. *The Financial Aspects of First Level Education in Iran*, J. Hallak, M. Cheikhestani and H. Varlet, Unesco: IIEP, 1972.
9. Government of Nepal publication, 1970.
10. *Education in the USSR*, N. P. Kuzin and others, Progress Publishers, Moscow, 1972.
11. 'Main lines of education and population policies in Tanzania', M. J. Kinunda, in *Population—Education—Development in Africa South of the Sahara*, Unesco Regional Office for Education in Africa, Dakar, 1972.
12. *Planeamiento Integral de la Educacion en Mexico*, Angel Palerm, Centro Nacional de Productividad, Mexico, 1969; and *Education in a Changing Mexico*, Clark C. Gill, U.S. Government Printing Office, Washington D.C., 1969.
13. *Learning To Be*, Unesco-Harrap, 1972, p. 193.
14. See Chapter 4, References, No. 2.
15. 'A crash programme for the education of out-of-school youth in the age group 14–21', J. P. Naik, in *Education and Development Reconsidered*, Vol. II, Conference at Bellagio, 1972 sponsored by the Rockefeller and Ford Foundations.
16. 'Education and employment for youth in developing countries', H. M. Phillips, in *Assignment Children*, No. 9, Unicef, 1969.
17. *Non-Formal Education for Rural Development—Strengthening Learning Opportunities for Children and Youth*, Unicef Document E/ICEF/6. 1284; and *Building New Educational Strategies to Serve Rural Children and Youth*, Unicef Document E/ICEF/L. 1304; both reports prepared for Unicef by the International Council for Educational Development.
18. 'Opportunities in non-formal education for rural development', Philip Coombs, in *Education and Development Reconsidered*, Vol II. Conference at Bellagio, 1972, sponsored by the Rockefeller and Ford Foundations.
19. *Non-Formal Education in African Development*, J. R. Sheffield, and V. D. Diejomach, African–American Institute, New York, 1972.
20. *Innovating Experiments in Cuba*, Raul Ferrer Perez, International Commission on the Development of Education, Series C; *Innovations*, No. 4. Unesco, 1971.

# SELECTED FURTHER READING

*education and the Employment Problem in Developing Countries*, Mark Blaug, International Labour Office, Geneva, 1973.

*Bulletin of the Unesco Regional Office for Education in Asia*, Vol. IV, No. 1, September 1969.

*Action-Training for Development*, Round Table, Dakar, 7–12 February, 1972, Unesco Regional Office for Education in Africa, Dakar.

'The mobile teaching package in Africa', Richard Marshall, in *Prospects*, Vol. II, No. 1, Unesco, 1972.

*The Mother Tongue as a Means of Prompting Equal Access to Education in Nigeria*, C. O. Taiwo, Unesco Document ED/WS/307, 1972.

*Human Resources and Development Planning in Africa*, Proceedings of an Expert Group Meeting held at the African Institute for Economic Development and Planning, Dakar, Feb. 26–March 1, 1973, OECD, 1973.

*Unemployment in an African Setting. Lessons of the Employment Strategy Mission to Kenya*, Hans Singer and Richard Jolly, International Labour Office, 1973.

*Adaptation of the Curriculum to the Zambian Environment*, J. R. Moris, V. L. Griffiths and P. Van Rensburg, Unesco Serial No. 2878/RMO.RD/ED, March 1973.

*International Conference on Education, XXXIInd Session, Recommendation No. 66*, to the Ministries of Education concerning the Improvement and Effectiveness of Educational Systems, Unesco: IBE, Geneva, 1970.

*Preparation of the Child for Modernization*, P. E. Mandl, United Nations Research Institute for Social Development, Geneva, 1969.

*Children and Their Primary Schools*, The Plowden Report, Her Majesty's Stationery Office, London, 1966.

'Primary education and employment in the rural economy with special reference to East Africa', Guy Hunter, in *The World Yearbook of Education*, 1967, ed. George Z. F. Benday, Joseph A. Lauwerys and Mark Blaug, Evans Bros., London, 1967.

'Environment education in the school curricula: the Swedish example', Sten Forseluis, in *Prospects*, Vol. II, No. 4, Unesco, 1972.

*Non-Formal Education in African Development*, James R. Sheffield and Victor R. Diejomach, African–American Institute, New York, 1971.

'The non-graded school in the United States', John Goodlad, in *Prospects*, No. 1, Unesco, 1969.

'Education for self-reliance: the Litowa Experiment', S. Toroka, in *Rural Africana*, No. 9, 1969.

*Enhancing the Contribution of Formal Education in Africa*, John W. Hanson, Overseas Liaison Committee, America Council on Education, Washington D.C., 1971.

On An Integrated Approach to the Primary Curriculum, Unesco ED/WS/253, September 1971.

'Employment policy in tropical Africa. The need for radical revision', Guy Hunter in *Employment in Africa—Some Critical Issues*, ILO, 1974. *Building New Educational Strategies to Serve Rural Children and Youth*, Case studies by the ICED, Unicef Document E/ICEF/Misc. 225, August 1974. *Attacking Rural Poverty. How Non-Formal Education Can Help*, Philip Coombs with Manzour Ahmed, A World Bank Publication, John Hopkins University Press, 1974.

CHAPTER 10

# Opportunity: Ladders, Buffer Cycles and Bridges

It was indicated in Chapter 8 on planning that the right to education was not only to have a minimum package of teaching and learning needs provided, but also to have a measure of opportunity. This measure is bound to vary according to the country's state of educational development. In the countries with complete educational systems the argument for greater equity in education centres round the length of secondary education, access to higher education and means of compensating for conditions produced by home circumstances or other reasons which place pupils at a disadvantage.

In countries with incomplete educational systems where the minimum needs of large sections of the population are not met, the problem of equity has to be met at the first level. It is necessary, therefore, to face the question how to restructure present types of first level cycles which are constructed on the basis of the movement to the second level, having regard to two requirements. On the one hand, the State should provide for the minimum needs of those who have to terminate owing to local conditions after about four years; on the other hand, it must provide, both for purposes of national and personal development, for a requisite stream to move on into the higher reaches of the system.

Ideally, this would take place by compensating the automatic selection which takes place by reason of family income, social status and home conditions, by extra education, and by broadening the basis of examination tests so that they assess not only the forms of talent expressed in the more verbal and bookish skills which children from families of higher social status acquire more rapidly, but also other types of intelligence, personality and creativity. These ideal conditions are not met anywhere and what can be done to progress towards this goal will depend on socio-economic, historical and political factors, and the capacity of educators to introduce changes which are acceptable to parents and society at large and which are at the same time viable educationally. Certainly, however, more can be done that at present; suggestions are made below as to some measures which might be used for the purpose.

To focus the problem, however, let us take a typical expression of how a developing country sees its own problem in regard to opportunity. We find, for instance, the Uganda National Commission for Unesco stating:[1]

One of Uganda's main educational challenges, as for many other countries, is to devise a curriculum that will serve the best interests of the 70 to 80 per cent of the school leavers who will not be able to go on to any formal post-primary education or training in either the public or private sector. The present syllabus achieves some degree of Ugandization, but leaves much of the general organization of curriculum and orientation of syllabuses as they were in the past—overcrowded and insufficiently related to the child's actual experience and interest.

Uganda has a 7 year primary cycle and there were 294,000 children of the age to enter the first grade in 1971. Out of these, only 133,000 were enrolled and these were engaged in a kind of obstacle race, with heavy repetition of grades as pupils failed to achieve promotion and only a small proportion obtaining the school leaving certificate, which is a passport to employment as well as to further education.

Obviously there are other opportunities in countries like Uganda for self-advancement which could be opened by types of education, if they existed, which were different in kind to the full seven year cycle. The country is not made up of wage employers on the one hand and drones on the other. The people in the sub-sistence economy, the women in the home and in the fields, need education too, but of a different sort. Similarly, one cannot suppose, having regard to the distribution of individuals' potentialities for success over the population at large, that those who emerge after successfully completing the seven year cycle are necessarily the cream of the nation's talent.

The main opportunities which a minimum or basic education provides by a four year terminal cycle are not usually measurable in economic terms in countries where employment is limited. They centre rather on the capacity to increase sub-sistence production so as to move over the margin into the cash economy, to make better use of the physical environment, to enjoy better health and nutrition as a result of the knowledge and ways of thinking acquired through basic education, to understand family planning, to participate in cooperative and community activities, and to command the satisfactions and utilities, personal and social, of literacy.

The adjustment of the cycle to provide for this kind of opportunity, as well as that at present offered by the employment market for the full primary school certificate, involves changes of the kind we have indicated already in the preceding chapter, the continuum between the short and the longer cycle being maintained by treating the latter years of the primary cycle as guidance years during which some options are still open. Let us look at the extent to which there are likely to be such options and what measures are required to realize them.

The guidance cycle over the last few years of the primary level is a mechanism intended to provide the opportunity for the pupils to be selected, both by the teachers and by their own selection, as to whether they usefully could, or would wish to, continue into secondary (assuming places are available and they pass the examination). It contains a sufficient number of practical or terminal type of features in the curriculum so that those who do not go forward into the second level can be equipped to enter employment after leaving primary school.

This is certainly an advance on the homogeneous, more bookish type of cycle which is geared to hypotheses of mounting to the second level even though few do so. But the opportunity requirements are still not met unless there are means by which talented children from incomplete rural schools, where the latter part of the cycle does not exist, and where teaching may be poor, can connect into the guidance cycles and receive compensatory courses to catch up. Nor does it provide for the child who in the course of the guidance cycle wishes to leave school, but at the same time maintain his literacy and receive some pre-employment education even though he is not yet strictly of working age.

These missing pieces of mechanism we may characterize as ladders, buffer cycles and bridges, since what is involved is a structural problem of passing from one level to another, of reducing the shock of re-entry into a more advanced course and of being able to move backwards and forwards between formal and non-formal education, or to move in and out of the educational system as a whole.

To explain what is in mind, let us give some examples. We take first the case of the child who is living in a poor rural community with a rather poor school which perhaps only provides for the first three or four grades and may be a one-teacher school. This is the only educational facility available to him, although he may have exceptional talent. What he needs is some kind of ladder leading into the full primary cycle. This ladder has to both be institutional and surmount the difficulties arising from family circumstances and geographical location.

Such ladders can only, in the present state of resources, provide for a limited number of children with talent. The requirement is that there should be a number of places for such talented children in the nearest school which offers the full cycle and that there should be a system by which talent can be spotted and children selected. The first requirement is purely a matter of resources, which would not be large. The latter is difficult to organize.

A possible selection procedure might be for teachers or headmasters of schools which are complete in their cycle to visit periodically the smaller incomplete schools and to identify talent based on teachers' reports and on special tests. These tests should not be those based on the curriculum in the longer cycle schools, but should be specially devised to suit local conditions and to discover aptitude even when the teaching received has been poor, when textbooks may have been lacking and when conditions in the home not been favourable to education. It is not beyond the capacity of educators to devise such tests if some funds and skills were devoted to the purpose in each major educational district.

It is, however, one thing to institutionalize a procedure for ladders of this kind and another to make it work in the case of the individual. The difficulties that may arise from his home environment, the demands made upon him by his family for usefulness in the home or work in the fields, and the problem of providing the necessary lodging and keep for him in the village or town where the more complete school is located, may be insuperable in a number of cases.

But in other cases it will be possible if agents of the welfare worker type are appointed to deal with this matter and to keep under review the various cases and devise means of trying to overcome the difficulties. If a sufficient number of talented children can be brought up ladders in this way, the cost of such agents, like the cost of working the selection procedure, is likely to be well worth while.

Alfred Marshall, the great neo-classical economist, not given to exaggeration, wrote in his *Principles of Economics* (page 216):[2]

> We may then conclude that the wisdom of expending public and private funds on education is not to be measured by its direct fruits alone. It will be profitable as a mere investment to give the masses of the people much greater opportunities and to get the start needed for bringing out their latent abilities. And the economic value of one industrial genius is sufficient to cover the expenses of the education of a whole town.

(This was more true in his era—the end of nineteenth century England—than in many developing areas; but the basic point holds, especially if we include leadership skills.)

Undoubtedly, chance will play a part in this upward movement as well as ability. Some children may have connections in the village where the more complete school is located, others will have some means of having their responsibilities in the home assumed by brothers or sisters. Some will benefit from voluntary arrangements which might be set up in the village where they are received, provided there is local initiative to organize this, others may not.

The existence of institutional ladders of this kind may make more acceptable the necessary changes in the curricula in rural schools which parents now oppose because it seems to them to limit the opportunity of their children to move up the social scale. Rather than let all of the children take out, so to speak, a ticket for a lottery which few will win and in a very haphazard way, they may be willing to accept changes which organize the chances more equitably.

Educational ladders which create opportunity for the poor but talented pupil have a long history in Europe going back to medieval times when living levels were as low or lower than in today's developing countries. While the numbers covered were small, structurally (the grammar school, for instance, in England) the process was a successful one. It would be worth testing out the possibility of setting up such arrangements as described, supported by inexpensive subventions in some suitable locations.

Solutions have already been sought in certain countries of grouping smaller schools under others which offer the full cycle. Examples exist in the 'godfather' schools of Madras and the 'nuclear' or 'consolidated' schools of Latin America. Examples also exist in the more remote rural areas in other countries, e.g. Poland. Few indications are available in the form of detailed research and published studies as to how these nuclear or godfather systems work in practice and ways in which the difficulties of selecting the pupils and housing them at the central school have been overcome.

The problem of housing and feeding is met in some African countries by boarding schools. This is one of the reasons why unit costs in some African countries are high compared with other developing regions where population is less dispersed over wide areas. What are required are more economical alternatives to full boarding schools through using local community effort, tribal allegiances and obligations etc., and additional sources of finance raised locally, nationally and internationally to develop this type of educational structure.

The Indian Education Commission's Report[3] deals with the question of school complexes but primarily in terms of planning rather than opportunity, though this point was also in mind. A convenient and expanded account of the proposals can be found in a monograph by J. P. Naik.[4]

The Commission pointed out that about one third of all Indian primary schools had an enrolment of less than 40 pupils, about a quarter of the Indian population living in villages of under 300 inhabitants. They urged that small neighbouring village should be persuaded to share a bigger and more efficient school, instead of insisting on their own schools however small, and that public opinion should be encouraged in this sense. The idea advanced was to link three or four higher primary schools with ten to twenty lower, the higher primary schools providing extension services to the lower.

Only limited progress has been made since the Education Commission's Report was issued in 1966, but the basic idea is clearly necessary not only for planning purposes but to promote opportunity. Undoubtedly, a great number of exceptionally talented Indian children are still not finding expression to their capacities under the present system.

The conclusion on educational ladders is that it would be desirable for each country to make an inventory of its present inter-school connections of this kind and of its scholarship or subvention facilities for bringing talented children forward, and the feasibility of increasing them. This might be combined with a survey of the distribution and location of schools and a mapping of prospective connections between them at the district level based on the varying stages of completeness of the cycle offered. This survey would have to be conducted in a realistic rather than encyclopaedic manner; it would be idle to put forward suggested networks of ladders which it would not be feasible to operate because of cost and lack of resources.

On the other hand, the survey could not fail to throw up a number of pieces of feasible action, as has been seen in the examples of certain countries mentioned, and the effort would be worthwhile as a first step in a long-term plan which might spread over a generation to increase educational opportunity. It would also open a new field of possible activity by educational aid agencies, multilateral, bilateral and voluntary, since both the construction of the ladders and their maintenance would, at any rate in the least developed countries, call for additional resources of finance and educational organizational skills.

For a ladder to a higher educational standard to be effective the child has to be able to step off into his new class with the possibility of becoming integrated into it fairly rapidly. This period may be overlong and lead to failure, not through lack of talent on the child's part, but through poor teaching and lack of textbooks and teachers' aids in his primary school and through conditions in the home. The latter might include, as they often do, the more regular use by the family of a language or dialect other than the national language used in the school, which places the child at a disadvantage.

Thus, another piece of educational mechanism is required, namely compensatory courses which will serve as buffers and diminish the harsher impacts of more efficient higher primary schools on pupils coming from less efficient lower ones. These courses may be part of the ordinary school day, though this is frequently difficult to arrange. They may alternatively take place out of school time and be conducted by teachers for overtime rates, by retired teachers, or when language and cultural assimilation are key factors, by voluntary workers or monitors. Some additional funds would be entailed, but of relatively small dimensions compared with the overall costs of the school.

The bottleneck, as we saw in other cases, is primarily the necessary educational and community organization rather than finance. Much will depend on the particular headmasters and on how in each situation the local educational authorities and inspectors react.

The concept of compensatory schooling is well understood in respect of local handicapped or backward children, but less so in the case of talented children from other villages, with whom these relations may in any event be factious rather than cooperative.

Indeed the problem of the handicapped and the backward is a shadow behind the whole conception of universal primary or basic education. Governments usually take the position that so long as masses of normal children are schoolless, special work for the handicapped cannot have the priority for public funds, but must be left largely to voluntary effort. The shortage of educational resources also makes it unlikely that large-scale compensatory courses could be set up to reduce the differentials created by family circumstances. This has not yet been achieved in the most socially and educationally developed countries.

While the case for compensatory courses for talented pupils who go up the state ladders is justifiable on national development grounds and would cost much less than a general effort for social compensation in the educational system, it may encounter problems of acceptance. The Indian Education Commission speaks of a programme to educate public opinion regarding the need for different villages to pool their facilities for educational cooperation, and cooperation would certainly have to be sought among village leaders.

We therefore conclude that, as discussed earlier, the whole process involved, starting with the encouragement (and payment) of headmasters from the full primary schools to go out and find talent in the incomplete ones, continuing with the selection and the organizing of ways, both official and voluntary, of getting the child moved and installed and boarded in the more advanced primary school, and going on finally to compensatory buffer courses, be supervised by special district agents appointed for the purpose. This would add to the cost but might make all the difference for success or failure of such efforts.

Such an agent might also have responsibilities for occupation guidance in the schools in the district, or might absorb the duties of existing counsellors. In particular, he could help in the problem of bridges between formal and non-formal education. Such bridges could be created even at the small village school level if there were available in the locality youth schemes or other community development projects of an educational character in which older children could participate.

A supplementary but also important role for such an agent would be to watch the situation of children who are on the threshold of entering school but cannot do so for family reasons, who are too far off from the nearest school, or who have dropped out through discouragement. While in many cases the reasons for non-attendance or drop-out are based on extreme poverty, there certainly will be a substantial number of cases where marginal action, if organized locally through such an agent, can push the children over the threshold of basic education. For this purpose both a certain limited amount of funds and a good deal of voluntary effort would be required, but the allocation of certain funds from the educational budget itself might have a higher return than simply opening new schools, if what is in mind is not an increase of facilities but the actual output of children with basic education which the educational system is producing. The agent working in this field would have to have close connections not only, as we have indicated, with the leaders of possible sources of voluntary effort in the villages, but also with the government departments running social services parallel to the educational system, such as health clinics and community services.

The effect of deprivation in the home is apparent even in the advanced countries; a study by the US Office of Education,[5] suggests that the deprived pupil needs 0·43 years of additional educational effort per year of the cycle to catch up with the non-deprived. Clearly, compensatory education to this degree is out of the question, especially in developing countries with incomplete primary enrolment, and a principal means of attack must be to reduce deprivation in the home.

Deprivation is, of course, relative, and what is in mind is not bringing every child up to an identical standard, but creating a situation in which the average child of different social groups has a comparable level of educational opportunity. The comparisons between non-deprived and deprived children made in the advanced countries are spread over a different scale of living levels. The steps to be taken by a deprived child to equal a non-deprived child may be greater in the United States than in a low income developing country. Accordingly, there may be in the developing countries quite a large number of children who are on the threshold of equality with the average child, who could be brought over the threshold by welfare measures of the kind mentioned above and discussed earlier as ways of dealing with drop-out.

If a talented child who has moved to a more complete school cannot remain for any particular reason to complete the course, he should be able to move over into non-formal education. Similarly, there will be children who have left earlier and are now in apprenticeship who could later come back into the formal system. In the case too of adolescents who have missed schooling, it is desirable that present non-formal education, which is usually for older youth, should be extended downwards in age admittance to enable them to attain literacy and pre-employment training. However, here too there should be the possibility by means of an institutional bridge for them to move into the educational system after attaining literacy when they show the capacities required to go up the normal second and perhaps higher level avenues.

The difficulties of establishing such a series of arrangements are easy to visualize by those who know the way matters are conducted at present and the conditions which would have to be changed. However, if the idea gains ground and efforts are made, and some funds are allotted to the purpose—a great deal of finance is not required, a certain amount of progress would be made and even this would be valuable.

If started now, even in embryo, it might be the germ of a system of intermittent or recurrent or lifelong education, which in the end must be one of the main solutions, not only in the educational field, but in the economic development and the overall raising of levels of living of the developing countries.

The difficulties of introducing the structural innovations involved in the foregoing proposals should not be underestimated since there will be a variety of views held and pressures made, as we saw in Chapter 5, by the forces influencing the universalization of primary education. First, there is the difficulty of bringing public opinion in the villages themselves to favour a more efficient system. The necessity of providing for both mass literacy and for opportunity, which is necessarily limited initially by shortage of resources, as compared with a system which provides on paper a full cycle to be extended eventually to everyone, but in fact leave behind a mass of illiteracy, is not readily understood.

A further group which will have to support the proposals if they are to be a success are those educators in the developing countries especially concerned with quality who are anxious to apply advances in performance in the schools as they are. They will have to balance the social, as compared with the pedagogic factors involved.

Equally, the foreign expert, whose views are frequently needed, and usually listened to with respect, has to make a mental break with the situation in the developed countries where democratization of education is the trend in the sense of lengthening the cycle for everyone since universal literacy is general.

Finally, at the decision making level, there are the educational Ministers themselves who have to make a choice between extending the existing apparently democratic type of cycle, which is likely to be the most popular step to take because of lack of information as to the extent of drop-out and repetition, or to face up to the educational and social reality, which is to combine the maximum amount of mass literacy and basic education with the maximum possible amount of development of opportunity.

It is easy to believe that the building of more schools with the existing educational structure is the way to add to educational output, whereas, in fact, in a great number of cases, action to reduce drop-out would give far larger quantitative and more important qualitative results for the child population as a whole and for the future of national development.

Some other aspects of opportunity and of the problem of meeting minimum needs while providing maximum possible access to further education are discussed in the following chapter which deals with educational methods. That chapter discusses, among other methods, the possibilities of applying the 'mastery' rather than the 'selective' approach to learning, a course recommended by many educators and psychologists. A further chapter pursues the problem more specifically at the rural level since it is there that most of the children live.

The present chapter on opportunity should not be closed without seeing the problem in its world perspective. Systems favouring educational opportunity in the developed countries which can be applied and made viable in the developing countries are few, and educational assistance is not yet adequately geared in amount or type to the developing countries' needs. Gaps in the basic education of the populations of so many countries is an impediment to full and equal nationhood and the development of opportunity on a global scale.

A reminder of both the disparities between countries and of the meaning of lack of educational opportunity to the individual were forcefully conveyed in a statement by Paul Gerin-Lajoie, President of the Canadian International Development Agency to the Canadian Council for Research in Education.[6] It reads:

I need not emphasize to this group who are concerned with change in education that the rich country model of development is now being challenged on a global scale. During the late '60's it became evident that less than 10 per cent of the human race consumes more than 50 per cent of the world's resources and produces 90 per cent of the physical pollution that threatens to extinguish the biosphere; life expectancy which had risen for decades now started to decline in some of the most affluent countries; crimes of violence increased; youth became alienated; some affluent countries had fearful racial problems; there were hard cores of poverty unaffected by high average incomes and so on. The rich country model became slightly more than tarnished.

Education cannot, of course, take all the blame for the current malaise of our society. It is one expression of a philosophy of life that is increasingly open to question. The functions which education performs in an industrialized society are now being challenged at the very time that the western education pyramid serves as a predominant model for less advantaged countries. If our rich country model is inappropriate even in purely economic terms for western societies, how much more so for societies of the Third World.

Fundamental to the western concept of education is the general accessibility of the school to all children. But on this very point, the identity between advantaged and less advantaged societies breaks down.

... No child, regardless of the part of the world in which he lives, fails to learn from school. Those who never get in learn that the good things of life are not for them. Those who drop out early learn that they do not deserve the good things of life. The later drop-outs learn that the systems can be beaten, but not by them. All resolve that their children shall climb higher on the ladder than they did.

## REFERENCES

1. *Educational Development in 1971/72 in the Republic of Uganda*, Uganda National Commission for Unesco, International Bureau of Education.
2. *Principles of Economics*, Alfred Marshall, p. 216.

3. See Chapter 5, References, No. 3.

4. See Chapter 4, References, No. 11.

5. *Analysis of Education for the Disadvantaged*, Office of Programme Planning and Evaluation, US Office of Education, Washington, D.C.

6. *Educational Innovation*, Paul Gerin-Lajoie, President of the Canadian International Development Agency, Canadian Information Office, 1971, p. 14.

# CHAPTER 11

# Methods and Technologies of Teaching and Learning

The measures described in the previous chapter dealt with how to increase the population coverage and improve the structure and content of the primary cycle. Types of change were discussed which would help to make primary education become universal in the developing countries, which were social in the sense that they changed the impact and distribution of primary education on the population, organization in the sense that they altered the way the system functioned and which were educational in the sense that they changed the content of the knowledge and capacities imparted to the pupils. Non-formal education was also discussed, in its role as an addition to and, in some circumstances, a substitute for the formal system.

Since it is the actual learning achieved which is touchstone of all educational development, the rest being means to an end, we need to reflect further both on what is desirable and feasible as regards actual learning needs and on possibilities in terms of curricula, methods and techniques. Thus, in the present chapter we shift our perspective to what may be called the more strictly pedagogical measures to be taken, such as patterns of teaching and learning, curriculum improvement, teacher training, and the use of teaching aids, notably the audio-visual media.

In educationally advanced societies a period of as long as ten years can be granted at public expense to practically all of the country's young citizens. In most developing countries, education of this length cannot be universalized and attempts to do so result in long cycles for the privileged and incomplete cycles for the underprivileged. The desirable and the feasible do not coincide.

In the former case the threshold of an educational poverty line has long been passed and the whole child population in effect obtains at least elementary standards of literacy. In the latter case a basic period of instruction and a system of content and methods has to be worked out to bring the whole of the child population over the threshold.

In the latter case, which is our concern, the learning needs have to be seen in terms of minimum but adequate possibilities. The higher the level set, the slower the process of universalization. At the same time, adequacy, as we saw earlier, has to be interpreted to mean a measure of opportunity to move up the educational ladder. This too has to be seen in terms of minimum standards to be extended progressively as development takes place. These two considerations affect not only the organization and structure of the system and the educational content, but also the methods and technologies. We need therefore to specify minimum needs.

Any attempt at a common definition of minimum learning needs for the 93 developing countries could only be highly general and schematic. Each situation can in reality only be tested against the local cultural and economic and social circumstances which in fact condition a large part of a child's psychology and learning power. In a rural Buddhic community, for instance, where the family and community have a cultural background of learning associated with the temple, the child's mind is different from in an urban setting where the conditioning is towards action and aggressiveness. What is a minimum learning package in an urban slum is different from what it is in a traditional rural community, which in turn is different from a rural area undergoing rapid changes in productivity through the 'green revolution' or through the creation of small industries.

In the urban slum or shanty towns, containing new immigrants from other areas, an increase of community spirit is usually needed to overcome difficulties and over-rapid disintegration of value systems. In the rural areas, however, it may be desirable that the minimum basic education be designed to create a certain independence from over-reliance on traditional community ideas which hold back progress.

If we concentrate upon a minimum education for every deprived child, we have therefore to accept flexibility of definition between countries. There would seem, however, to be a certain common features to all civilized societies which constitute a floor.

The author's own definition, contained in a paper prepared for the Rockefeller-Ford Bellagio Conference already cited was:

Minimum needs in developing countries would normally be literacy, numeracy, adequate verbal expression, and some knowledge of citizenship and of the physical and social environment, of health and nutrition learned by methods which rouse curiosity, develop self-reliance, and encourage physical and mental adaptability. In the case of adults, knowledge of family planning, and some conditioning for local employment, or in the subsistence sector for raising productivity, would be included.

An extended definition of minimum learning needs given in New Paths to Learning, (pp. 13–17) a publication prepared by the International Council for Educational Development in 1973 for Unicef, is:

(a) Positive attitudes, toward cooperation with and help to one's family and fellow men, toward work and community and national development, and not least of all toward continued learning and toward the development of ethical values. Such attitudes should find concrete expression in one's daily behavior—in the family and the community, at work and in all learning environments.

(b) Functional literacy and numeracy, sufficient (i) to read with comprehension a national newspaper or magazine, useful agricultural, health, and other 'how-to-do-it' bulletins, or manufacturers' instruction sheets; (ii) to write a legible letter to, for example, a friend or to a government bureau requesting information; and (iii) to handle important common computations—such as measurement of land and buildings, calculation of agricultural input costs and revenues, interest charges on credit and rental rates on land.

(c) A scientific outlook and an elementary understanding of the processes of nature in the particular areas, as they pertain, for example, to health and sanitation, to raising crops and animals, to nutrition, food storage and preparation and to the environment and its protection.

(d) Functional knowledge and skills for raising a family and operating a household, including the essential elements of protecting family health, family planning where appropriate, good child care, nutrition and sanitation; cultural activities and recreation; care of the injured and sick; intelligent shopping and use of money; making clothes and other consumer goods, house repairs and environmental improvements; growing and preserving food for family consumption.

(e) Functional knowledge and skills for earning a living, including not only the skills required for a particular local occupation, but also a knowledge of a variety of locally useful common skills for agriculture and nonfarm use.

(f) Functional knowledge and skills for civic participation, including some knowledge of national and local history and ideology, an understanding of one's society; awareness of government structure and functions; taxes and public expenditures; available social services; rights and obligations of individual citizens; principles, aims and functioning of cooperatives and of local voluntary associations.

One of the countries which, as mentioned earlier, has pioneered the provision of minimum basic education for the whole of a population which previously had heavy illiteracy is the USSR. The elementary school system in the USSR, as pointed out earlier, has changed recently from a four-year to a three-year period of study. The elementary cycle of three years is designed to

teach the child to read, write and do sums, to provide an introduction to nature study and the social sciences, as well as to aesthetic, vocational and physical training, to develop the child's powers of reasoning and self-sufficiency. The subjects studied in elementary school are: native language, mathematics, nature study, shop, music and physical training.[1]

It will be noted that the definition in *New Paths to Learning* goes further than the other two quoted as regards raising a family and functional skills for work and civic participation owing to the fact that it covers adults as well as children. Without these items the three definitions broadly coincide. However, to have a definition of minimum needs is only the first step, since there looms the important pedagogic issue of the logic, order, psychology, and system under which knowledge is best conveyed during the period chosen. There is also the further issue of at what age the instruction can best be given. in addition there is the question of the material means (radio, school gardens, visits to factories or to the countryside, recreational and cultural facilities) which are necessary to supplement work in the classroom.

The advantages of supplementary action of this kind outside the classroom is generally recognized and only limited by the lack of facilities in the developing countries and of teachers' incentives. They may, however, be inhibited by the feeling that valuable time is lost at the desk; it is of interest to note that the new USSR system of shortening the elementary cycle has been achieved without weakening this side of the child's education. The interest of Soviet experience is not only in the pedagogic research on which it is based but also in the fact that it covers, in the Asian Republics of the USSR, states with environments not dissimilar from those of other developing Asian countries.

The reason for the successful reduction of the elementary cycle in the USSR appears to be not so much the condensation or streamlining of content as changes in methods designed to increase the capacities of and incentives for children to learn rapidly, especially by arousing curiosity and linking the instruction given to interesting practical problems.

A factor which may have intervened to a considerable extent is also one which may not be reproducible in most of the areas of the bulk of the developing countries. This is that pre-school education paid for by the State has been well established for many years, permitting mothers to work in the factories or in the fields and the children to begin their effective education earlier than the school entry age.

A further factor which should be reproducible in the developing countries in due course, since it is where major learning obstacles lie, is instruction in the native language. The fact that so many children in the developing countries are instructed in a language different from that they use in the home obviously extends the period required. In the USSR elementary education is given in languages and the children in non-Russian schools have the option to study Russian during the second half of the first year of school or the beginning of the second year; it becomes compulsory only after the fourth grade.

This kind of pattern may be reproducible under a drive for universalizing basic education in developing countries. It would, however, involve considerable effort in the development of some of the indigenous languages, the production of textbooks, and compensatory teaching for pupils with language handicaps. The Education Ministry in the Soviet Union claims that at present Soviet publishing houses have put out children's books in the languages of 36 nationalities and peoples which in Czarist Russia did not have a written language.[2]

Perhaps the largest single element in the success of the three-year cycle has been the improvement in the logic and psychology of learning and the organization of teaching material. The measures adopted were preceded by several years of research and experimentation. Some illustrations of the approaches adopted are as follows. Let us take, for instance, the case of language arts. These are normally the largest items in the consumption of school time (see Table 4.4, Chapter 4, for Asia,

showing the percentage of time allotted to different subjects) and are of key importance as they lead to literacy. In the new Soviet elementary cycle that pupils are introduced in the first three grades to the basic aspects of the language such as
phonetic and lexical phenomena, morphological word structure and parts of speech,
according to summaries made by Unesco's Abstraction Service of publications by
the USSR Academy of Pedagogical Sciences.

This report, based on the draft proposals produced in 1966 which were subsequently adopted, states:[3]

> But only the most essential elements of this subject are included in the primary
> education programme. The programme is not supposed to burden children
> with the intricacies of the language or spelling which are exceptions to the
> general rule, or of exclusively theoretical significance, or are difficult to grasp
> at this stage of instruction. Only that information which can be clearly un-
> derstood and assimilated by children will be considered useful for the
> children's intellectual development, as well as for the development of their
> speech habits . . . . Lexical exercises take up more space in the new programme
> than in the current one. The reading course takes into consideration not only
> cognitive but also affective aims.

In the elementary mathematics curriculum

> the programme material is re-distributed over grades and complemented with
> new themes related to the children's mathematical development. The
> arithmetic of natural numbers is the pivot of the course. A deeper notion of the
> number is provided. The children are familiarized with the names of the com-
> ponents of arithmetical operations. In the third grade, the programme
> provides for the study of the changes in the results of addition, subtraction,
> multiplication and division in connection with the changes in the components.
> Numerical formulae are introduced in the solution of problems.

As regards natural history,

> systematic observations of, and experiments on, plant and animal life, excur-
> sions, the use of maps at school and in the field, and independent work in the
> study of literature and other sources of knowledge promote the pupils' power
> of observation, arouse their spirit of curiosity and enquiry, and enable them to
> make objective analyses, comparisons, and conclusions. The development of
> these qualities is moreover accompanied by a corresponding enrichment of the
> pupils' natural science vocabulary.

As regards the natural sciences, these are based on the principle of local studies.

> This implies that the first-graders study nature around their school and the
> work carried out by the people living next door to them; the second-graders
> study nature and the work of the people living in their district; third-graders
> study nature and the work of the region which incorporates their district and
> their town or village. For a deeper understanding of the peculiarities of local
> nature the pupils compare it to the nature of various zones of the Soviet Union.

As an example of the form of experimentation on which the reform was based, it is interesting to see from L. V. Zankow[4] that an experiment was made in the USSR in which difficulty, speed and comprehension of theoretical principles of learning were the major criteria. Primary-level students who had participated in the experiment were to identify an unknown stuffed bird. The results showed that their comments as compared to their initial observations before having taken the course, increased by 100 per cent while the increase was only 33 per cent for ordinary pupils.

Educational methods and technologies consist of curricula and syllabuses (to conform with the educational objectives which have been chosen), teaching (which normally means teachers, but might also mean machines), learning (which normally means assimilation, but also means 'learning how to learn'), teaching and learning aid (e.g. books, audio-visual media and material equipment of all kinds), together with systems of evaluating pupils' progress (examinations, tests, etc.).

Changes in methods and technology do not necessarily have to involve reform of the system or alteration of its structure and content. Some of them are neutral from a normative standpoint and may be used to strengthen the *status quo* rather than bring about reform; but in practice, when major changes of methods of instruction are introduced, a rethinking usually takes place of overall objectives and performance. Others are closely linked to reform, the method itself being an objective, e.g. the promotion of an enquiring and questioning attitude in children as distinct from one of over-ready acceptance of conventional views.

Systems of evaluating pupils' progress, like methods of teaching, may also be objectives as well as instruments. Changes where both objectives and means are mixed are particularly important, since they exercise a leverage on the whole system.

An example is the adoption of a system of evaluating pupils' progress by their degree of mastery of a subject, rather than by their performance as compared with other pupils, and the development of curricula and methods for this purpose. This is an important approach in furthering the spread of basic education as well as for aiding personality development. While selective tests are necessary for entry to secondary education, which is bound to be fairly closely restricted by lack of resources, no such restrictions are required up to the level of a minimum basic education, since this is a human right. It will be recalled that we made earlier the suggestion that certificates of basic education should be issued in order to encourage the completion of the last years of the elementary part of the cycle, and the 'mastery' rather than the 'competitive' method is clearly indicated for this purpose.

The 'mastery learning' approach, which has been given prominence by Bloom and Carroll in the United States and by Freire in Brazil, has therefore particular application for the closing of the education gap. The 315 million educationally deprived chidren are, as we saw earlier, mostly located in disadvantageous circumstances.

Not all educators are agreed about the desirability of adopting the mastery technique. It may be criticized as diminishing the incentive of the less good learners in the class to imitate and compete with the more able pupils, and as diminishing both opportunity and excellence. Much depends on whether the problem is predominantly quantitative or qualitative and whether the introduction of this method is accompanied by measures to promote opportunity for the more able to move ahead more quickly. Clearly, its desirability can only be judged in each case after full study.

An example of how this approach may be studied and then applied in a modified way to suit local conditions is the case of Korea described by Hogwon Kim.[5] Kim quotes B. S. Bloom as follows:

> The most wasteful and destructive aspect of our present educational system is the set of expectations about student learning each teacher brings to the beginning of a new course or term. The instructor expects a third of his pupils to learn well what is taught, a third to learn less well, and a third to fail or just 'get by'. These expectations are transmitted to the pupils through school grading policies and practices and through the methods and material of instruction. Students quickly learn to act in accordance with them, and the final sorting through grading process approximates the teacher's original expectations. A pernicious self-fulfilling prophecy has been created.
>
> Most students (perhaps over 90 per cent) can master what we teach. Our basic intructional task is to define what we mean by mastery of a subjects and to discover methods and material to help the largest proportion of our students reach it.

Kim then states:

> In applying the strategy of mastery learning in the Korean schools, it was found inevitable to make some adjustment and reorganization of various procedures initially suggested by Carroll and Bloom. One reason for doing so is the fact that classes in our schools have large pupil/teacher ratios, which prohibits the use of multiple and individualized approaches in teaching. It was also evident that introducing an abrupt and complete change into the practices used for so long would create extreme difficulties and frustrations for the teachers. Our task, then, was to formulate a modified model of mastery learning which fully recognized and took into consideration the specific characteristics and needs of our classrooms. The modified model should be one which, while providing assistance to the classroom teachers—incorporating the principles of modern instructional theories—would not impose an unduly heavy overload on them.
>
> The resulting strategy may be schematically shown in a flow chart describing a unit of instruction. The major principles of instruction for mastery learning are incorporated in the flow chart shown in Figure 11.1.

The results of the Korean project have been very successful:

> This project was a large-scale expansion of the earlier experiment on mastery learning. Nine middle schools (approximately 5800 seventh graders) in Seoul participated. The experiment covered eight weeks of learning in mathematics and English.

The results indicated that the percentage of experimental students attaining varied widely across the sample schools. On the average, however, 72 per cent of the students reached the mastery criterion by learning English under experimental conditions compared to only 28 per cent learning under ordinary instructional conditions. In mathematics, an average of 61 per cent of the mastery compared to 39 per cent of the non-mastery students attained the summative achievement test criterion. Two schools did not follow the prescribed procedures. If the results for these schools are ignored, then 75 per cent of the mastery students attained the criterion level in English and 67 per cent in Mathematics.

Beginning from March 1970, the mastery learning project was further expanded with respect to the time, which now covered the entire academic year; and with respect to the number of participating schools and students, which now encompassed 45 schools, including 13 schools in the rural areas, with a total of 25,887 students in the seventh grade. The results indicated that the percentage of experimental students attaining mastery had generally decreased to around 50 per cent, but the differences in the mastery percentage between experimental and control groups remained 20 per cent to 45 per cent in favour of the experimental group.

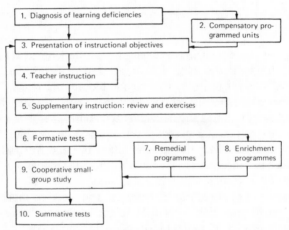

Figure 11.1

This experiment was applied to the middle school grades, but it also has implications for the earlier key learning years in primary education. These implications may be expected to be social as well as pedagogic, since it obviates the sense of failure and dependency on the part of less favoured sections of the population. Similar considerations apply to curriculum reform in general.

Curricula for primary education have to meet three needs—first, those of the majority of children for whom basic or minimum education will be terminal, secondly, those of the children who will complete the whole of the primary cycle and, thirdly, the children who will proceed to secondary education.

This presents a difficult problem to which the ideal solution is individualized instruction, which is, unfortunately, quite impracticable at present to any substantial degree, owing to teacher load.

The alternatives after a basic elementary education stage of between 4 and 5 years to take care of the early leavers, are: (a) to divide pupils into practical and academic streams on the basis of ability or inclination, (b) to continue with a basic cycle in which the practical and academic are combined, selection only taking place at the end of the full cycle. Sri Lanka has chosen the latter course. Its curriculum after grade five (now called 'junior secondary' education) includes a new area named 'pre-vocational studies'. These include some manual skills, an understanding of some selected vocations and their role in the community, linkages between studies at school and vocational aptitudes, e.g. the relevance of science, and inculcation of values connected with production and development. This constitutes in effect a guidance cycle without actually dividing the pupils into two streams. The selectivity test begins after the ninth grade and it is at that stage that the selection for academic attainment takes place.

Unesco, for its part, has been stressing for a number of years what it calls the 'integrated approach' to curriculum development. This means in the first place that curriculum change must not be seen simply as an alteration of the syllabus, but as a new approach to methods as well as content. It means further that curriculum change has to be systematized with the retraining of teachers and the making of the necessary alterations in examination requirements.

Inside education administrations there have been examples of sections concerned with curriculum change not being in close enough contact with those concerned with teacher training and examination policy leading to a lack of coordination. Slips, therefore, can and have occurred in applying an integrated approach, and educational administrations are not always organized for such a purpose.

Unesco has, therefore, been stressing the importance of setting up curriculum development centres. A chart setting out the design of such centres is shown in Figure 11.2, taken from the Unesco Conference of Asian Ministers of Education held in 1972.[6]

The problem is well illustrated in a comment by the British Centre for Educational Development Overseas (CEDO) on a science teaching project in India:

> In the past, a change of syllabus has involved the deletion of some content, the accretion of other; methods remained a constant parameter. Here, the development of the new syllabuses, even though they involved substantial additions of unfamiliar material, is the minor change: the major change lies in the revolution proposed in method. Unless teachers, through thorough retraining, are made familiar with the demonstrational, experimental and other teaching techniques involved, they will fail in using the syllabuses, learning will again take place by rote, and the basic aims of the Project will not be achieved.

A model which brings in all of the main factors involved in integrated curriculum development (though curiously it leaves out the evaluation system) is one by Marklund, Head of the Research and Development Bureau of the Swedish National

Board of Education, referred to in the Report of a conference sponsored by the United States National Science Foundation and organized by the Centre for Educational Research and Innovation (CERI) of the OECD.[7] The Report states:

Marklund put forward a series of what he called 'squares'—the school, the class, the lesson, the subject, the teacher, and the textbook. To be effective, development had to modify each of these squares—thereby changing what he called the 'frame factors'. These squares must be prised up with 'educational crowbars'.

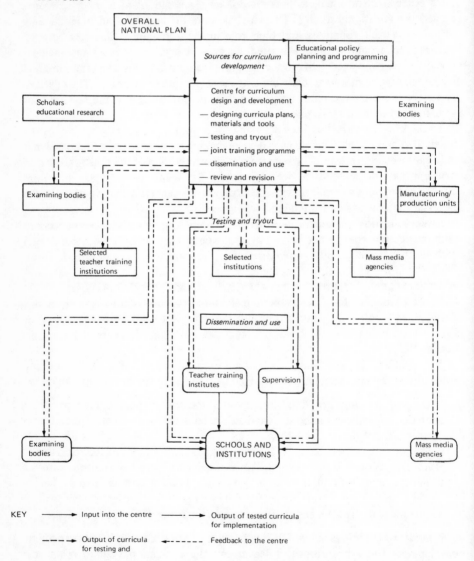

Figure 11.2   Centre for curriculum design and development, input–output chart

Modern curriculum development should replace the squares by a more dynamic and flexible framework on the following lines:

| | | |
|---|---|---|
| School | _____ | system of school units |
| Class | _____ | flexible groutping of pupils |
| Lesson | _____ | system of shorter time modules |
| Subject | _____ | study units |
| Teacher | _____ | teacher team |
| Textbook | _____ | educational materials system |

For a listing and classification of actual methods to be employed in teaching–learning situations, reference can usefully be made to Table 11.1, taken from the report of a workshop held by the OECD Centre for Educational Research and Innovation.[8] This classification is self-explanatory except to note that most of the operations have to be teacher inspired where they are not actually teacher directed. From the curriculum and the methods it is necessary, therefore, to move to the teacher.

A model which shows the stages of development of primary education in terms of teachers is that of Beeby,[9] who sees primary education passing through four stages of development.

The first is the Dame School stage in which the bulk of the teachers are ill-educated and mostly untrained. The syllabus consists mostly of mechanical teaching of reading, writing, and arithmetic, and memorization of fact. The second is the stage of Formalism in which the teachers are still ill-educated, but are trained. Conceptions are added to facts, but in a lifeless way, conceptions being memorized like facts.

The third stage is that of Transition in which teachers are better educated than in the second stage and are also trained. They will have completed secondary school, or its equivalent, and since their knowledge is considerably in advance of that of the pupils, they will be more secure intellectually and less inclined to avoid risking discussion with the pupils. There will be scope for the more able and advanturous teachers to use more stimulating tactics and methods than in the second stage, though the formalism of the examination system will still set the overall tone.

The fourth stage in Beeby's model is the stage of meaning at which teachers are well-educated and well-trained. At this stage questions of what are the real objectives of education become crucial and different views will prevail; but briefly it may be said that the child is taught to think and that meaning replaces memorizing both of facts and concepts.

On the basis of this model, action to increase quality and relevance consists of passing as many schools as possible into the fourth stage as soon as possible, which means in effect increasing the training and educational level of the teachers.

While the Marklund presentation is more complete, the advantage of the Beeby model is that the capacity of the teacher is likely in the end to be the decisive factor in educational reform in the developing countries.

This is clear in the Peruvian reform referred to in the previous chapter. Salazar

**Table 11**   Classification of teaching—learning methods

Dimension I:  social,setting

| | |
|---|---|
| 1.  working individually | (a) free |
| | (b) teacher directed |
| | (c) programmed |
| 2.  working in pairs | (a) teacher—student |
| | (b) student—student |
| 3.  working in groups smaller than the class | (a) groups on the same work |
| | (b) groups on different work |
| 4.  working in class | (a) teacher — class (primarily one-way) |
| | (b) teacher — class dialogue (two-way) |
| | (c) discussion (several ways) |
| 5.  working in groups larger than the class | (a) lecture, film etc. |
| | (b) team-teaching |

Note:  this classification leaves the matter of homogeneous or mixed-ability groups to be decided.

Dimension II:  learning processes and situations

| | |
|---|---|
| 1.  free play | |
| 2.  discovery and enquiry | |
| 3.  creative and imaginative work | (a) aesthetic |
| | (b) technological |
| 4.  learning of facts, skills and attitudes by | (a) trial and errors |
| | (b) identification and imitation |
| | (c) rote |
| 5.  problem solving and structured discussion | |

Note:  this classification leaves the question of motivation, competition and rewards to be
       considered.

Dimension III: media

1.  human resources (teachers, peers, assistants, visitors, etc.)
2.  print in all forms (books, sheets, graphs, reproduced material)
3.  static visual material (blackboard, overhead projector, slides, photographs)
4.  sound media (tapes, discs, radio)
5.  moving visual and audio-visual material (film, TV, CCTV, videotapes)
6.  situational information (drama, role-playing, educational games, case studies)
7.  apparatus and tools (as in workshops, laboratories; including models and simulators)
8.  computers

Bondy, in the description of the reform already cited,[10] draws attention to the links
with teacher training in the following terms:

> ... the Government made the teachers the main target of its strategy. In
> teacher training curricula, the accent was put on the continuous retraining of
> teachers, to enable them to teach the new curriculum; involvement of teachers
> in the actual preparation of the school curriculum; involvement of teachers in

non-formal programmes (i.e. adult education). In the villages they very often function as a link between community and Government. The measure of progress is to be seen most clearly at the primary level, rather than at the secondary level, where the inputs are still the outputs of the old system.

We turn now to the physical (or hard) forms of technology, such as audio-visual media, and discuss the extent of their present use and their utility. We also refer to programmed instruction and teaching machines and to the redesigning of school buildings to make open schools. These items are treated for convenience under 'hard' rather than 'soft' technology, but in fact they involve both.

An important survey of the state of audio-visual instruction is given in a Workshop Report[11] of the National Institute for Educational Research in Tokyo, which collaborates with Unesco on educational problems in Asia.

The actual state of the use of instructional materials, including the new media, was set out in the report as shown in Table 11.2. Commenting on the evolution of audio-visual instruction in the region, the Report, states:

The development of audio-visual instruction or the effective utilization of instructional technology in any country has to pass through four distinct stages ... These steps are the crossing of psychological barriers with regard to the utilization of audio-visual materials on the part of teachers and teacher educators, visible and effective practice of preparation and utilization of inexpensive materials in the teaching–learning process, development and production of commercially produced materials and finally the distinct emergence, availability and popular utilization of audio-visual materials, equipment and hardware.

There is a wide and easily perceptible divergence of production, availability and utilization of audio-visual materials in the countries of Asia. Countries which have advanced economically have a fully developed audio-visual technology. Hardware like projectors, TV sets, tape recorders are easily available and their purposeful utilization is increasing. While there are some countries where even the teachers have yet to be fully trained to improve their own materials and to use the inexpensive aids. The gaps in the status of utilization of audio-visual materials in different countries are appalling.

The Report adds:

Perhaps there is a common fallacy among developing nations that an effective audio-visual programme must necessarily incorporate the sophisticated softwares and hardwares of the developed and technically advanced nations such as Japan. Developing countries in Asia should be encouraged to develop an adequate audio-visual programme initially in their own traditional ways—improvising and utilizing locally available aids and materials. Subsequently, a more ambitious plan can be evolved with the assistance of an international body like Unesco.

Among the interesting suggestions made at the workshop is one that an international production system of audio-visual aids and materials should be set up. The

Table 11.2  Utilization of Instructional

| | Afghanistan | Ceylon | China Rep. of | India | Indonesia | Iran |
|---|---|---|---|---|---|---|
| Chalk and blackboard | c | c | c | c | c | c |
| Chart and diagrams | c | c | c | c | c | c |
| Maps | c | c | | c | c | c |
| Wall pictures | x | c | | | | x |
| Pictures | | x | c | | c | c |
| Photographs | x | | x | x | | c |
| Bulletin boards | | c | c | | | |
| Flannel boards | x | x | c | | | |
| Felt boards | | | | | | |
| Flash cards | | x | x | | | c |
| Picture-story show | | | | | | x |
| Models | x | x | c | c | | |
| Specimens of rocks, etc. | x | c | c | | | x |
| Globes | c | x | | | x | c |
| Objects | | x | | | x | |
| Mock-ups | | | | | | |
| Diorama | | | | | | |
| Planetarium | | | | | | |
| Science kits or apparatus | c | | | c | | |
| Demonstration equipment | | | | | | |
| Weight pieces | | | | | | |
| Filmstrips | x | | c | x | | x |
| Slides | x | | c | x | | x |
| Records | | | c | | | x |
| Sound film-strips | | | | | | |
| 8 mm film loops | | | | | | c |
| Films | x | x | | x | | c |
| Projectors | | | c | | | c |
| Opaques projectors | | | | | | c |
| Epivisor | | | | | | |
| Epidiascope | | x | | | | |
| Overhead projector | | | | | | |
| Radio | | x | | x | | x |
| TV and telecast | | | | | | |
| Tape recorder | | x | c | | | c |
| Video tape recorder | | | | | | |
| Magnetic sheet recorder | | | | | | |
| Supplementary reading books | | x | x | c | | c |
| Resource books | | | | x | | |
| Teacher's handbooks | | x | c | c | | c |
| Workbooks | | | | c | | c |
| Cuisennaire rods | | | | | | |
| Locally made materials | x | x | | x | | |

*The information given in the table is supplemented by the participants.

importance of such action if it could be taken would be that there is at present a vicious circle between the lack of demand for audio-visual aids and the high cost which is due to insufficient demand.

At the same time we have some cautionary remarks in the contribution of Indonesia to the report, where it is stated:

Aids and materials*

| Japan | Korea Rep. of | Laos | Malaysia | Nepal | Pakistan | Philippines | Thailand | Viet-Nam, Rep. of |
|---|---|---|---|---|---|---|---|---|
| c | c | c | c | c | c | c | c | c |
| c | c | c | c | c | c | c |   | c |
| c | c | c | c | c | c | c | c | c |
| c |   | c | c |   | x | c |   | c |
|   | x |   | c | c | c | c | c | c |
|   | c | c | x | x |   | c |   | c |
|   |   |   | c | c | c | c |   | c |
|   |   |   | c | c |   | c |   | c |
|   | c |   | c |   |   | c |   |   |
|   |   |   | c | c |   | c |   |   |
|   | c |   | x |   |   | c |   |   |
| c | c | x | c | c | x | c |   | c |
| c | c | x | x | c |   | c | c | c |
| c | c | x | c | c | x | c | c | c |
|   | x |   |   | x | x | c |   | c |
|   | x |   |   |   |   | c |   |   |
|   | x |   |   |   |   | c |   |   |
| x |   |   |   |   |   | c |   |   |
| c | c | x | c | c |   | c | c | c |
|   | c |   | c | c |   | x |   |   |
|   | x |   | c | c |   | c | c | c |
| c | x |   | x | x |   | x | x | x |
| c | c |   | c | x |   | c | x | x |
|   | x |   | c | x |   | c | x | x |
|   |   |   | c |   |   | x |   |   |
|   |   |   | x |   |   |   |   |   |
| c | x |   | c | x | x | x | x | x |
| c | x |   | c | x |   | c |   |   |
|   |   |   |   |   |   | x |   |   |
|   | x |   | x |   |   |   |   |   |
|   |   |   | x |   |   |   |   |   |
| x | x | x |   |   |   |   |   |   |
| c | c |   | c | x | x | c | c | x |
| c | x |   | x | x |   | x |   |   |
| c | c |   | c |   |   | c |   |   |
| x | x |   |   |   |   |   |   |   |
| x | x |   |   |   |   |   |   |   |
| c | x | c | c | c | x | c |   |   |
| c |   |   | x |   |   | x |   |   |
|   | c | c | x | c | x | c |   |   |
|   | c |   | c |   |   | c |   |   |
|   |   |   |   |   |   | x |   |   |
|   | c | c | c | c | x | c |   | c |

The distribution of materials, the lending of apparatus and materials would be very costly, due to the great distances in Indonesia, the possibility of loss and damage, the poor communications and inavailability of copies. As for machines and apparatus, like cameras, projectors, tape recorder, films, tapes and books, since these articles are all imported goods, the loss or damage of machines and tools would result in insuperable difficulties. To import machines would need years because of lack of funds and intricate administrative procedures.

... For the same reasons as stated above, the Government has no government assisted machinery or agencies. Occasionally an order is placed for the production of materials, at local manufacturers of school materials. The manufacturer stops production as soon as the order is carried out.

For the same reason, there is no nationwide private machinery. A manufacturer cannot live on orders, occasionally placed, while there is no demand from private schools either.

The situations in local areas are even worse. There are provinces outside Java which could not even buy materials locally. They have to order everything from Java, or establish manufacturer plants only for the period it is needed to meet the demand. These are mainly workshops, improvised from local entrepreneurs.

No local independent machinery can exist without continuous demand from the public. Therefore no local entrepreneur would be easily persuaded to establish any manufacturing enterprise.

These observations point to the limitations of the use of audio-visual media in countries where there is no substantial consumer market.

In India the situation is different because of its experience in the production of feature films, documentaries etc., the large amount of research which is taking place in audio-visual aids and the availability of producers. The Indian contribution to the seminar noted:

There is a mushroom growth of producers and dealers of audio-visual materials and teaching aids in India and at present over 200 such sources and agencies can be listed. Producers who are pouring out materials of a fairly good quality are few. Some time back in our all-India search for audio-visual materials for an international exhibition at Bangkok, we could select suitable materials from about a dozen firms in India. Commendable graphic materials in the form of charts, maps, auto-didactic playway materials, models, and allied three-dimensional materials are being produced. There is a dearth of good filmstrips and instructional films.

The growth and popular utilization of instructional technology is closely linked up with the availability of audio-visual equipment and hardware. The average monthly production of 16 mm sound projectors by two and sometimes by three firms in India totals up to 160 projectors. Half of these go to educational institutions and are used for direct educational purposes. It is estimated that at present there are more than 9000 projectors in educational institutions in the country.

The problem in India as elsewhere comes back to the question of the training and status of the teachers and indicates how wise it has been in the Ivory Coast project to accord such a large part of the additional investment to better training and remuneration for teachers. The Indian contribution to the Tokyo Workshop Reports the reactions of teachers as follows:

Following is an analysis of the major problems in the proper utilization of audio-visual aids in schools, as viewed by teachers.

Lack of finance

(1) The school has no funds for audio-visual aids.

(2) Most of the funds are used for laboratory equipment for Science.

(3) My poor emoluments hinder my use of personal funds.

Lack of time at the disposal of the teacher

(1) There is no spare time in schools hours.

(2) There is no spare time after school hours.

(3) There is no time with other teachers to assist me in preparing aids.

Overcrowded curriculum

(1) Time allotted for different subjects is limited.

(2) The syllabus is heavy with so many subjects.

(3) There are so many extra-curricular activities.

No relationship with the system of examination

(1) Aids do not prepare the students for the examination in general.

(2) The use of aids does not allow me to cover all topics in a subject.

(3) They have no relationship with the descriptive type of examinations.

Lack of skill on the part of the teacher for improvising aids

(1) I have no previous training.

(2) I am not an artist.

(3) I do not think it necessary for a teacher to prepare his own aids.

Non-availability of aids

(1) I do not know the sources.

(2) Proper aids are not available.

(3) Aids are not available when required.

Lack of skill on the part of the teacher for the utilization of aids

(1) I have never used these aids.

(2) I have not been properly trained in their use.

(3) These aids do not facilitate learning at the proper time, when used.

The Tokyo Workshop made a number of important recommendations as regards immediate needs which may be summarized as follows:

(1) Setting up of an Asian Centre for audio-visual instruction with assistance from Unesco.

(2) Development of a basic corps of teacher educators in audio-visual instruction. There would be an optional paper in audio-visual instruction in teacher training institutions and a certain amount of information should be integrated into most of the papers.

(3) In-service and training programmes in audio-visual instructions should be developed for administrators, teacher educators and producers of materials.

(4) A literature giving information on the subject should be developed in the form of a directory of aids and materials and handbooks for their use.

(5) Prototypes of materials of instruction and inexpensive aids should be produced and circulated as prototypes.

(6) Research studies and evaluations of educational films should be established both nationally and internationally.

(7) An international production system should be established under the auspices of the United Nations or Unesco which would provide techniques on local production methods and as much international aid as possible should be harnessed to this purpose wherever it was clear that the possibilities of their use were viable and effective.

While radio programmes are in fairly wide use in developing countries for instructional purposes, usually at the post-primary and adult level, they do not have more than a small marginal impact at the primary level. It is rather with television, with its greater visual stimulus, that the future lies; but this medium remains still largely unexplored. The main problems are the expense and the upkeep of the hardware, the cost of the supplementary training or retraining of teachers which is required and the shortage of well organized television materials to be incorporated in the school curriculum.

Full-scale programmes have, however, been tried or are in progress in a limited number of countries, notably Niger, the Ivory Coast, Tunisia, El Salvador and Western Samoa. The Niger television project was scarcely a success owing to its high cost in relation to output. The costs of televised education are only competitive with the normal methods when there is a large coverage of population, since, basically, television is an aid to the teaching force and does not substitute. Its utility depends on the increase in efficiency it brings in the form of shortening course, reducing wastage and achieving high performance levels of both teachers and pupils.

The Niger Experience was taken into account in the design of the most far-reaching programme for the use of the new media in primary education, which is that now being carried out in the Ivory Coast as from 1971, after three years of preparation and considerable assistance from external sources (five donor countries, six international agencies, and one Foundation). The programme provides for televised education in the primary schools to become general by 1980 and embrace the whole primary school curriculum by 1985–86.

Although not especially associated with social change as in the case with the reforms in Peru and Tanzania, the Ivory Coast programme to have television as a main educational instrument in all of its primary schools is conceived as having a much wider impact than a drastic change in method. This can be seen from the material put out by the Government[12] which reads as follows:

The introduction of educational television in the Ivory Coast is more than just the application of modern technical facilities to the teaching of children. The Ivory Coast education venture is an integrated programme based on experiments and achievements almost everywhere in the world: school broadcasts in European countries; the Italian *telescuola*; seven educational television channels in Japan; the pilot projects in El Salvador, Niger, and the American Samoas.

It is nevertheless an original undertaking because it keeps in touch with and adapts to developments, and seeks to achieve what educationalists call 'the unity of school and life' and which, in the case of the Ivory Coast, is more in the nature of 'comprehensive education' reaching all inhabitants and inducing them to participate actively, from childhood to old-age in the nation's harmonious development and its political, cultural, social and economic evolution.

Television and radio (the use of which will start in 1972) are 'instruments' in the service of education. Their combination and the system's reliability make it possible to hasten the introduction of the use of the most modern methods and additional educational content. Direct communication between the Production Centre and the pupils and teachers makes the use of new methods an immediate possibility. To achieve that aim, the re-training of the whole teaching profession, which begins in 1972, is of vital importance. The re-training is supplemented by the 'Teacher's Diary' and the 'pedagogic support' broadcast three times a week.

In addition, the existing structure, thanks to the Operating Service, the feedback system and the conclusions of the Evaluation Unit, makes it possible to correct the way in which the methods are applied, and even to correct the methods themselves. Modern technology is already proving that it can confer on the education system the adaptability necessary for the rapid evolution of socio-economic conditions in countries where far-reaching changes are in progress.

A reproach often made is the cost of the operation, yet one of the reasons which prompted the Ivory Coast Government to adopt the system was the economic advantage it brings with it. Studies have shown that the transformation of the Ivory Coast school system with a view to the eradication of illiteracy by traditional methods would not only take more time but would be far more costly.

At the outset, of course, the infrastructure for transmission, and the system of production and maintenance, demanded considerable cost in proportion to the relatively few pupils reached in 1970–72 (20,517 pupils in 447 classes). *A fortiori*, if the renovated primary education enables a child to complete primary schooling in six years, that is to say without having to repeat a class, it is clearly cheaper. In fact, not only do children repeating a class occupy the place of children who attend school if the repetition could be avoided by more effective teaching, but there are so many who do have to repeat that the cost to the Ivory Coast is about two thousand million CFA francs annually—a third of the primary education budget. Television would never cost so much.

It is true that in the early years, the effort was made possible thanks to the surge of international solidarity with a Government which shouldered its responsibilities; but that solidarity was manifest precisely during the initial period when the largest investments were made in specialists and equipment.

It must be stressed that in the calculation of the economics of the operation, account must be taken of the fact that the reception network will be an incomparable medium of popular culture and civic education.

The fact that the operation is justified by the overall impact of the television network on adult and civic education and culture somewhat reduces the value of this example as an experiment in primary education as such. But it is clearly an ambitious programme of great importance not only for the country itself, but for those who will wish to see how the question of cost in relation to output finally works out, whether wastage will in fact be reduced as much as hoped, whether problems of maintenance of equipment which are liable to be troublesome will be solved, whether the retraining of teachers can be made effective and contained in the estimated cost of the project without considerable salary increases, whether at the same time as introducing a major new costly mechanical input output can be redirected in learning and teaching content towards a wider conception of education as is hoped.

From the standpoint of its contribution to the technology of primary education, the most interesting feature is the extent to which it adds to the skills of the teachers. Pauvert, the French educator, who was closely associated with the Ivory Coast Project, writes:[13] 'The cost of recycling and teacher training, and the salary increases involved in raising the qualifications of the teachers represent 80 per cent of the additional unit cost per pupil. Contrary to what is usually supposed it is not the additional cost of the television itself which is the highest'.

This would indicate that the real innovation which is taking place is not so much a question of new media but of a massive change in teacher qualifications. This in turn inevitably raises the questions whether such a massive retraining without the aid of television might have comparable results and what is being done about the use of audio-visual material limited to teacher training.

In addition to improving teacher qualifications in the more academic sense, measures are needed to improve the face-to-face and behavioural aspects of classwork. A valuable step is utilizing schools near teacher training centres for demonstration lessons after which discussion could be held using tape recorders and films to evaluate performance and to study and correct the various procedures and techniques used to create good learning situations. The latter is particularly important since being able to pass the teacher training diploma from an intellectual standpoint is not necessarily reflected in classroom behaviour.

It would be desirable in the long run for every teacher training college to have a laboratory attached in which the teacher can observe and appraise his own methods at work. Procedure for such laboratories have been worked out in detail at Stanford University under the heading of 'Micro-Teaching', the essence of which is to show on a microscopic scale the impact of the teacher by reconstituting classes with a few volunteer pupils. The originality of the procedure is that it eliminates factors, present in the class as a whole, such as the pupils' reactions to each other and to the teacher having to handle a whole subject, and it focuses instead upon smaller situations which are 'blown up' for close analysis. A further element of it is that the teacher can undertake his own feedback and correct himself without necessarily relying upon the supervisor, which often means that the changes he introduces himself become more lasting.

This practice, if extended, would help to defeat the widespread use of 'survival' techniques by teachers who restrict the scope of the development of learning situations in class owing to their own inability to cope with them, provided that the requisite training and status improvement is also brought about. Survival techniques cannot be eliminated without a set of other specific measures to improve the teacher's capacity and the curriculum and tools with which he is working.

Television is being used for teacher training in some countries, notably in Cuba, but it is not usual unless there is also television in use in the schools. The extension of the audio-visual techniques in teacher training, both before and during service, may be one of the most fruitful fields for the new more sophisticated media, since the recipients have a greater degree of maturity than classes of primary school children. Certainly, short films of demonstration lessons in actual classrooms should be an essential tool in use in teacher training institutions; and television programmes, in addition to their actual educational value for teachers, can also contribute to the adoption of nationwide standards.

This still leaves us with the question, raised earlier, whether, since the main effort and expense is on teacher training, the same results could not be obtained by massive teacher training programmes without classroom television.

The answer given by the planners of the Ivory Coast project is that there is a greater learning activity created by television. This is the key to the issue, since the extra cost of the new programme is expected to be met largely by the reduction of repetition of pupils of grades due to the better quality of the instruction. But here too the question has to be asked whether the repetition could not be reduced, as it has been successfully in a number of other countries, by automatic promotion.

The Ivory Coast Television Project has been carefully costed, but it is as well to illustrate some of the difficulties involved. In the Report of the International Commission on the Development of Education the project is cited as a means of reducing unit cost as follows:

> In the Ivory Coast, the introduction of television instruction in primary schools, with the accompanying necessary upgrading of teachers' qualifications, increased the unit cost per student from $60 to $80 per year. But the increased efficiency expected from the revamped system aims at reducing the present expenditure (average fifteen school years) per student completing the primary cycle to eight years' expenditure. That is, cost per completed student, now 15 × $60, or $900, will drop to 8 × $80, or $640.

Commenting on this[14] Michel Debeauvais writes more cautiously. He states:

> ... the introduction of this technological innovation (apart from its efficiency as a teaching tool, which the arguments for the project do nothing to prove) would be more likely to lead to an over-all increase in expenditure rather than to a reduction, because: (1) the ban on repeating is not necessarily linked with the introduction of television, any more than it is with an improvement in educational efficiency. (2) Calculation of the 'unit cost per certificated student' means that the total cost of all the years of education dispensed to a whole batch of students is ascribed only to those who finish the course, since that total includes the cost of the years spent by those who have dropped out. The Report even goes so far as to speak of 'reducing the present expenditure (average of fifteen school years) per student completing the primary cycle to eight years' expenditure'.
>
> This interpretation of an index of educational efficiency as a concept of 'the cost of wastage in non-monetary terms' thus creates the illusion that a saving could be made simply by putting a ban on repeating. It would be better not to confuse the educational aspects of school wastage with financial considerations.
>
> Dealing only with these latter considerations, it would seem more correct to say, according to the data given in the Report, that in order to attain the growth target of 94 per cent in enrolment at public primary schools, and taking into account the one-third increase in unit costs, expenditure would increase (all other things being equal) by 150 per cent, given constant prices, between 1969 and 1980.

Debeauvais adds: 'Specific objections could probably be made to each of these arguments, which do not go beyond a brief and superficial quantitative analysis'. He goes on to make the point that research aimed at evaluating educational and economic efficiency is still at an exploratory stage and that further investigation is necessary.

An example of one of the factors extremely difficult to measure is the indirect benefits from the operation, which, it will be recalled, was described above as 'an incomparable medium of popular culture and civic education'. Frequently the justification for the large-scale use of the new media, such as television and radio, in the developing countries is based by their governments on the general development of the communications system as well as the specific gains for education in school.

Since knowledge is still in the exploratory stage as regards the contribution to school education which could be made by a large-scale use of the communications products of the electrical industries, there are naturally differences of assessment as to the prospects. Dragoljub Najman in his essay already cited,[15] says 'Thanks to electronic devices we are probably heading towards a new Golden Age of education'.

An opposite opinion on the same points is that which appears in a study prepared by the International Council for Educational Development for the World Bank.[16] Under the heading 'Improving educational technologies', it is stated:

> Out thoughts on this subject will disappoint those who dream of great breakthroughs in educational technologies involving satellites, computerized instruction and such, that will enable the deprived rural areas of the world to be saturated almost overnight with rich learning opportunities. Such bold ideas seem unfeasible, at least for this century. Not only would these sophisticated technologies be economically impossible on a large scale for poor rural areas (they would be less so for densely populated and more affluect cities), but the inherent limitations on the kinds of programme content they could handle, not to mention the myriad of organizational, logistical, and personnel problems that would have to be solved (and which have scarcely been solved for the educational use of films, radio, and printed materials)—all these sobering considerations prompted us to consider less flamboyant means to enhance rural learning opportunities.

Further, the Unesco: IIEP study, *The New Media: Memo to Educational Planners*,[17] states that

> ... there have now been over four hundred separate research investigations comparing the relative effectiveness of TV versus live classroom instruction. Essentially all of these studies have had the same result: the students in the remote classrooms learn as much or slightly more, than the students in the live classrooms. Very similar results have been obtained in experiments with good programmed instructional materials. There is strong evidence to show that students learn as well and in less time than with conventional classroom practice. Yet these techniques have not received wide acceptance. The basic question is: Why not?

The answer we would suggest ourselves is that the result that pupils learn 'slightly more' is not a sufficient inducement to embark on prospects of using educational hardware on a large scale.

Can these different views be made compatible if we differentiate their time perspective? If Najman is looking forward a hundred years, will his assessment be realized? Supporting Najman's view of the extent of the long term educational change which may be expected from the spread of electronic devices is the research, already quoted in our first chapter, of the possibilities of the introduction of shoulder carrels linked to computers and to a 'town brain'.

It is, however, possible that in the long term there will also have been changes in the value systems in the industrialized countries which will turn more towards, rather than away from the person to person approach, characteristic of humanist attitudes to education. There are already many manifestations of a search for sensitizing, rather than mechanizing, the communications process and some fundamental questioning of the values associated with technological progress.

The major issue is action in the next decade or two. During this period points of no return may be reached on which future electronics can have no influence. The fact that this is sensed by educators is no doubt one of the principal reasons why the demand for innovation in the form of hardware is relatively quiescent, while that for software is acute.

The greatest single leverage in technological change is therefore likely to come at present from changes in structure and content and teacher training rather than from mechanical aids. This is partly because education is by nature 'soft', becoming a psychological and social process, and partly for economic reasons, as well as the time pressures we have indicated.

Similar in kind to the possibilities and problems presented by school television are those of the use of satellites. They have additional advantages because of the very extensive coverage they can offer and especially because of their possibility of reaching sparsely populated areas and migrant populations. The problem of expense, however, looms large and, commenting on the prospects for the use of satellites, the Report of the International Commission on the Development of Education states:[18]

> Certain countries facing serious educational difficulties may be tempted to put satellites into orbit for widespread diffusion of education programmes before precise objectives have been clearly defined and content carefully prepared. Outside the enormous expense of such projects, this would mean taking the risk—calculated or not—of a failure that would so break the budget and so shake the faith that it would block any other possibility for large-scale technological innovation. At the present time, considering the fact that audiovisual means—particularly local television and radio networks—have not yet been sufficiently developed and utilized, projects of this kind may well appear to be incompatible with the commonly prevailing situation in which resources are scarce and serious, balanced, educational plans are necessary.
>
> National spatial telecommunications systems are only of interest to linguistically homogeneous regions, to very large countries such as India, Brazil and Canada or to a few with very unusual geographical outlines such as Indonesia and Japan. Economically and technically, it would not be feasible to justify or to carry out nationally organized programmes virtually anywhere else.

On the other hand a form of hard combined with soft technology which is not over-expensive, if its use can be justified pedagogically, is programmed instruction.

The software aspect is that it utilizes the results of experiments by psychologists of the processes which condition the mind's retentivity. The hardware aspect is that it can be used in the form of teaching machines. The pedagogical advantage of such machines is that they permit individualized instruction, since the pupil can choose his own paths of learning and remedy his particular weaknesses. Limitations of programmed instruction are that while valuable for the acquisition of knowledge of facts and ways of thinking, it may work in ways which do not stimulate the creative and personality-forming functions of education. These take place better in face-to-face contact with teacher and other children, in classes or in small groups.

Pocztar[19] states:

While it is true that programmed education has many advantages, its general use cannot be envisaged immediately. This is certainly not desirable so long as teachers have not been given the necessary training to familiarize them with educational technology and make them aware of the problems still raised by its inclusion in the educational system.

An area of soft plus hard technology where the prospects are clearer and the difficulties fewer is in school building, e.g. the 'open' schools, now being built in considerable numbers in Sweden, and also in England, the United States and Canada. They provide the physical surroundings in which team teaching and learning and more individualized instruction in small groups can replace the standard classroom methods.

On this point a Swedish authority, Birgit Rodhe, writes:[20] 'the classroom school, the "egg-crate school" or, to use another metaphor, the school of "little boxes all the same", seemed both to hinder pedagogical innovation and to further a state of education an scoeity, in which the *status quo* is happily preserved from one generation to the next'.

She comments on the English open schools as follows:

In recent years special attention has been directed towards the English primary school, which seems to embody many of the educational objectives sought elsewhere. In England, renewal in school building has its origin both in building techniques and in educational methods, and initiatives have come both from the national and the local level. The new English primary schools are mostly small and intimate, with 200–300 pupils between 5 and 11 years of age (e.g. the Prior Weston School, London). The design aims at achieving a combination of open space and intimacy in order to further the maximum of activity, creativity and security for each child. The children are constantly encouraged to inquire and discover for themselves.

There seems to be a very happy interrelation in these schools between school design and an education, full of imagination and constant discovery for children. Parents are closely engaged with the life of the school and sometimes also have facilities of their own on the school premises.

A point in favour of the application of this method in the less developed countries is its saving in costs which is about 10 to 15 per cent less than for traditional types of school. Difficulties, as with all innovations, are the teacher training and organization experience required to make a flexible system of this kind work smoothly. In the developing countries many schools are open schools by duress rather than by choice. In India, for instance, it is estimated that about 40 per cent of primary schools are single teacher schools, while the proportion having the multiple class system is much higher.

The development in less developed areas of open schools, with well trained teachers, interlocked with the life of the community, but at the same time providing competency in literacy and numeracy, would be a big step to attaining universal minimum basic education. There would be a period of time needed for this system to acquire the necessary prestige to gain parents' support but measures could be adopted to encourage this. One might be, as suggested earlier, the granting of certificates of attainment of basic education so that the children who cannot complete the full cycle would have an incentive to attain at least a good level of literacy.

These certificates would have to be accepted by employers and governments as a first evidence of preparedness for employment. Such certificates might be a useful bridge for movement between formal and non-formal education as well as removing the stigma attached to drop-out, since this term is at present applied to all who do not complete the full primary cycle even if they attain literacy.

The most important type of technological change is when teaching methods, content and teacher training, and the structure and output of the system, are all changed in an integrated way. An example of this is the reduction of from four to three years of the elementary cycle in compulsory education in the Soviet Union. The content and the instructional methods were changed as a result of research and experiment, which had taken place over a preceding period, and teacher supply and training adjusted accordingly. The system is one of 'form masters' teaching the whole class up to three years, followed by subject teaching by various teachers after the third year.

The USSR experience leading to the adoption of a three-year course of elementary education is described by two leading USSR educators, A. Arsenyev and A. Markouchevitch, as follows:[21]

Preparations for the transition from a four-year to a three-year period of elementary schooling began in 1966. Experiments along the above-mentioned three lines of research had already been conducted in the experimental schools of the Academy of Pedagogical Sciences or by enthusiastic individual teachers at some of the regular schools .... A series of experiments involving a far more generalized trial of the new elementary programme was necessary in order to confirm its validity .... The results of these experiments are currently available only for schools in twelve districts of the R.S.S.F.R. and in a few districts of other Soviet Republics—in all, 617 schools with some 15,000 first-year and 10,000 second-year pupils. These results confirm the hypothesis that elementary schooling can be completed in three years.

They have been widely extended since 1969. What was done was to place less emphasis on developing automatic skills and on rote learning, and to provoke aptitudes for comparison and comment. This innovation was aided by the extensive pre-primary education which is part of the Soviet Union's system, but this was not a decisive factor, since the favourable results also covered some children without pre-primary schooling.

Western observers at one time believed that the political restrictions in the USSR would have a dulling effect on the production of enquiring minds with a bent to research and innovation. This has been disproved by the remarkable advances in science which have taken place under the Soviet system. The reason is perhaps that the scientific approach is encouraged at the earliest years (see the reports of the Soviet Academy of Pedagogical Sciences, *Programma srednej skoly, Nacal'nye klassy*). Each of the three primary grades is taught the application of the natural sciences to a successively more complex environment. Whereas the first graders are concerned with their very immediate surroundings, the children in the third grade are already able to compare the nature and work of their town to that of the various zones of the USSR (see also L. V. Zankow, *Razvities ucascibja v processes obucenija*).

Bassett, in his book *Innovations in Primary Education*,[22] comments on the important research in the United States on the same matter and states:

> The development of knowledge is usually away frm primary experience to abstractions, away from particular objects or events to general propositions. Accordingly, it is to be expected that the order in which knowledge is taught, particularly in the elementary school, will differ from the order in which it is most systematically expressed.
>
> Dewey makes this distinction the basis for two different kinds of teaching, which he calls the logical and the psychological methods. The former is described by him as follows: 'Pupils began their study of science with texts in which the subject is organized into topics according to the order of the specialist . . . . Laws are introduced at a very early stage . . . . The pupils learn a science instead of learning the scientific way of treating the familiar material of ordinary experience'.
>
> The psychological method he describes in these words: '. . . by following in connection with problems selected from the material of ordinary acquaintance, the methods by which scientific men have reached their perfected knowledge, [the student] gains independent power to deal with material within his range, and avoids the mental confusion and intellectual dictates attendant upon studying matter whose meaning is only symbolic'.

Bassett goes on to say,

> Countless commentators, adherents and opponents of Dewey have taken up the same theme and dealt with it in their own way. In the hands of some the psychological method, with its emphasis on the children (and with a rather sentimental psychology to match), has resulted in needlessly undisciplined learning and low levels of scholarship. In the hands of others the logical method, with its emphasis on the subjects to be learned (and with a rather

ruthless or uninformed view of children to match), has resulted in undue pressure on children, and the setting up of undesirable attitudes to learning.

The three year elementary cycle, when it has been in operation long enough to be subjected to large scale evaluation, may throw an interesting light on this area of pedagogy, and have important implications for children in developing countries still struggling with rote learning.

## REFERENCES

1. *Education in the USSR*, Progress Publishers, Moscow, p. 39.
2. *Education in the USSR*, Progress Publishers, Moscow, p. 81.
3. Unesco Cooperative Educational Abstracting Service, *Abstract No. 6-67/E*, September 1968.
4. *Razvities Ucascibja v Processe Obucenija*, L. V. Zankow; see also *The New Curriculum*, UK Schools Council, HMSO, 1967.
5. 'Mastery learning in the Korean middle schools', Hogwon Kim, in *Bulletin of the Unesco Regional Office for Education in Asia*, Vol. VI, No. 1, Bangkok, 1971.
6. *Development of Education in Asia*, UNESCO/MINEDAS 3, 1971.
7. See Chapter 4, References, No. 10.
8. *The Nature of Curriculum for the Eighties and Onwards*, Report on a Workshop held at Kassel, Germany, OECD (CERI), 1970.
9. *The Quality of Education in Developing Countries*, C. E. Beeby, Harvard University Press, 1966, p. 72.
10. See Chapter 9, References, No. 6.
11. *Audio-Visual Instruction in Asia*, Workshop Report of the National Institute for Educational Research, Tokyo, Japan, 1971.
12. *Television in the Modernization of Education in the Ivory Coast,* Secretary of State for Primary Education and Educational Television, Ivory Coast, 1969.
13. *Stratègie Nationale de l'innovation (Côte-d'Ivoire)*, J. C. Pauvert, International Commission on the Development of Education, Series C: *Innovations*, No. 6, Unesco, 1971.
14. 'Problems of costs and opportunities', Michel Debeauvais, in *Prospects*, Vol. III, No. 3, Unesco, 1973.
15. See Chapter 4, References, No. 2, p. 67.
16. *Attacking Rural Poverty*, prepared by the International Council for Educational Development for the World Bank, 1973, Section 13, para. 77.
17. *The New Media: Memo to Educational Planners*, Unesco: IIEP.
18. *Learning To Be*, Unesco-Harrap, p. 123.
19. *The Theory and Practice of Programmed Instruction*, Jerry Pocztar, Unesco, 1972, p. 23.
20. 'A two-way open school', Birgit Rodhe, in *Prospects*, Vol. II, No. 1, Unesco, 1972, pp. 88–99.
21. See Chapter 1, References, No. 8.
22. See Chapter 7, References, No. 2.

## SELECTED FURTHER READING

*Educational Technology. Bulletin of the International Bureau of Education*, Geneva, No. 177, Unesco, 1970.

207

*New Educational Technology and its Implications for the Efficiency of Educational Systems*, Michael Schmidbauer, International Commission on the Development of Education, Series C: *Innovations*, No. 5, Unesco, 1971.

*Modernization of Education, Teaching Media and Technology*, International Meeting of Experts, Dec. 4–8, 1972 convened by Unesco, The Pedagogical Research Institute, Prague, 1973.

*Research and Development in Teacher Education in Asia*, Report of a Working Group, Baguio City, Philippines, 11–20 January, 1972, Asian Institute for Teacher Educators (sponsored by Unesco), University of the Philippines, 1972.

*Further Education of Teachers in Service in Asia: A Regional Survey*, Unesco Regional Office for Education in Asia, Bangkok, 1973.

*To Improve Learning*, a report to the President and the Congress by the Commission of Instructional Technology, Washington, D.C., 1969.

*New Methods and Techniques in Teacher Training*, Final Report, ED/CONF.14/3, Unesco, 1969.

*Better Teachers*, an experiment with in-service teacher training conducted by the UNRWA/Unesco Institute of Education, Unesco, 1970.

*Conference on Policies for Educational Growth, Background Study No. 7*, OECD, 1970.

*A Structural Foundation for Tomorrow's Education*, Jean Piaget, in *Prospects*, Vol. II, No. 1, Unesco, 1972.

*Education and Technology*, Louis Ziegle, International Commission on the Development of Education, Series B: *Opinions*, No. 14, Unesco.

*Educational Technology*, Henri Dieuzeide, International Commission on the Development of Education, Series B: *Opinions*, No. 30, Unesco.

*Out-of-School Education: The Mass Media*, Joseph Rovan, International Commission on the Development of Education, Series B: *Opinions*, No. 32, Unesco.

*Education and the Computer*, Claude Saury and Michel Scholl, International Commission on the Development of Education, Series C: *Innovations*, No. 8, Unesco.

*Mastery Learning: Theory and Practice*, ed. James H. Block, Holt, Rinehart and Winston, New York, 1971.

*Report of the Missions for the Evaluation of Educational Television in Niger, El Salvador and American Samoa*, Publication on the Educational Television Programme, Vol. III, Ministry of Education of the Republic of the Ivory Coast.

*The Teaching of Reading*, ed. Ralph C. Staiger, Unesco-Ginn, 1973.

*The New Mathematics and an Old Culture: A Study of Learning among the Kpelle of Liberia*, Case Studies in Education, Holt, Rinehart and Winston, New York, 1967.

*Vers une Politique en Faveur des Jeunes en Milieu Urbain*, P. Kuenstler, secretariat paper for Second United Nations Congress on the Prevention of Crime and Treatment of Offenders, London, 1960, Unicef, 1969.

*The School and the Child in the Third World*, R. Van Waeyenberghe, Assignment Children, Unicef, 1968.

'Africa: education from within', Roland Colin, in *Ceres* (FAO Review), Vol. IV, No. 3, 1971.

International Children's Centre, Paris. Various documents and reports on conditions affecting child learning in the developing countries.

*Use of Radio and Television for Rural Development in Africa*, Conference on Educational Radio and Television, Algiers. Unesco, 1969.

*Educational Technology: A First Look*, John Leedham, Pitman Education Library, 1973.

*SEPEXTE '73. Analysis of the Preparatory Questionnaire addressed to experts in Educational Technology*, Unesco ED/WS/442, October 1973.

*SEPEXTE '73. Field Staff Retraining in Educational Technology: Study of an Operational Multimedia System*, Unesco ED/WS/448, November 1973.

CHAPTER 12

# Rural Basic Education

The great majority of the population of the developing regions (except in the case of Latin America, where the proportion is about a half only) live in rural areas. Education for the children of rural areas is beset with most of the general problems which have been described in earlier chapters, but also with many special difficulties. These difficulties vary greatly from country to country but have some common features.

The first of these, unfortunately, is the shortage of tested solutions which can be applied, despite many experimental projects launched by various countries often with external assistance. Two succinct analyses of the problems are contained in brochures published by the International Institute of Education Planning (Unesco), prepared respectively by Griffiths[1] and Hawes.[2] Both are pessimistic.

Beeby in his Foreword to Griffith's brochure remarks that some people will consider the author's views unduly pessimistic. However, it is to be observed that in the Report of the Director General of Unesco on the activities of the Organization in 1972[3] it is stated that 'in general the studies show that attempts to adapt education to rural needs have not met with great success because of lack of concurrence between educational planning and potentialities for educational development and employment in villages'. Further, a review of experience which supports the view that most of the programmes which have an agricultural bias to rural primary schools have failed is contained in *Educational Programmes in Rural Areas* by Brembeck and Hovey.[4]

The difficulties described by Griffith and Hawes are that the teachers are poorly paid and trained and insufficiently motivated towards rural life and that they use 'survival' rather than 'activating' teaching (i.e. they tend to give rote-like instruction which is the easiest to operate in overcrowded classes without equipment, and which involves no risk to the teacher's status of imparting information the pupils do not have). Further, they point out that there are few good jobs for rural areas and the clerical type of skills are the best passport or lottery ticket to break out of a poor environment. Parents and pupils are therefore inclined to prefer literary to practical types of teaching and are in any event sceptical of the capacity of schoolteachers to deal with agricultural and domestic problems.

Effective curriculum development, they say, has to be thought of as requiring 'decades rather than years' and a heavy expenditure of funds which are not likely to be available. Terms used to describe really effective curriculum change are 'a very long and complex operation' (Hawes) and 'the achievement of maximum reform would therefore take a long time, perhaps thirty years or more . . .' (Griffiths). Both, however, as will be shown below, recognize the need for minimum and intermediate as well as maximum objectives.

Brembeck and Hovey draw attention particularly to their failure to satisfy parents' motivations commenting for instance on the failure of the Indian project (Wardha) for free and compulsory seven year courses of manual and productive work for village life state. 'Many reasons are given for the failure but basic among them is that the programme went against what the parents saw as the function of education.'

The minimum programme proposed (by Griffiths) consists of requirements that could be satisfied without much change, i.e. to teach in the upper classes of primary the capacity to read agricultural instruction, write letters, keep records, calculate crop yields. Without scrapping existing books and teachers' work schedules, new material could be inserted related to rural life, or could supplement existing content. Science, and agriculture itself, is not included in the minimum objective since they would require a radical change in the methods of teaching. Nor is there included significant advances in attitudes and habits, though he believes an increase in accuracy and reliability would be brought about in the pupils' present work by an intensive campaign to improve standards in village schools and enforce them.

A suggestion which has been made frequently is that as well as including some rural science in the science syllabus, primary education should be used as a direct vehicle for agricultural education. This would help to break down the estrangement of the education system from the environment; the necessary productive or didactic facilities (school farms or gardens) would be provided for the purpose.

For many years now there has been much discussion and a certain amount of experience of this. The results of experience to date are on the whole negative and most authorities recommend a rural bias to the curriculum and teaching methods rather than agricultural teaching. In some areas, however, especially those highly dependent for their lifelihood on single crops, or specialized agricultural skills, actual practice training in upper primary is not to be ruled out and exists in some countries.

The extent of the rural bias possible in the curriculum in first level education is in fact linked to the prevailing type of educational structure. In the first four or five elementary years which are terminal for most rural children little more can be done than to create in the pupils a feeling for the value of practical work and the problems and possibilities of rural development and to teach ways of avoiding the hazards of health and malnutrition which abound. This can be done as part of the general teaching (e.g. the choice of examples in teaching literacy, arithmetic and history) or through cultivation of school gardens, visits to successful farms, talks and demonstrations by social workers concerned with health and malnutrition, etc.

At the upper primary level the rural bias can be made more intensive as part of a guidance cycle in which some rural science related to the local crops and environmental conditions would be alternated with some practical exposure to working and living conditions and some time passed under controlled conditions in suitable farms. For those who are clearly able to go up the educational ladder the scientific content would be greater but the links with production work would be maintained.

An important reform in this sense has been introduced in Peru. Two streams of basic education (*basica regular* and *basica laboral*), the first more scholastic but linked to the world of work and the latter directly oriented to work, are interlocked in a system of planning by districts which includes nuclear schools for those in the district who can go beyond what the local education offers.

The French-speaking countries of Africa and French aid agencies have also been very active for some time now in seeking solutions to rural education problems. The concept of a two-part cycle of primary education was developed at the 1966 Conference of Ministers of Education of the French-speaking countries. Important experiments of ruralization have been that in Upper Volta (in principle at the post-elementary school level but, in fact, covering many primary age pupils) and, in respect of ruralized elementary education, those in Madagascar, Dahomey and Niger.

Madagascar introduced experimentally in 1962 a rural four-year basic cycle un-der which rural communities would participate and lower salaries would be paid by them than under the standard system. By 1970 the experiment was intended to cover 660 classes or 10 per cent of the elementary school pupils. In fact, only about a hundred were covered. The villages clamoured for 'real schools' and considered the plan undemocratic, as it would tie their children to the peasantry. Dahomey and Upper Volta experienced similar difficulties.

The Upper Volta rural education programme has been a valuable experiment but has been the subject of considerable controversy. In the early 1960s Upper Volta adopted a dual system. As a result some villages now have standard primary schools which give a six-year course ending in a primary school certificate examina-tion which provides entry into the six-year secondary cycle. In other villages the arrangement is for a combined literacy and vocational course in agricultural skills, the age of entry is intended to be between 13 and 15, but in fact some younger children enter.

In the standard primary schools only one out of five pupils gets the certificate, the majority repeat one or two classes and less than one out of ten enters the first grade of secondary. In the centres for rural education the course lasts three years only and there is no promotion or repetition. About half of the time is devoted to teaching literacy and numeracy about the level of lower primary and the rest is spent on prac-tical agricultural skills in fields and workshops attached to the school. The drop-out rate is about one in five.

A study evaluating the dual system is being made by the ICED and its first con-clusions (made by Sven Grabe) can be summarized as follows:[5]

Children who completed the full primary cycle acquired lasting literacy and have mastered the French language, but show alienation from the rural communities. Those who dropped out even after four or five years, and even most of those who stayed the course but failed in the examinations, relapsed into illiteracy. All of those who had some schooling in the standard primary system showed signs of wanting to leave the community and look for work in urban areas. The children who passed the school leaving certificate seek work in commercial or artisan apprenticeship in their own or nearby countries.

In the case of the ruralized education system, the better centres obtained good functional literacy among about half of their students. Although their literacy is in the French language it differs from that of the standard school in the sense that it is more locally orientated from a cultural standpoint than the former. There is great variation between the efficiency of the different education centres depending upon supervision and the time since the teachers had left the teacher training college. Newly trained teachers had better results and better social contacts than those who had stayed in the same village for several years. In one district where supervision was lax the relapse into illiteracy was nearly 100 per cent.

It would seem that although the rural centres are not working as well as had been hoped, they have favourable features which counteract some of those which are unfavourable in the standard primary system. On the other hand, there is evidence of the population taking an increasingly negative attitude towards the centre on the ground that it gives 'second best' education. The paradox is that the pupils emerging from the centres seem better orientated towards the local community's culture and values and are more useful to it, yet the community itself seems to want its children to go to schools which alienate them rather than integrate them with the local community, but which given them the possibility of going to urban areas.

The conclusion to be drawn is an important one for educational policy makers and for overall development strategy. If it is the case, as it would seem, that the future of the country is going to remain for a long time in the level of development of the rural local communities, industry and commerce and urban employment being very small, this would indicate that the government should persist, even if the local population disfavours it, with encouraging the rural centre approach.

However, it would also mean that this approach should be better implemented. It should not only be supervized more uniformly but should be given more financial support, and the land and training facilities provided should be better. If this is done, and if the creation of additional standard primary schools is tapered off in the rural areas, there would be a good chance of the population accepting the rural system progressively as it becomes part of their community life.

There is evidence that the Upper Volta programme for rural education did not have a fair chance. It was prepared hastily was under-financed and the agricultural land given to the schools by the communities was often bad and usable only with excessively fatiguing labour by the pupils.

Another interesting new type of programme in operation in French-speaking Africa, which is one which employs a comprehensive approach in which great attention is given to the problem of local participation is the Mandoul experiment. The comprehensive aspect of the project was that it was part of a programme for the overall development of the Mandoul Valley, and not an isolated education project. Both isolated projects and those on a broad national scale are often exposed to failure, while those built round poles of overall development have more chance of success. In a description in an official report of the French aid authorities,[6] it is stated:

many difficulties were encountered, both on the side of the villagers and the teachers. One of the first obstacles to be overcome is certainly resistance on the part of a certain section of the population astonished by the novelty of the project. On one occasion this resistance took the form of open hostility, and one villager challenged us in front of the whole meeting by saying that 'school is something for teachers and white people and is no concern of the villagers. We don't ask the teachers or the whites to plait sekos'. While this sort of opposition was exceptional it sometimes took the form of equivocation, lateness at meetings or delay in implementing action even when jointly decided upon. To overcome this obstacle we believe it essential that the population be fully briefed on the aims of the project and of the potential advantages to them, and that efforts should be unceasing to disseminate information inside the village compounds.

Two conditions are necessary for this:

—information should be circulated within the village by individuals whom the inhabitants trust, i.e. by respected villagers rather than by the teachers, who at first are regarded as strangers and at best can obtain polite agreement but no wholehearted support;

—it is also essential to associate the official village leaders with the project, to obtain their backing and support. It is not enough to obtain a formal agreement or authorization from the chief of the village—the entire administrative and traditional leadership must be approached. There are various reasons for this: they possess a highly developed grapevine, while owing to their status in the village they can just as easily slow down as speed up the forces of change. Knowing the importance of their role in the village, we organized a meeting with the chiefs and leaders so that they could share directly in the project. The chief of Matekaga I, Matekaga II, compound chiefs, land chiefs, initiation chief, the Ngonbang, the Mohs, elders, the PPT-RDA political delegate, and two women delegates attended the meeting together with the village leaders chosen to deal with the school. The discussion was long but fruitful; we explained the aims of the project and asked them to help directly in discovering new schemes, get people to attend the meetings, promote the wider dissemination of information and to speed up action.

It is not a question of providing information out of politeness but of discussing both broadly and in detail, the aims of the project and the methods to be adopted. The traditional chiefs are responsible for the main aspects of the children's education and it would be a serious mistake to neglect their requirements or to deprive oneself of their knowledge. They are not necessarily hostile to innovations, as shown by the following remark: 'The children must understand everything which has happened in the village so that they should not lose their roots. They learn about everything that happens elsewhere without knowing what takes place in their village. The children used to go to Bangui for their schooling. Now they have a school here in the village and this is a good thing, but the elders must also go to the school and give advice to the children, talk to them about the past so that the customs continue with the young'. These words were spoken by a traditional chief at the end of the meeting referred to, showing a dual concern, that the village should be able to develop by accepting progress while at the same time retaining its culture.

The village selected 18 representatives to go regularly to the school to check on attendance and to give instruction in the school's cotton field. A mimeographed newsletter was also produced with the help of the villagers.

It is clear from the problem of relating education to felt needs, that self-help projects are in principle particularly advantageous. However, they vary in aim and in efficacy and need scrutiny. Some spring from democratic origins and represent original nuclei of self-government by tribes and villagers; others spring from feudal concepts and are sometimes charged with using cheap unpaid labour of the less privileged, while the more privileged contribute money. Some are centred on new and progressive concepts of self-reliance; others reflect the wish of the local population to remain in dysfunctional types of education.

Another approach is to try to create community schools in which both villagers and children participate. This has rarely been implemented in French-speaking Africa so far, except in the private sector in Dahomey. An example of this community school based on the cooperation principle and involving the participation of the children in production is the Litowa school in the Ruruma district of Tanzania. The case for community schools, with examples of the rare experiments which have been made, is contained in *Community Schools in Developing Countries* by Houghton and Tregear.[7]

In most programmes the problem of language is an additional difficulty since local vernaculars abound and there may be two official languages. Language learning may be the main ladder to higher forms of employment for the rural worker, as well as an important contribution to national unity. The teaching of the languages required has to be efficacious and consume as little time as possible, so as not to take up too much of the syllabus. It must be followed up by the provision of reading material. Interesting new methods of the teaching of Swahili are being introduced in Zambia with United Kingdom assistance. There are valuable models for resource centres for literacy materials in some countries, e.g. Indonesia.

The various suggestions which have been made need to be incorporated in a strategy of starting with the most receptive areas, which are the most ready for primary education, and then extending the effort out into those where the prospects are less favourable. In the less favourable areas small primary schools, usually one-class schools, which give a minimum basic education can be effective with trained teachers who receive suitable incentives, provided they are linked to some degree with the nearest full primary school. Thus there would be a double effort extending the full national cycle outwards and at the same time extending a minimum basic and ruralized education inwards. As development increased in the country the two movements would eventually coalesce.

The hope would be that over the twenty years the national formal system as a whole would also have been changed through reforms which would make it more practically orientated, more flexible and continuous in the sense of a start towards lifelong education.

During this process, in order to avoid the restriction of educational opportunity to which parents so much object, it would be necessary to develop the system of ladders and bridges and buffer cycles described in Chapter 10.

It is to be expected that negative attitudes of parents to ruralized or non-formal education would change over time as development takes place (since the mere process of economic development has an impact on the prestige accorded to different types of education and employment) and if new approaches to village participation are used.

Governments need perhaps have fewer qualms about a policy running counter to rural parents' present attitudes if it became clear, as emerges from the ICED research in Upper Volta, that the ruralized education does in fact promote the cultural life of the village, whereas primary education alienates the children from their national culture which is basically rural.

The participation factor will also be accentuated if the effort is linked to existing traditional forms of education, such as the Moslem and Buddhic schools which do in fact act as primary schools and are responsible for making many children literate, though not always with the more modern methods available in the country and with content not geared to development values.

In this connection, Mauritania is interesting. According to the Unesco statistics, only 15 per cent of the population is enrolled, but it is also reported that more than half of the population is literate. The reason for this is the existence of the Koranic schools which do not figure in the official statistics.

An important factor influencing the difficulties and possibilities which have been discussed up to now in this chapter is, of course, the supply and training of suitable teachers. We saw earlier the criticism that teachers in rural primary schools were ill-adapted to their task: that, if trained, they lacked identification with village aims and needs and, if not trained, as is so often the case, employed 'survival' techniques of teaching by rote to avoid problems they could not cope with rather than stimulating the pupils.

A thorough examination of the role of teacher education in promoting rural transformation is contained in a publication with that title published by the National Institute of Education, Makerere University, Kampala, Uganda.

A valuable source of reference is also the article by Bhunthin Attagara.[8] He describes the steps being taken to include work and study in community development in the curriculum for training rural teachers. He states: 'We have tried to use the total environment, and not just the formal instructional period, as an educational instrument to cultivate attitudes of responsibility and hard work'. About a quarter of the instruction time at the teacher colleges is devoted to practical work.

In Tanzania, as part of the Ujaama policy already described in Chapter 9, rural teacher education has been deepened to stress ways of developing attitudes of leadership and social conscience among the teachers, including the promotion of local cultural and community activities.

Additional costs would be involved, since there would have to be more supervision, more training of teachers, better land and material available for demonstration purposes, as well as audio-visual aids and other devices to make the education prestigious as well as effective. The Mexican innovation of prefabricated schools containing living quarters for the teacher will be possible in some areas.

It is impossible to provide in the immediate future schools of rural areas with newly trained teachers or to recycle in a short time those already at work. Further, although the teachers' degree of integration and engagement has to be increased if primary education is to serve rural areas adequately, it is both desirable and unavoidable that teachers of urban origin and urbanized motivations should serve periods in rural areas; otherwise there will be a dual system and educational opportunity will be prejudiced. A period of service in rural areas can be made a requirement, an alternative to military service, or a form of national service. But it would be best that the bulk of the teachers come from the rural areas themselves.

To increase the number of locally recruited teachers would help to reduce the lack of rural jobs and provide avenues for local talent. The extension of rural primary education could thus be an interesting source of employment opportunity to which the average rural child could aspire. This would call for a type of teacher training and selection based on proficiency in conveying minimum basic learning attainments and in practical demonstration, based on activation rather than encyclopaedic teaching methods.

It would also mean applying to teacher education for some years to come the same principles of minimum basic education in teaching combined with opportunity ladders and bridges and buffer cycles which we have recommended for basic education itself.

The qualifications for selection of basic education teachers from those at present expected of the standard primary teacher and would mean some reduction of the years of formal education expected at present for trained teachers, and selection based more on qualities useful for rural life. Local teacher training institutions would need to be set up with opportunity ladders to district and national colleges.

We made earlier the suggestion that certificates should be issued for minimum basic education so that drop-outs who did not complete the full cycle and children who failed the school-leaving examination should not be discouraged. Certificates could also be issued for teachers with proven capacity in basic education, to be accompanied by further training possibilities later. The concept of recurrent education and of ladders and bridges between the non-formal and the formal system and between the minimum of full basic educational streams could be applied to teachers as well as to pupils.

While any system must provide for the requisite degree of mobility of talent from rural areas into cities and other focal points of national development, action is needed to reduce unproductive migration to unemployment in marginal urban areas.

The estimates made by the United Nations show that the worldwide process of urbanization is likely to continue and the proportion of the population in rural areas is likely to decline, although their absolute numbers will increase. For this reason a balance has to be struck in educational policies between, on the one hand, a healthy movement from rural areas to better life in the towns, which means migration of talent from rural areas, and on the other hand, a conservation of talent in the countryside to promote rural development—especially as rural conditions will remain for a long time the circumstances in which most school leaders in the developing countries will live.

The problem of the division of the educational output in the rural areas between the two different needs is not at present being solved, leading to migration to urban unemployment and shanty towns, and we have suggested in the earlier chapter on opportunity and educational ladders and bridges, approaches which may offer some partial solutions. They do not, however, cover the bulk of the problem which is to provide for rural areas and their marginal populations, forms of development and services which will raise both their educational and their living levels. Concerning marginal populations, the United Nations Study on Education, Human Resources and Development in Latin America states:[9]

> None of the countries attaining effective universal education in the past has faced, on a scale comparable with that indicated by present Latin American population trends, the problem of adapting education to the needs of 'marginal' masses, although some of these countries are still struggling with such problems in relation to minorities. Marginal status is compatible with strongly felt needs for education; indeed, some marginal families seem to invest exaggerated hopes in education as an avenue towards higher status for their children, and appreciable proportions of low-income families that have been questioned about reasons for migration to a city mention the attraction of better urban educational opportunities.

We can therefore pull together the threads of this chapter by concluding that the problem of rural primary education has to be solved as part of overall development policies which provide physical investment to raise rural productivity and social services to raise the living levels of the populations, with provision for desirable forms of migration to the towns combined with incentives for the finding and development of talent to remain in the countryside to lead rural development. At the same time, at the level of mass education, both formal and non-formal education have to be extended on a strategy of proceeding along a scale of feasibility. The underlying educational concept should be to maximize literacy and basic education wherever it can be well used and maintained and to relate rural education to the conditions of life and work. This should be combined with the overall view of the child, since it is the primary age group with which we are concerned, and this means the expansion of the services in the fields of health and nutrition which are not only important in their own right, but also play a key role in the child's learning capacity and thereby in educational productivity.

An important measure at all times is bringing the enrolment of girls to equal proportions to those of boys. In rural communities women not only play a key part in the home, in the fields of health and nutrition and family planning, but also have a great influence on the motivation towards development of the family as a whole. Economists, like sociologists, believe that if the impact of the expansion of primary education results in the reduction of the inequalities between the education of boys and of girls, a substantial step will have been taken to improve living levels and motivations for development even on existing levels of income.

Most of the difficulties which have been described we may list under four factors:

Factor A: The attitudes of villagers to the school, and to the function of education.

Factor B: The attitudes of teachers to the rural environment, and their capacity to activate rural children towards its development.

Factor C: The material development which plays an imprtant role in determining these attitudes.

Factor D: The management and 'human engineering' capacities of administrators and project leaders to improve the functioning of the educational process and to devise good educational patterns which will both meet local needs and be actively adopted by local opinion and, at the same time, serve national development objectives.

The greatest chance of success lies in combined action, which ought frequently to extend over into adult education, since this may be the chief way of influencing village attitudes, and into physical development projects, since visible material change is required to spark development incentives.

The strategy has to be one based on feasibility since the difficulties are so great. On the concept of feasibility, which can easily be misused to hold up progress, the United Nations have written:[10]

It must be acknowledged that certain social standards, however desirable, may not be technically feasible, or may be costly to achieve. In such cases, instead of investing tremendous efforts and resources in areas where there is little hope of success, the same resources could be invested more effectively in other areas where they could bring more obvious benefit to a greater number of equally vulnerable people. A certain 'scale of feasibility' could well be developed on the basis of international experience for the guidance of national planners. It should be noted, however, that the level of feasibility of certain programmes is bound to change depending on further methodological or technological progress.

Since the number of children below the educational poverty line is so large it is necessary to deal first with those areas where poles of development exist, but where nonetheless many children are still below but on the margin of receiving a minimum basic education. Initial action to push these children 'over the hump' will yield quicker and more tangible results than attempts to lift all the children at once up to the desired level.

# REFERENCES

1. *the Problems of Rural Education*, V. L. Griffiths, Unesco: IIEP, 1968.
2. *Planning the Primary School Curriculum in Developing Countries*, H. W. R. Hawes, Unesco: IIEP.
3. *Report of Director General*, Unesco 18 C/3, 1972, p. 51.
4. *Educational Programs in Rural Areas*, Cole S. Brembeck and Richard L. Hovey, Unesco SC/W5/507, 1972, pp. 5–11.
5. See Chapter 9, References, No. 17.
6. *Information Report to Development Assistance Committee*, OECD, 1970. See also 'Africa, education from within', Roland Colin, in *CERES* (FAO Review), Vol. IV, No. 3, 1971, p. 63.
7. See Chapter 4, Reference 4.
8. 'The challenge of innovation in teacher education in Thailand', Bunthin Attagara, in *Teacher Education*, International Council on Education for Teaching, Washington D.C., 1972.
9. *Education, Human Resources, and Development in Latin America*, United Nations, 1968, p. 74.
10. *Social Welfare Planning in the Context of National Development Plans*, United Nations ST/SOA/99, New York, 1970, pp. 80–81.

## SELECTED FURTHER READING

*educational Documentation and Information. Bulletin of the International Bureau of Education*, Geneva, No. 183, Unesco, 1972.

*Prospects*, Vol III, No. 2, Unesco, 1973.

*Prospects*, No. 2, Unesco, 1969.

*Education and Training in Botswana*, Swedish International Development Authority, 1972.

*Social Research and Rural Life in Central America, Mexico, and the Caribbean Region*, Unesco, 1966.

*Social Research and the Problems of Rural Life in South-East Asia*, Unesco, 1963.

*Building New Educational Strategies to Serve Rural Children and Youth*, prepared by the International Council for Educational Development for Unicef, E/ICEF/L. 1304, 1974.

*The Mandoul Project—A Rural Education Experiment in Chad. Note by the French Delegation*, OECD DAC) (72)47, September, 1972.

*The Role of Teacher Education in Promoting Rural Transformation*, ed. Carl J. Manone, National Institute of Education, Makerere University, Kampala, 1972.

*World Conference on Agricultural Education and Training. Report, Vols. I and II*, Copenhagen, Denmark, 28 July–8 August, 1970, FAO, Unesco and ILO, RU: AET/70.

*Education in Africa: Research and Action*, Richard Jolly, East African Publishing House, Nairobi.

*Education in a Rural Environment*, Unesco, 1974.

'Education and research in rural development', Theodore W. Schulz, in *Rural Development in Tropical Latin America*, eds. K. L. Turk and L. C. Crowder, New York State College of Agriculture, 1967.

*Education in Rural Areas in the Asian Region—A General Review*, Bulletin of the Unesco Regional Office for Education in Asia, Vol. V, No. 1, September 1970.

'The school as an agent for rural development', David Zarembka, in *Rural Africana*, No. 9, African Studies Center, Michigan State University, 1969.

*Reforms for Rural Primary and Middle Schools; A Draft Program in Communist China*, S. E. Fraser, Society for the Advancement of Education, New York, 1971.

'Education and economic opportunity in Africa', Guy Hunter, in *Development Digest*, Vol. VIII, No. 4, Government Printing Office, Washington, D.C., 1970.

'Education for self reliance: a critical evaluation', Philip Foster, in *Education in Africa: Research and Action*, ed. Richard Jolly, East African Publishing House, Nairobi, 1969.

'Education for the rural community', Guy Hunter, in *African Education: Research and Action*, ed. Richard Jolly, East African Publishing House, Nairobi, 1969.

'Out-of-school education and training for primary-school leavers in rural Kenya: a proposal', Walter Elkan, in *International Labour Review*, Vol. 104, No. 3, ILO, 1971.

# CHAPTER 13

# External Aid: International Cooperation

The Specialized Agency of the United Nations responsible for education is Unesco. It has programmes of its own, largely of a normative and advisory character, but also is the administering agency for other sources of funding in the United Nations system of agencies and for some bilateral agencies under Funds in Trust Agreements.

The overall development of the child is the concern of Unicef, the United Nations Children's Emergency Fund and the Social Affairs Department of the United Nations. Unicef, as a result of a policy review made in 1972, now allocates all its educational aid to basic education and is phasing out its assistance to the second level.

The International Bank for Reconstruction and Development and its associate body, The International Development Association, known together as the World Bank Group, is the largest single international provider of total educational aid, which amounted to $726 million over the period 1969–73, of which only about $18 million, was for basic education. The Bank has, however, recently decided that for 1974–78, out of a lending programme of just over $1400 million for education and training about 27 per cent or $370 m:llion would go to basic education with a proportionate decrease for the other levels. Their aid is in the form of loans, or long term credits at very low rates of interest with a long period of exemption before interest is payable. The Inter-American Development Bank is also a large lender for educational purposes, but has mostly supported higher education.

The United Nations Development Programme, the UNDP, is the largest provider of educational aid of all kinds after the World Bank Group within the United Nations system and its affiliated agencies, but has allocated a small proportion of its resources to primary education. However, it provided $11 million for the Unesco Experimental Literacy Programme which covered a million people 1967–72, whose average age was 24 but many of whom were under 18.

The World Food Programme also helps primary education with substantial sums to provide meals for school children, which permits the funds saved in the recipient countries to be used for other means of the development of primary education. The International Labour Organization, the ILO, and the Food and Agricultural Organization, FAO, also support out-of-school education for older children and adolescents in non-formal education.

The Organization of American States through the Inter-American Council for

Education, Science, and Culture, and the Commission of European Communities have substantial educational assistance programmes. The European Development Fund has also provided capital aid for education. The Colombo Plan also has supplied assistance to Asian countries, and the Commonwealth Fund for Technical Cooperation helps Commonwealth countries. Other Commonwealth activities provide technical assistance under various regional funds, e.g. the Special Commonwealth African Assistance Plan (SCAAP), the plan for Technical Assistance to Non-Commonwealth Countries in Africa (TANCA), and the Commonwealth Scholarship and Bursary Scheme. A new source of aid recently established is the Programme of the United Nations Volunteers set up by the UN General Assembly as from January 1971.

The Rockefeller, Ford and Carnegie Foundations have very substantial educational aid programmes.

Of the individual countries which give educational aid to developing countries on a bilateral basis, the largest single donor of educational aid at all levels is France, followed by the Gerhan Federal Republic, the United States, the United Kingdom and a number of other countries, notably Belgium, Sweden, Canada and Australia. Most large bilateral donors have, like the international agencies (with the exception of Unicef) largely concentrated upon the second and higher levels of general education, and upon technical education, and have given little support to primary. This has largely resulted from the view that educational aid had to be linked to the immediate problems of nation building and economic development in the newly developing countries by meeting the needs for cadres of people trained at the second, technical and third levels.

This view, as indicated elsewhere, is gradually changing. Unesco has revived its interest in primary education and the Commission on International Development of Education (the Faure Commission) which it set up, recommended that basic education should be given top priority for the 1970s.

At one time bilateral donors were concerned with providing teaching staff at the primary level, but this has now become unnecessary as the countries have set up their own teaching forces.

Accordingly, today the aid given consists of assistance in modernizing their primary educational systems rather than the actual supply of effectives or materials. Unicef, and also some bilateral donors, do provide equipment, but it is usually in the form of material supplies needed such as paper and printing machinery for textbooks, equipment, jeeps etc., as part of pilot projects or other programmes designed to produce improvements in educational organization and content, in methods and teaching aids and in teacher training.

Among the bilateral donors. Sweden, France and Canada show special interest in primary education. In addition, there is a very substantial educational aid effort going to the developing countries from non-governmental organizations. The proportion of this overall aid which goes to primary education is considerably higher than in the case of the international or bilateral donors, since the voluntary organizations, mostly religious groups, have traditionally been concerned with education at the local level and the establishment of missionary schools.

Many of the innovatory projects mentioned in earlier chapters have been assisted by external aid and often started off by them.

The joint Unicef-Unesco guidelines governing their new policy states:[1] 'New approaches are essential to provide the mass of educationally deprived children and youth with basic and continuing educational opportunities. Unicef in collaboration with Unesco should place a priority on this field which includes out-of-school education and the use of new media'.

Among the types of project to be aided are those which bring about changes of educational structures and patterns; curriculum reform; the training of educational personnel; the improvement of the school environment such as community schemes to expand the enrolment of girls, improve nutrition, etc.; and other educational services of a technical nature such as the improvement of the production of teaching material and assistance for new textbooks etc.

Unicef is also continuing its aid, under its joint programme with Unesco, to ongoing needs of the educational system such as the training of teachers, whether pre-service or in-service and the production of science equipment suitable for use at the primary level; and it has a special interest, in view of the role of women in child welfare, in encouraging the education of girls.

The aid given by the UNDP through Unesco, which is its executive agency, is mostly for the training of teacher educators and teacher training. Projects are also assisted which deal with rural education, especially pilot projects which may have a multiplier effect.

The World Bank Group is becoming increasingly concerned about the deficits in primary education and basic education for adolescents and adults who missed schooling. The annual report of the World Bank Group for 1973 indicates the policy trend as follows:[2]

The greater emphasis on objectives of social equity is reflected in several of the education projects which have been financed during the last five years. It is reflected also in the studies and research which are being done. Both actual operations and studies reflect a new strategy, with greater stress on people in the traditional-transitional sectors of the economy which have hitherto been left outside education systems. The aim is to find appropriate ways to enable education systems to promote both economic growth and social justice. This has required a comprehensive approach at all levels and areas of both formal and non-formal education and training.

It also states:

In the education sector, the Bank and IDA for the first time supported projects—in Indonesia and Lebanon—devoted mainly to the development of primary education. In both a central aim was to make educational opportunities more widely available to all population groups in the country.

The assistance took the form in the case of Lebanon of a loan for primary education of $6·6 million at $7\frac{1}{4}$ per cent repayable as from 1978. This was provided by the World Bank in the form of what is known as a 'hard' loan. In the case of Indonesia, the assistance was given by the IDA in the form of a 'soft' credit of $12 million with only a nominal service charge of $\frac{3}{4}$ per cent, and repayment to be spread over the period 1983 to 2023. The Sector Working Paper on education, published by the Bank in December 1974, which heralds the new policy, states:

> In countries where mass education can be achieved through the expansion of the primary system, the Bank will give particular attention to curriculum and other reforms which take into account the needs of the many who will not continue beyond the primary cycle. A review and revision of education structures will be encouraged to provide low-cost, minimum, mass education in poor countries with low primary school enrtlment ratios. A variety of programs for youths and adults will also be supported as a follow-up, or, when necessary, as an alternative to primary education.

The World Bank under the presidency of Robert MacNamara intends to react to the fact that the development which they have been aiding, like other agencies, over the last decade has not been equitably distributed and is not reaching the poor.

In his address to the Board of Governors of the World Bank Group in Nairobi in September 1973, MacNamara stated:[3] 'Experience demonstrates that in the short run there is only a limited transfer of benefits from the modern to the traditional sector. Disparities in income will simply widen unless action is taken which will directly benefit the poorest'. While recognizing that the problem is basically for the governments themselves, he stressed the need for development of the rural areas where 70 per cent of the population of the developing countries lives and where, by the year 2000, the percentage will still be as high as 50 per cent. Efforts should be made, assisted by international resources on a world scale, to reduce the number of people, estimated at 40 per cent of the total, who are living below the poverty line in the developing countries.

In his earlier address in September of 1972 in Washington, he had stated in regard to the poor farmer:[4] 'His nation may have doubled or tripled its educational budget and in the capital city there may be an impressive university. But for 300 million children of poor farmers like himself there are still no schools—and for hundreds of millions of others if a school, no qualified teachers—and if a qualified teacher, no adequate books'.

These remarks are significant coming from the president of a group which approved development lending totalling $3555 million during the year ended in June 1973.

In international educational circles, notably in Unesco, as was witnessed by an important intervention by Rene Maheu, the Director General, during the United Nations Economic and Social Council Session in the summer of 1973, the same shift of emphasis is taking place. There are, therefore, prospects for increased attention to aid to primary education.

In the aid agencies such a shift of policy requires a period of adjustment and a series of measures of redeployment. For aid to be switched from one educational level to another the technical 'backstopping' has to be changed since it varies according to the different levels of education. Agencies have to strengthen their expertise, documentation and research and development activities in the field of primary education which has hitherto been somewhat neglected. Further, the type of external assistance required is different.

In higher and technical education and general secondary education the component of capital equipment and outside expertise required is higher than in the case of the primary level. There is thus a greater need to use local rather than imported resources, both material and human. An essential feature of aid to primary education must be assistance directed more closely to aiding the countries to help themselves.

Further, in view of the need to find new patterns of teaching and learning and to adopt innovation in structure and content, it will be particularly important that aid should concentrate upon research and development and experimentation. This means assistance for the training of research workers, educators and administrators, so as to develop the country's capacity to innovate. It will also involve some direct financing of the local costs of experiment.

At present aid agencies do not normally finance local costs, expecting the recipient countries to carry this expenditure. The governments of most developing countries, however, like those elsewhere, are disinclined to take risks in experimentation, which may run counter to the traditional wishes of parents, where success is not assured by sound precedents.

There is, therefore, an important role for external aid in helping countries in risk-taking, which is essential, as we saw earlier, to bringing about the necessary reform, innovation and renovation of primary education.

At present, external aid represents about 15 per cent of the total educational budgets of the developing countries. The amount of assistance going to primary education, however, is only about 1 or 2 per cent of the total expenditure of the developing countries on education at the first level. We may, therefore, hope to see a substantial increase in assistance to primary education from the redeployment of present educational assistance, even if the total amount does not increase.

Increased aid to primary education should be prepared and carried out in the spirit of the approach which substitutes the words 'international cooperation' for the expression 'aid'. Rene Maheu, the Director General of Unesco, described the evolution of the aid process in his speech to the Economic and Social Council of the United Nations in July 1973. He stated:[5]

The situation which had existed in the 1960s no longer prevailed, and a new phase was opening with needs, possibilities and responsibilities which required new attitudes.

Firstly, it was now better realized that financial and technical assistance were especially useful if their aim was to facilitate the establishment or strengthening of the recipient countries' structures and cadres for their own development. Since it was intended to increase their potential rather than their present performances, such aid was necessarily medium-term or long-term and was therefore particularly suitable for action by the specialized agencies.

Secondly, it was becoming increasingly evident that international assistance, though naturally provided at the request of and in cooperation with the governments concerned, should not contribute to the systematic consolidation of the economic and social *status quo*. The distribution of the gross national product among the citizens of individual countries should be as much a matter of concern as inequalities in the gross national products of different countries. Development was therefore objectively linked to change, and assistance from international organs should be channelled principally towards innovation enterprises. That was where it would pay the greatest dividends and where international organizations could best serve Governments.

Thirdly, international systems should be adapted to the new concepts and profound changes which had emerged in the situation and attitudes of recipient countries. The contribution of international organizations should increasingly be seen as a means of promoting the maximum mobilization and optimum utilization of national resources. On an average, the national effort accounted for about 80 per cent of the development process; the 20 per cent which international assistance represented was best used in furthering that national effort and should therefore be increasingly integrated into the national system.

The value of cooperation in the preparation and adoption of policies, strategies and plans was becoming increasingly apparent. Unesco has had experience of such cooperation for some years in the key areas of educational, scientific and cultural policies. That new relationship between national authorities and international organizations could no longer be referred to as aid or assistance, but constituted cooperation in the form of joint research, in which the role of the international organization was primarily to encourage and perhaps to expand that research, but not to direct it.

A summary of suggestions for improving the aid process for education, which apply to primary as well as to the other levels was set out in a recent publication by the International Institute for Educational Planning.[6]

## REFERENCES

1. U.N. Documents E/ICEF/L) 1279 and Add. 1, 1972.
2. *Annual Report*, World Bank/International Development Association, 1973.
3. *Address to the Board of Governors*, Robert S. McNamara, President World Bank Group, September 1973.
4. *Address to the Board of Governors*, Robert S. McNamara, President World Bank Group, September 25, 1972.
5. Speech to the Economic and Social Council of the United Nations, Rene Maheu, Director General, Unesco, July, 1973.
6. Planning Educational Assistance for the Second Development Decade, Paris, Unesco: IIEP, 1973.

226

# SELECTED FURTHER READING

*Annual Reports* of Director General to the Unesco Executive Board and to the Economic and Social Council of the United Nations on the Activities of the Organization, Unesco.
*Annual Reports*, World Bank/International Development Association.
*Reports* of the Main Bilateral Aid Agencies to their Legislatures.
*Inducing Social Change in Developing Communities, An International Survey of Expert Advice*, Herbert H. Hyman, Gene N. Levine and Charles R. Wright, United Nations Research Institute for Social Development, 1967.
*Development Assistance Review*, Edwin M. Martin, Chairman of the Development Assistance Committee, OECD, 1970.
'International aid for educational development in the form of technical assistance and real resources', H. M. Phillips, in *The Economics of Education*, eds. E. A. G. Robinson and J. E. Vaizey, MacMillan, 1966.
*Aid in Uganda—Education*, Peter Williams, Overseas Development Institute Ltd., 1966.
*The Integration of External Assistance with Educational Planning in Nigeria*, L. Cerych, Unesco: IIEP, 1967.
*Evaluating Development Assistance*, OECD, 1972.
*Education Renewal Fund*, World Council of Churches and World Council of Christian Education, Geneva.
*The Final Report of the Joint Study Commission on Education, 1964–1968*, The World Council of Churches and The World Council of Christian Education, Geneva, 1968.
*Education in Developing Countries, A Review of Current Problems and of British Aid*, Ministry of Overseas Development. Her Majesty's Stationery Office, London, 1970.
*Voluntary Foreign Aid Programs*, Reports of American Voluntary Agencies engaged in Overseas Relief and Development registered with the Advisory Committee on Voluntary Foreign Aid, Department of State, Agency for International Development, Washington, D.C., 1971.
*Oikoumene. Service Programme and List of Projects, 1973*, World Council of Churches.
*Education: Sector Working Paper*, World Bank, September 1971.
*New Trends in Service by Youth*, United Nations Department of Economic and Social Affairs, New York, 1971.
*Aid to Education in Less Developed Countries*, Note by the Secretariat, OECD, April 1971.
*La France et l'Aide a l'Éducation dans 14 États Africains et Malgache*, Andre Labrousse, Unesco: IIEP Occasional Papers, No. 22, 1971.
*International Cooperation in Education*, H. M. Phillips, International Commission on the Development of Education, Series B: *Opinions*, No. 49, Unesco, 1971.

CHAPTER 14

# Summary and List of Suggestions

There follows a summary and a list of the principal points suggested for action or research and experiment in the various chapters. They inevitably oversimplify many intricate issues discussed in the text and not all of the suggestions are applicable to every developing country.

Several hundred million children and youth in the developing countries were growing up in 1975 without the prospect of obtaining literacy, owing to lack of school places and high rates of drop-out. For 1985 the estimate is higher.

This is a serious socio-political, as well as pedagogic, situation. It is part of the fundamental issue of mankind's economic and social development, and the historic dilemma of the division of the world between the 'haves' and the 'have nots'—a division particularly unfortunate in the case of education, since it is both one of the stepping stones to worldwide development and also a basic human right.

While the extent of basic education in any given country is closely influenced by the country's overall level of development, there is substantial room to manoeuvre. This is evident from the large variations, in the proportions of children enrolled, between countries at similar levels of development.

The governments of the developing countries aim to universalize primary education; but the projections for the developing countries as a whole suggest a period of stagnation and even regression of progress on the existing basis, owing mainly to a bulge in the rate of population growth which is passing through the school age population, relief from which will not be felt until the middle 1980s.

Further the burden of the increase in world oil prices on the economies of most of the developing countries may cause delays in implementing both present and future programmes. Nevertheless planning and initial action should take place now, as what is required is a vital long-term investment, the cost of which is relatively small. Given the political will on the part of governments to reshape, where necessary, their educational priorities (which are in any event now moving in many cases towards basic education owing to some over-production at the other levels), and given the capacity of educators to make the necessary innovations (which would be mainly organizational), mass educational poverty in the sense described could be to a large extent alleviated within the next two decades, though there would remain some particularly difficult countries, and areas of countries, which are least developed.

The challenge is how to hasten the process of universalization and also to improve the education given. Qualitatively, the situation is dominated by poor methods of teaching and learning and lack of relevance to the environment. Large proportions of the teaching force remain untrained, despite important efforts made for teacher training.

Reform of structure and curricula is on the move but primary education is still for the most part designed to serve the few who continue up the educational system rather than the great mass of children for whom the primary cycle is terminal (half of them leave before having four years of education). Insufficient effort is made at present to offer these children a minimum package of teaching and learning needs, suited to their personal development in their environment, which would bring them above the educational poverty line.

New conceptions of the role of primary education as a social instrument are under discussion, and these need to be applied without harming its role as the underpinning of the educational system as a whole. Difficult problems pedagogic and organizational have to be solved but while there are an increasing number of adherents to the new ideas, there are not enough statesmen, educators or administrators applying them. Nor is there enough applied research and experimentation—an important process for which funds, both national and international, are woefully inadequate.

Developing countries with large proportions of children below the educational poverty line would need to concentrate, for the next two decades, on a drive to universalize basic education in the sense of four or five years to provide a minimum package of learning needs, rather than on attempting to universalize a full 7- or 10-year cycle.

This does not mean that as part of their normal educational development the late primary and early secondary grades, which are so important in laying the basis for skills in industry and commerce and for the effectiveness of the other educational levels, should not also be nurtured. They must continue to be extended to a larger section of the population in accordance with economic requirements and possibilities and subject to the priority of at least a minimum basic education for all as a human right.

A nation cannot be built on minimum education alone and the right to at least minimum education includes at least minimum educational opportunity. There is thus a task of educational 'engineering' to produce a minimum set of ladders, bridges and buffer cycles to facilitate movement between schools which have varying degrees of completeness of curricula in order to develop educational opportunity. An important effort of educational planning, of the kind applied to the educational system as a whole, is needed within the primary cycle.

A stock-taking is required as a first step and a new diagnosis of needs in each country, taking into account their present enrolment ratios, their population growth, their financial capacity to support universal basic education and their overall development plan.

This should be followed by a plan for universalizing at least basic minimum education and opportunity throughout the country. The plan should set out the options and time spans involved.

Execution of the plan should be phased along a scale of feasibility, the most promising areas, where developing is occurring or is in view, being taken first for the expansion of the existing system. The least developed areas, where enrolment is very low, must be dealt with on a more long-term basis and with perhaps entirely new methods. Improvements and innovations in educational methods, technology and management, as well as in structure, are needed to increase efficiency and to speed progress over the whole front.

Considerable external aid from the more advanced countries is required to help countries to face the challenge with new efforts and methods, to tide them over immediate deficiencies in finance, expertise and materials and to increase their longer term capacity to plan, undertake and manage the necessary improvements and innovation: in structural organization and pedagogic methods. They must be helped less than in the past by expertise and institution building based on Western patterns and more by direct aid to them that they may find solutions fitted to their own needs and aspirations and undertake local research and development in regard to new learning and teaching patterns.

Factors both positive and negative which will determine the pace of progress are numerous.

*Positive factors* are: the difficulties of financing universal basic education of a minimum kind tend to be overrated in all except the very least developed countries and, in reality, more leeway exists in most countries than is usually supposed—the average finance devoted to education as a whole in 1971 was not more than 15 per cent of the national budget and 3·0 per cent of GNP. The total yearly expenditure of the developing countries on primary education covers three-quarters of the world's children but is, in total, only about half their annual military expenditure, only about a tenth of the sales of the world's two largest motor manufacturers in 1973, and only about a half of the gifts of funds made annually by Americans to religious causes; only half the educational budgets of the developing countries went to primary education and some internal switch of resources should be possible in view of the over-production at the other levels; a number of financial arguments commonly used are fallacious, e.g. that costs are becoming unbearable, whereas the proportion of GNP spent on education is declining and current costs are often for overlong primary cycles, some countries, e.g. India already have four-fifths or nearly four-fifths of their children in school for a four-year period; the momentum among educators in favour of innovation and reform is mounting, as for example in the recent setting up by Unesco of the Asian Programme of Educational Innovation for Development (APEID), the earlier creation by the South East Asian Ministers of Education Organization (SEAMEO) of INNOTECH, and the findings of the International Commission on Educational Development (the Faure Report), and political pressures are growing; some national examples of reform and innovation in the required direction, important though few, are appearing, e.g. in Peru, Tanzania and Sri Lanka (Ceylon).

230

*Negative factors* are: the population bulge, although temporary, is increasing the backlog of unschooled children and adolescents becoming adult; further, it is to be expected that, as the effort to universalize education extends into less developed areas, an increasing number of difficulties will be experienced; national income, though growing, is generally maldistributed, as are educational services; unit costs are hard to change, as cost is made up 90 per cent by teachers' salaries—too high, relatively to *per capita* income, in a few countries, too low in most; innovation and reform in education are difficult and slow; too much adaptability cannot be expected from teachers who are often untrained, poorly paid and under-qualified; the environmental conditions causing drop-out will take a long time to improve and they are, in some cases, stagnating at low levels; poverty will continue to take its toll on the schooling of children; not all countries are politically motivated to giving priority to primary education and, where the motivations exist, there is not always available the necessary expertise to execute reforms; the organizational and management issues involved are difficult ones; there is a paucity of documentation, and adequate statistics, of research and experimentation in new methods; population growth is exceeding enrolment in both Africa and Asia.

These sets of factors may well balance each other out unless action is taken to tilt the balance. *The danger, and here lies the heart of the challenge*, is that both the policies of the developing countries and the aid given by the advanced countries will be based on continuing on existing lines. This would be serious, because educational change is by nature slow to be accepted and, even when adopted, the maturation period of its benefits is long.

What is required now is the stock-taking already mentioned and the planning of actual measures and innovations to be taken as early as possible, which will aim at a large measure of universalization of basic education in the next two decades. A set of suggestions for such measures is contained under the different chapter headings of Part 3.

## LIST OF SUGGESTED MEASURES

**Planning and Finance; Population Coverage**

(1) Make a map of the population of children and youth under 18 who are below the educational poverty line, that is those who are growing up illiterate and without the chance of a minimum basic education; show the causes by type of area; make projections of the present rate of progress and estimated growth of the school age population over the next 20 years to show the time required to obtain minimum basic education for all.

(2) Evaluate the results of (1) in the light of the economic and social importance of basic education, as compared with that of the other educational levels and other social and economic objectives; take into account that a minimum basic education is a fundamental human right.

(3) Replace the prevailing concept of 'access to education' by that of 'delivery' of at least minimum basic education and minimum opportunity for further education for

all children; no longer treat the human right to education as conditional as some authorities do, but regard it as an absolute right to a minimum basic education limited only by supply possibilities; take overall view of child development including health, nutrition and family planning.

(4) Improve statistics so that they show regularly the chances of children in different localities of receiving at least four years of education and indicate the extent and distribution of unenrolment and drop-out.

(5) Consider necessary reforms of educational structure, content and methods to assure universal population coverage with relevant basic education by the target date, set up the necessary medium- and long-term plans to provide schools and teachers; include 'crash' programmes for illiterate youth in areas of rapid development.

(6) Consider additional financing of basic education by a combination of the following measures: (a) increasing the educational budget; (b) redistributing resources between the educational levels within existing expenditure; (c) using more local resources (e.g. earmarked local taxes and levies on employers) accompanied by district planning; (d) improving cost efficiency.

(7) Eliminate the cost of education falling on disadvantaged parents in the form of fees, uniforms etc.

**Educational Organization**

(8) Reduce drop-out by providing or organizing school meals, school transport and visits to parents in the home.

(9) Set up non-formal education projects which will create literacy and elementary education for those adolescents, who missed primary schooling or dropped out too soon, who are in areas where development is active or imminent.

(10) Utilize the various means of public communication and cooperation in the community (radio, cooperatives etc.), as links with the school programmes.

(11) Create or adapt district nuclear schools to be outlets for pupils from incomplete rural schools; set up district production centres for simple teaching aids.

(12) Construct subsidized ladders for selected pupils to move from low or incomplete primary to upper primary schools and organize public and private facilities to assist the geographical movement of children for the purpose, such as boarding, utilizing religious, tribal, family and other group affiliations as well as public services.

(13) Devise selection tests for the purpose which offset as far as possible the deficiencies due to poor teaching and shortage of textbooks in incomplete rural schools; include qualities required for contribution to the local community as well as intellectual quotient; give success under new types of selection the necessary

prestige for recruitment to the public services with the provision of follow-up and buffer courses during employment.

(14) Give compensatory or buffer courses to ease the transition of children from poor lower primary schools to higher or from non-formal to formal education.

(15) Use self-help subsidized or cooperative programmes to build or improve schools and provide school gardens and organize transport to school.

(16) Vary school hours and years of attendance to suit local conditions.

(17) Create links with the world of work and facilitate them by adopting intermittent and part-time education in suitable cases.

(18) Experiment with community schools, covering both older children and adolescents and adults.

(19) Create intermittent movement between formal and available non-formal education in the later years of primary.

(20) Allocate funds and seek external support for setting up such 'nuclear' networks, even in embryo, and set up small district planning offices, each including an agent to stimulate local cooperation of population.

(21) Extend such embryo networks along a scale of feasibility.

(22) Adapt traditional education (e.g. Koranic schools, tribal initiation procedures etc.) to developmental as well as cultural needs by advice and subsidies.

**Teachers**

(23) Undertake programmes of the necessary initial and in-service training of the teaching force and review salaries and status.

(24) Examine the benefit to be derived from a much larger investment than at present in improving the status, qualifications, training and salaries of teachers in the light of the evidence of the economic value of primary education.

(25) Consider offering teachers delayed future benefits, to come into operation in easier times, when the backlog of unschooled children has been reduced and there is only population growth to be met.

(26) Recruit rural teachers increasingly among rural people and set up district training centres for teachers; include part-time teachers who can give practical training for the second half of the primary cycle and for non-formal education.

(27) Apply the principle of minimum basic training to the supply of rural teachers and progressively replace untrained teachers by the output of district training institutions, set up especially to give such training.

(28) Link such district teacher training institutions to the national system by oppor-

tunity ladders, bridges and buffer cycles, for rural teachers as shown above for pupils of incomplete rural schools.

(29) Hold seminars on educational change in teacher training colleges and give special consideration to the promotion of teachers who excel in them; give extra remuneration for headmasters of more advanced primary schools to visit and advise the more backward.

(30) Establish teacher training curricula which include both rural and national needs, but with a rural bias in the district training institutions, and arrange selection of teachers in cooperation with rural district leaders.

(31) Ensure greater teacher participation in primary educational policy and execution, as well as the local community.

(32) Use the new media and mechanical aids to assist the teaching force where the cost benefit is favourable.

(33) Use the so-called 'micro' or 'clinical' techniques in teacher training colleges to enable teachers to see their own weaknesses and correct them.

## Content, Curricula, Methods, Research and Development, Administration

(34) Work out the optimum package of minimum learning needs for different districts and regions and how they can best be blended with national requirements.

(35) Evaluate how these learning needs are met at present in the content of curricula and the changes necessary.

(36) Adopt an integrated approach embracing the main factors involved in curriculum reform, notably research and evaluation, the retraining of teachers, the consequent alterations required in the examination system, the supply of new teaching materials, etc.

(37) Set up the necessary administrative coordination arrangements to ensure an integrated approach to curriculum development and establish curriculum development centres.

(38) Train curriculum development personnel and other specialists to give more attention to the first level of education.

(39) Increase the link between the school and agriculture by inserting more practical work in the curriculum, especially in every-day science, without trying to train children prematurely for agricultural work.

(40) Consider establishing certificates for basic education as an incentive for pupils to stay and so reduce drop-out in the fourth year.

(41) Retrain and recycle teacher educators and inspectors, as may be necessary, in addition to teachers in reformed curricula.

(42) Increase inspection and the quality of inspectors, but encourage local innovatory initiatives on agreed lines in the classrooms.

(43) Consider new educational methods which may be applicable, e.g. the ungraded school, the use of monitors and team teaching, the mastery method, programmed instruction, etc.

(44) Apply the new methods and kits for science teaching, adapted to basic education.

(45) Study the results of repetition of grades and consider automatic promotion combined with compensatory courses, particularly for children not speaking in the home the language of instruction.

(46) Allocate more resources to research and development and to experimentation; seek external aid for this purpose with a view to training more local cadres of educators and administrators in the capacities required and for experimental projects locally designed but stimulated by assistance from outside sources.

(47) Set up the required programmes of research and development and experimentation to define (a) types of minimum learning needs for children and youth related both to local and to national needs; (b) alternative methods of instruction and types of teaching–learning patterns to be followed, e.g. mastery learning as compared with the competitive approach; (c) the minimum qualifications and types of training for teachers to carry out such programmes; (d) the examination, selection and certification processes required to meet both the objectives of minimum basic education and of minimum opportunity and to make the system function both pedagogically and socially; (e) the action to be taken with parents, employers and community leaders to facilitate acceptance of the changes involved and to secure their participation in the organization and promotion of the programme.

(48) Make the research essentially of an applied rather than a theoretical nature in view of the difficulties which abound; improve diagnosis of needs and preparation of programmes and projects by using research institutions both national and provincial or district, as well as provincial or district authorities, to establish data and recommend action.

(49) Set up check-list of points to be studied and verified for establishing viable programmes and projects for minimum education, both formal and non-formal, especially for rural areas.

(50) Adopt measures to increase the commitment of local population to viewing and using education as an instrument of rural development.

(51) Exchange information on innovation both within the country and internationally.

(52) Undertake information work with rural parents to reduce drop-out due to child employment and to reduce bias on their part in favour of clerical education for their children; ensure their participation in projects for educational changes.

(53) Diminish obstacles to the education of girls, e.g. by increasing the number of women teachers, providing group transport to school, persuading parents by visits to their homes, etc.

(54) Set up 'watchdog' committees at the various administrative levels, central and regional, to check on progress on the spread of basic education and provide them with the necessary statistical data.

This list of suggestions as Mr. Platt indicates in the Preface is by no means a prescription and only a set of pointers but certainly the steps described in the first 7 points should be undertaken by all countries.

The main obstacles in most countries would be likely to be (1) the time required to design and apply the necessary changes; (2) deficiencies in the financial inputs needed to generate educational change (such as expenditure on educational research and development, experimentation and staff training and 'pump priming' funds to start new programmes and projects); (3) shortages of the planning, organizing, pedagogic and managerial skills required; (4) difficulties of a political or traditional nature in developing the social as distinct from the pedagogic role of education.

In the least developed countries and provinces which have very low enrolment ratios and poor economies, but which fortunately cover only a small part of the total child population of the developing countries, these obstacles will be particularly difficult. What seems to be required is a simple work-orientated form of instruction, mostly non-formal in type, which should be founded in the villages and move out towards the formal system as development took place and as the formal system itself was effectively able to extend itself outwards. The measures in this sense which were discussed are still largely experimental and these areas present a special challenge to education to continue to experiment with innovatory solutions.

# APPENDIXES

# Indicators for 93 Developing Countries

1. Educational and financial statistics taken from *Unesco Statistical Yearbooks, 1972* and *1973* and the World Bank Sector Paper, December 1974. Certain figures from *Bulletin of the Unesco Regional Office for Education in Asia*, No. 14, June 1973 and *Progress of Education in the Asian Region: A Statistical Review*, Unesco Regional Office for Education in Asia, 1969.
2. GNP figures and population size are taken from 1973 *World Bank Atlas*.
3. Other population statistics from *Unesco Statistical Yearbook*, from UN Population Division estimates, and from papers prepared by Unesco Statistical Office for World Population Conference, 1974.
4. Statistics on tax ratios taken from 'Measuring tax effort in developing countries', by Jorgan R. Lotz and Elliot R. Morss in *Staff Papers, Washington, International Monetary Fund*, Vol. XIV, No. 3, November 1967.
5. Enrolment figures, financial figures and pupil/teacher ratios are for 1970, 1971 to 1974, excepting those marked * which are for 1969 or between 1965 and 1968; those marked † are for years before 1965. Illiteracy figures are particularly varied as to their dates; see *Literacy 1969–1971*, Unesco, 1972.
6. There are a considerable number of gaps since statistics are not available for some countries or are too early in date to use—places have been left which the reader may wish to fill as statistics become available from, for example, the next edition of the Unesco *Statistical Yearbook*. In using the figures regard should be paid to the footnotes in the Yearbook describing the nature of the figures and their basis.
7. The enrolment ratios are 'gross' in the sense that they include, as we pointed out in detail in Chapter 3, over-age pupils and repeaters. Thus, the total number of children in school at any given time is compared with the number of pupils in the age group for the cycle (Item D). Net enrolment ratios, which show the proportion of children in the declared age group for the cycle who are actually in school are lower. These are shown in the Unesco *Statistical Yearbook* for 1971. For the purpose of showing the actual education taking place the gross figures are preferable even though they inflate the enrolment ratios.

## LIST OF INDICATORS

A. Gross Enrolment Ratio (first level)
B. Average Annual Rate of Growth of Enrolment, age group 6–11, 1960–70

C.  Projected Enrolment Ratio, 1985, age group 6–11
D.  Number of Grades of Primary Cycle
E.  Pupil/Teacher Ratio for first level
F.  GNP *per capita* ($US)
G.  GNP *per capita* Annual Percentage Growth Rate, 1965–71
H.  Population Size (millions)
I.  Average Annual Percentage Population Growth Rate, age group 0–4, 1970–85
J.  Average Annual Percentage Population Growth Rate, age group 6–11, 1970–85
K.  Percentage of GNP devoted to Expenditure on Education (all levels)
L.  Percentage of National Budget allocated to Education (all levels)
M.  Percentage of Total Current Public Expenditure on Education allocated to First Level
N.  Proportion of GNP raised in Taxation
O.  Percentage of Illiteracy

| Country | Bhutan | Yemen Arab Republic of | Somalia | Ethiopia | Mauritania | Upper Volta | Niger | Mali | Sudan |
|---|---|---|---|---|---|---|---|---|---|
| A | 7* | 9* | 10 | 11* | 12* | 13 | 14 | 20 | 20* |
| B | 24·0 | 7·1 | 4·6 | 11·4 | 12·1 | 5·5 | 13·0 | 9·0 | 8·8 |
| C | 16·1 | 14·6 | 6·4 | 13·7 | | 10·7 | 12·4 | 19·0 | 32·1 |
| D | 6–12 | 7–12 | 8–11 | 7–12 | 6–11 | 6–11 | 7–12 | 6–14 | 7–12 |
|   | (7 years) | (6 years) | (4 years) | (6 years) | (6 years) | (6 years) | (6 years) | (9 years) | (6 years) |
| E | 22 | 40 | 35 | 51 | 22 | 45 | 40 | 40 | 45 |
| F | 80 | 90 | 70 | 80 | 170 | 70 | 100 | 70 | 120 |
| G | 0·4 | 2·4 | 0·8 | 1·2 | 2·1 | 1·7 | −4·4 | 1·0 | −0·9 |
| H | 1 | 6 | 3 | 25·3 | 1·2 | 5·5 | 4 | 5·1 | 16·1 |
| I | 1·4 | 3·1 | 3·5 | 2·5 | 3·2 | 2·6 | 3·4 | 2·8 | 3·4 |
| J | | 3·6 | 2·1 | 2·8 | 3·0 | 2·8 | 3·6 | 3·0 | 3·8 |
| K | | 1·0 | | 2·8 | 4·5 | 4·0 | 1·9† | 4·6 | 4·5 |
| L | | 5·1 | 7·9 | 18·3 | 26·6 | 14·1† | 18·7 | 19·5* | 12·6 |
| M | 17·4 | | 64·0 | 56·7 | 69·1† | 38·8 | 60·0 | 52·2 | 40·3 |
| N | | | | 8·3 | | | 12·0 | 15·4 | 13·3 |
| O | | | | | 88·9 | | 99·1† | 97·8† | 88·0† |

| Country | Afghanistan | Portuguese Guinea | Burundi | Gambia | Nepal | Sierra Leone | Chad | Guinea |
|---|---|---|---|---|---|---|---|---|
| A | 22 | 25* | 26* | 26* | 28* | 29* | 30* | 33 |
| B | 12.4 | 4.7 | 6.3 | 9.6 | 8.0 | 8.3 | 10.7 | 7.9 |
| C | 17.8 | | 30.2 | | 30.8 | | 29.2 | 23.3 |
| D | 7–12 (6 years) | 6–11 (6 years) | 6–12 (7 years) | 6–11 (6 years) | 6–10 (5 years) | 5–11 (7 years) | 6–11 (6 years) | 7–12 (6 years) |
| E | 41 | 45 | 37 | 26 | 25* | 31* | 66 | 36 |
| F | 80 | 250 | 80 | 140 | 90 | 200 | 80 | 90 |
| G | 1.6 | 3.0 | 2.2 | 2.1 | 0.6 | 4.7 | 2.2 | 0.3 |
| H | 15 | 0.6 | 4 | 0.4 | 11 | 3 | 3.7 | 4 |
| I | 2.0 | 2.3 | 2.8 | 2.6 | 1.6 | 2.7 | 2.9 | 2.7 |
| J | 3.4 | 2.4 | 3.0 | 2.7 | 2.3 | 2.8 | 2.6 | 3.0 |
| K | | | 2.6 | 3.0 | 0.6 | 3.8 | 4.3 | |
| L | 11.1* | 7.9 | 18.5* | 15.2* | 8.4 | 17.9* | 18.5* | 20.8* |
| M | 26.8 | | 45.2 | 43.7 | 28.8† | 24.8 | 56.3 | 28.4 |
| N | 5.9 | | 13.0 | | | | 13.0 | |
| O | | | | | 87.5 | 93.3† | | |

| Country | Nigeria | Tanzania | Malawi | Angola | Dahomey | Haiti | Senegal | Pakistan |
|---|---|---|---|---|---|---|---|---|
| A | 34 | 34* | 37 | 40* | 40 | 40* | 40* | 44* |
| B | 3.1 | 7.7 | 1.6 | 15.0 | 7.3 | 3.9 | 7.4 | 8.2 |
| C | | 27.1 | 41.1 | | 33.6 | 24.1 | | |
| D | 6–12 (7 years) | 7–13 (7 years) | 6–13 (8 years) | 6–9 (4 years) | 6–11 (6 years) | 7–12 (6 years) | 6–11 (6 years) | 6–10 (5 years) |
| E | 37 | 45 | 42 | 44 | 44 | 45 | 46 | 35 |
| F | 140 | 110 | 90 | 370 | 100 | 120 | 250 | 130 |
| G | 2.7 | 3.3 | 2.3 | 5.4 | 1.8 | 0.8 | –1.2 | 3.0 |
| H | 56.5 | 13.3 | 5 | 6 | 3 | 4 | 4 | 62.7 |
| I | 3.2 | 3.1 | 3.1 | 2.5 | 3.0 | 2.9 | 2.8 | 2.7 |
| J | 3.1 | 3.1 | 2.9 | 2.9 | 3.3 | 3.0 | 3.0 | 3.6 |
| K | 3.2 | 4.5 | 3.3 | | 4.6 | | 4.0 | 1.3 |
| L | | | 12.7 | | 28.3 | | 16.1* | 4.1 |
| M | 40.3 | 51.2* | 42.4 | | 48.5 | 70.2* | 57.4* | 34.5 |
| N | 11.3 | 13.8 | 11.7 | | | 9.6 | | |
| O | 88.5† | | 77.9† | 97.0† | | 89.5† | 94.4† | |

| Country | Uganda | Mozambique | Laos | Morocco | Bangladesh | India | Guatemala | Iran | Kenya |
|---|---|---|---|---|---|---|---|---|---|
| A | 46 | 50* | 51 | 55 | 56 | 83 | 59 | 62 | 67 |
| B | 6·4 | 2·4 | 10·8 | 3·6 | 7·0 | 5·0 | 6·0 | 8·1 | 7·6 |
| C | 53·0 | | 56·6 | | | | | | |
| D | 6–12 (7 years) | 6–10 (5 years) | 6–11 (6 years) | 7–11 (5 years) | 5–9 (5 years) | 6–11 (6 years) | 7–12 (6 years) | 6–11 (6 years) | 6–12 (7 years) |
| E | 36 | 75* | 36 | 35 | 48 | 43* | 36 | 33 | 31 |
| F | 130 | 280 | 120 | 260 | 70 | 110 | 390 | 450 | 160 |
| G | 1·6 | 5·6 | 3·5 | 2·5 | −0·1 | 2·4 | 2·1 | 7·7 | 4·3 |
| H | 10·1 | 8 | 3 | 15·4 | 72·4 | 551·1 | 5·4 | 30 | 12 |
| I | 3·0 | 2·8 | 2·4 | 3·0 | | 1·6 | 2·7 | 2·7 | 3·4 |
| J | 3·1 | 3·0 | 2·7 | 3·9 | | 2·8 | 2·4 | 3·2 | 3·5 |
| K | 5·2 | | | 4·2 | 1·2 | 2·9* | 2·2 | 3·1 | 5·3 |
| L | 17·8 | 5·9 | 11·3* | 17·5 | | 19·7* | 18·8 | 7·1 | 18·4* |
| M | 48·8 | 31·5† | 61·1 | 44·8 | | 23·8 | 58·2 | 50·9 | 48·0 |
| N | 13·9 | | | | | 12·5 | 9·3 | 16·3 | 17·2 |
| O | 74·9† | 98·5† | | 78·6 | | 72·2† | 62·1† | 77·2† | |

| Country | Yemen, People's Democratic Republic of | Iraq | Burma | Egypt | Indonesia | Mongolia | Honduras | Liberia |
|---|---|---|---|---|---|---|---|---|
| A | 68 | 69 | 70* | 70 | 71 | 72† | 73* | 73 |
| B | 16·7 | 4·8 | 6·4 | 3·8 | 4·1 | 7·2 | 5·6 | 1·6 |
| C | | | | | | | | |
| D | 7–12 (6 years) | 7–12 (6 years) | 5–9 (5 years) | 6–11 (6 years) | 7–12 (6 years) | 8–11 (4 years) | 7–12 (6 years) | 6–11 (6 years) |
| E | 29 | 22 | 51* | 39 | 32 | 31 | 37 | 31 |
| F | 120 | 370 | 80 | 220 | 80 | 380 | 300 | 210 |
| G | −7·2 | 1·4 | 0·1 | 0·2 | 3·4 | 1·4 | 1·4 | 3·8 |
| H | 1·5 | 10 | 30 | 34 | 119·2 | 1 | 2·6 | 2 |
| I | 3·1 | 3·7 | 1·7 | 2·5 | 1·7 | 2·2 | 3·5 | 2·7 |
| J | 3·6 | 4·0 | 2·4 | 3·2 | 3·1 | 3·0 | 3·7 | 2·7 |
| K | 2·3 | 6·7 | 3·2 | 4·8 | 2·6 | | 3·9 | 3·7 |
| L | 10·9 | 20·9 | 18·4 | 18·3 | 18·9 | 15·6 | 19·4 | 13·8* |
| M | 87·5 | 58·1 | 33·9 | 78·8 | 47·8 | 58·8 | 64·7 | 47·9* |
| N | | 18·4 | 18·4 | 18·5 | | | 9·9 | 17·7 |
| O | 79·0† | 85·5† | 42·3† | 80·5† | 40·4 | 4·6† | 64·8† | 91·1† |

| Country | Khmer Republic | Rwanda | Algeria | Central African Republic | Togo | Ivory Coast | Botswana |
|---|---|---|---|---|---|---|---|
| A | 74* | 74 | 75 | 76 | 76 | 77 | 78 |
| B | 6·4 | 5·5 | 8·3 | 11·4 | 9·2 | 7·8 | 14·2 |
| C | | 61·5 | | | | | 58·9 |
| D | 6–11 (6 years) | 7–12 (6 years) | 6–11 (6 years) | 6–11 (6 years) | 6–11 (6 years) | 6–11 (6 years) | 7–13 (7 years) |
| E | 26 | 59 | 40 | 68 | 60 | 46 | 33 |
| F | 130 | 60 | 360 | 150 | 150 | 330 | 160 |
| G | −2·2 | 2·2 | 4·8 | 1·6 | 2·5 | 4·4 | 4·9 |
| H | 8 | 4 | 14·4 | 2 | 2 | 5·2 | 0·6 |
| I | 3·0 | 3·3 | 3·7 | 3·0 | 3·0 | 2·9 | 2·7 |
| J | 3·4 | 3·6 | 3·6 | 1·9 | 3·2 | 3·1 | 2·7 |
| K | 6·5 | | 9·0 | 4·0 | 2·2* | 6·7 | 3·5 |
| L | 14·2 | | 12·9 | 16·4* | 24·2 | 2·3 | 11·2 |
| M | 59·4 | 38·1* | 56·3 | 68·0 | 54·3 | 27·6 | 55·3 |
| N | | | 22·4 | | | | |
| O | 63·9 | | 73·6 | | | | 79·5† |

| Country | Equatorial Guinea | Bolivia | Nicaragua | Thailand | Viet-Nam, Republic of | Malagasy Republic | Swaziland |
|---|---|---|---|---|---|---|---|
| A | 78* | 79* | 80 | 80* | 82* | 84 | 84 |
| B | 3·7 | 6·3 | 6·0 | 4·0 | 7·9 | 9·0 | 7·4 |
| C | | | | | | | |
| D | 6–13 (8 years) | 7–12 (6 years) | 7–12 (6 years) | 7–13 (7 years) | 6–10 (5 years) | 6–11 (6 years) | 6–12 (7 years) |
| E | 78* | 24 | 38 | 29 | 55* | 65 | 38 |
| F | 210 | 190 | 450 | 210 | 230 | 140 | 190 |
| G | −1·8 | 2·2 | 1·3 | 4·7 | −0·7 | 2·5 | 0·9 |
| H | 0·3 | 5 | 2 | 39·8 | 19 | 7 | 0·4 |
| I | 2·4 | 2·6 | 3·7 | 2·4 | 0·8 | 3·1 | 3·3 |
| J | 2·2 | 2·8 | 3·2 | 3·0 | 0·6 | 3·4 | 3·5 |
| K | 1·1 | 3·2* | 2·3 | 3·6 | 1·4 | 3·1 | 4·7 |
| L | 2·4 | 26·1* | 18·8 | 18·1 | 5·0 | | 18·7 |
| M | | 59·8 | 63·0 | 58·5 | 57·5 | 54·4 | 39·6* |
| N | | 67·9† | 13·5 | 12·6 | | 15·7 | |
| O | | | 50·4† | 21·4 | | 66·5† | 77·2† |

| Country | Zambia | Colombia | Syria | Ghana | West Malaysia | Malaysia Sabah | El Salvador | British Solomon Islands |
|---|---|---|---|---|---|---|---|---|
| A | 85 | 88* | 88 | 89 | 89 | 90* | 90 | 91* (net) |
| B | 7·5 | 6·2 | 7·9 | 6·8 | 4·8 | 11·5 | 4·4 | 6·0 |
| C | | | | | | | | |
| D | 7—13 (7 years) | 7—11 (5 years) | 6—11 (6 years) | 6—15 (10 years) | 6—11 (6 years) | 6—11 (6 years) | 7—12 (6 years) | 5—14 × 7/10 |
| E | 47 | 36 | 37 | 29 | 31 | 27 | 37 | 24 |
| F | 380 | 370 | 290 | 250 | | | 320 | 200 |
| G | 1·0 | 2·3 | 3·1 | −2·1 | | | 0·5 | −2·0 |
| H | 4·2 | 22·3 | 7 | 9 | | | 4 | 0·2 |
| I | 3·5 | 2·9 | 3·8 | 3·5 | 2·4 | 3·3 | 3·8 | 2·9 |
| J | 3·4 | 3·4 | 3·9 | 3·2 | 1·8 | 4·0 | 3·9 | |
| K | 6·2 | 1·5 | 3·9 | 3·7 | 5·4 | | 3·6 | |
| L | 12·8 | 20·9 | 10·1 | 20·3* | 12·2 | | 27·6 | 15·0 |
| M | 44·3 | 26·9 | 55·1 | 39·0 | 40·7 | 54·6 | 57·9 | 32·4 |
| N | | 10·9 | | 13·9 | | | 10·9 | |
| O | 52·7 | 27·1† | 60·0 | | 39·2 | 55·7 | 51·0† | |

| Country | Ecuador | Western Samoa | Sri Lanka | Paraguay | Jordan | Lesotho | Guyana | Albania |
|---|---|---|---|---|---|---|---|---|
| A | 91* | 91 (net) | 92* | 93 | 94* | 95 | 99 | 103* |
| B | 5.6 | 2.9 | 2.6 | 3.5 | 3.3 | 4.4 | | 6.1 |
| C | | 95.5 | | | | 70.0 | | |
| D | 6–11 (6 years) | 6–12 (7 years) | 5–12 (8 years) | 7–12 (6 years) | 6–11 (6 years) | 6–13 (8 years) | 6–11 (6 years) | 7–13 (7 years) |
| E | 38 | 28 | | 26 | 38 | 45 | 33 | 26* |
| F | 310 | 140 | 100 | 280 | 260 | 100 | 390 | 480 |
| G | 2.6 | 0.3 | 1.8 | 1.3 | −3.5 | 0.5 | 3.3 | 4.8 |
| H | 6 | 0.1 | 13 | 2.4 | 2.4 | 1 | 0.7 | 2 |
| I | 3.1 | 2.7 | 1.3 | 3.4 | 3.4 | 2.5 | 3.1 | |
| J | 3.3 | | | 3.9 | 3.9 | 2.6 | 2.7 | 2.9 |
| K | 3.5 | | 4.1 | 2.3 | 3.4 | 3.9* | 4.0 | |
| L | 19.8 | 21.8 | 13.7 | 15.5† | 7.5 | 13.3 | 12.4 | 11.6 |
| M | 45.1 | 57.3 | 60.9 | 61.0 | 80.0 | 53.7 | 40.9 | 7.9 |
| N | 16.7 | | 18.6 | 10.2 | | | | |
| O | 32.5 | 2.6* | 19.1 | 25.4 | 67.6† | 41.4* | | 28.5† |

| Country | Korea, Republic of | Mauritius | Republic of China (Taiwan) | Dominican Republic | Tunisia | Cameroon | Southern Rhodesia |
|---|---|---|---|---|---|---|---|
| A | 104 | 105 | 105* (net) | 107 | 107 | 108 | 108* |
| B | 5·0 | 3·4 | 2·9 | 3·8 | 6·8 | 7·9 | 4·2 |
| C | | | | | | | |
| D | 6—10 (5 years) | 6—11 (6 years) | 6—11 (6 years) | 7—12 (6 years) | 6—11 (6 years) | 6—11 (6 years) | 7—11 (5 years) |
| E | 55 | 31 | 40 | 54 | 50 | 49 | 38† |
| F | 290 | 280 | 430 | 430 | 320 | 200 | 320 |
| G | 10·0 | −0·7 | 7·3 | 4·7 | 3·6 | 3·7 | 2·6 |
| H | 32 | 0·8 | 15 | 4 | 5 | 6 | 6 |
| I | 1·8 | 2·2 | | 3·5 | 3·1 | 3·1 | 3·7 |
| J | 1·2 | 1·6 | | 3·1 | 3·4 | 3·0 | 4·0 |
| K | 4·2 | 3·7 | 3·9* | 2·8 | 7·2 | 3·5 | 3·9* |
| L | 24·6 | 11·0 | | 16·6 | 25·2* | 19·7 | 16·6* |
| M | 65·5 | 67·8 | 39·0* | 42·3 | 50·3* | 38·1 | |
| N | 9·0 | | 15·0 | 17·9 | | 15·4 | |
| O | 12·4 | 38·4† | | 31·5 | | | |

| Country | Fiji Islands | Philippines | British Honduras | Turkey | Peru | Seychelles Islands | Zaire | Brazil |
|---|---|---|---|---|---|---|---|---|
| A | 109† | 109* | 110* (net) | 111 | 115 | 115 (net) | 115 | 130 |
| B | 4·7 | 5·2 | 3·6 | 6·3 | 6·9 | 4·6 | 5·4 | 5·2 |
| C | | | | | | | | |
| D | 6—11 (6 years) | 7—12 (6 years) | 8—10 (3 years) | 7—11 (5 years) | 6—11 (6 years) | 5—14 x 6/10 | 6—11 (6 years) | 7—10 (4 years) |
| E | 32 | 30 | 28 | 42 | 37 | 25 | 44 | 31 |
| F | 470 | 240 | | 340 | 480 | 70 | 90 | 460 |
| G | 2·6 | 2·7 | | 4·0 | 0·5 | 0·4 | 3·6 | 5·1 |
| H | 0·5 | 38 | | 36·2 | 14·4 | 0·05 | 19·3 | 93·2 |
| I | | 3·3 | 3·5 | 2·0 | 2·7 | 3·0 | 3·2 | 2·7 |
| J | 1·6 | 3·6 | | 2·7 | 2·8 | | 3·0 | 2·8 |
| K | 4·3 | 4·6 | 2·3* | 4·0 | 3·7 | | 4·1 | 3·3 |
| L | | | | 18·5 | 20·3 | 8·9 | 18·7 | 12·4 |
| M | 61·1 | 85·2 | 57·0 | 61·3† | 35·8* | 60·8 | 69·7* | 2·4 |
| N | | 10·8 | | 15·1 | 16·0 | | 22·5 | 21·4 |
| O | 35·6† | 16·7 | 13·4† | 48·6 | 39·4† | 42·3 | 84·6† | 33·8 |

| Country | Congo People's Republic of | Grenada | China People's Republic of | Maldive Islands | Sikkim |
|---|---|---|---|---|---|
| A | 145 | 148 (net) | | 18·9 | |
| B | 7·9 | 2·7 | | 17·5 | |
| C | | | | | |
| D | 6–11 (6 years) | 6–10 (5 years) | | | |
| E | 59 | 38 | | 26 | 80 |
| F | 270 | 330 | 160 | 90 | |
| G | 1·4 | 1·7 | 2·6 | 0·7 | 0·3 |
| H | 1·1 | 0·1 | 800 | 0·1 | 0·2 |
| I | 3·0 | | 0·4 | 1·3 | 1·1 |
| J | 3·0 | | | | |
| K | 7·5 | 5·7* | | | |
| L | 25·3 | 17·6 | | | |
| M | 45·1 | 81·3 | | | |
| N | | | | | |
| O | | 23·6† | | | |

# Convention Against Discrimination in Education

**List of countries which have deposited with Unesco instruments of ratification or acceptance of the Convention.**

The convention against Discrimination in Education came into force on 22 May 1962. By 25 May 1972 the following 58 Member States had deposited instruments of ratification or acceptance of the Convention: Albania, Algeria, Argentina, Australia, Brazil, Bulgaria, Byelorussian Soviet Socialist Republic, Central African Republic, Chile, China, Congo, Costa Rica, Cuba, Cyprus, Czechoslovakia, Dahomey, Denmark, Arab Republic of Egypt, Finland, France, Federal Republic of Germany, Guinea, Hungary, Indonesia, Iran, Israel, Italy, Kuwait, Lebanon, Liberia, Luxembourg, Madagascar, Malta, Mauritius, Mongolia, Morocco, Netherlands, New Zealand, Niger, Nigeria, Norway, Panama, Peru, Philippines, Poland, Romania, Senegal, Sierra Leone, Spain, Sweden, Tunisia, Ukrainian Soviet Socialist Republic, Union of Soviet Socialist Republics, United Kingdom of Great Britain and Northern Ireland, Venezuela, Republic of Viet-Nam, Yugoslavia; Swaziland, a non-Member State, had acceded thereto.

# Index

258